PUBLICATIONS ON ASIA
OF THE HENRY M. JACKSON SCHOOL
OF INTERNATIONAL STUDIES
Volume 40

SŪR DĀS

Poet, Singer, Saint

JOHN STRATTON HAWLEY

UNIVERSITY OF WASHINGTON PRESS
Seattle and London

This book is sponsored by the South Asia Program
of the Henry M. Jackson School of International Studies
University of Washington

The research for and publication of this book
have been greatly assisted by grants from the
Program for Editions and the Program for Publications
of the National Endowment for the Humanities.

Frontispiece: Sūr Dās. Detail from an illustration for a poem from the *Sūr Sāgar,* Mewar, 1720–1730 A.D. Courtesy of the Los Angeles County Museum of Art (Nasli and Alice Heeramanick Collection, M.71.1.11).

Library of Congress Cataloging in Publication Data

Hawley, John Stratton, 1941–
Sūr Dās : poet, singer, saint.

(Publications on Asia of the Henry M. Jackson School of International Studies, University of Washington ; v. 40)
Includes English translations of selected poems from Sūradāsa's Sūrasāgara.
Bibliography: p.
Includes index.
1. Sūradāsa, 1483?–1563?—Criticism and interpretation.
I. Sūradāsa, 1483?–1563? Sūrasāgara. English. Selections.
1984. II. Title. III. Series.
PK1967.9.S9Z68 1984 891′.4312 84-40327
ISBN 0-295-96102-3

Edition for South Asia
published by Oxford University Press, Delhi

In memory of my father,
Robert Charles Hawley,
who now sees face to face

Contents

Illustrations

Preface

IN MAY OF 1978, Indians from Calcutta to Bombay observed the five-hundredth anniversary of the birth of Sūr Dās, the famed blind poet of Hindi literature. In India the event was heralded by a burst of new publications celebrating the poet's life and works, adding to an already substantial store. These portraits of Sūr differ somewhat in perspective and detail, but their colors are always drawn from traditional life stories of the poet and from the great ocean of poetry attributed to him, the *Sūr Sāgar*.

This book will search for a portrait too, but it is a hidden portrait, an image that has heretofore been concealed behind centuries of encrustation and retouching. We shall attempt the task of cleaning that historical canvas, not only by critically examining the legends that have grown up about the poet's life, but by discriminating between those poems in the *Sūr Sāgar* that can reasonably be said to have come from circles not too far distant from the poet himself, and those that were added later. The latter are by far the majority, so the "Sūr" who emerges in our portrait—the author of these early poems, doubtless to some extent a collective entity—is thinner and sparer than the more ample Sūr that traditional scholarship depicts. Our profile of Sūr will, of course, be selective and subjective. When so much has been lost to time and so much added by it, nothing else is possible; photography is out of the question. But the techniques, concerns, and commitments evident in the old poems upon which we shall rely—compositions of our hidden "Sūr"—are definite and consistent enough to form a coherent image of the poet. A characteristic physiognomy emerges from the darkness at the edges.

This portrait will be not only literary but religious, for all of Sūr's poetry is devoted in one way or another to Krishna, the deft and mischievous cowherd god who has come more than any other figure to dominate the artistic and religious attentions of India in the last half millennium. The distinction between the realms of literature and religion is familiar to Westerners, and for purposes of this book we shall at times emphasize one, at times the other. But in regard to medieval India, where saints were singers and the greatest works of literature were devotional in tone and intent, this bifurcation is false. Sūr's religion, as we shall discover, had as much to do with art as with piety.

The opening chapters lay the groundwork. In the first we make our way through a halo of stories that now surrounds the poet-saint. We shall find that these hagiographical tales, though significant in their own right, tell us little about the poet himself. For that we must turn to his own words—or as close to his words as we can come—by consulting the early manuscripts of the *Sūr Sāgar.* These do reveal the consistent profile of a poet we can call "Sūr," for the early *Sūr Sāgar* has a shape and tone that is substantially different from what it later became as it was weighed down with numerous additional poems. In chapter two we describe this early *Sūr Sāgar,* the source for our portrait of Sūr, and analyze how it developed over the years.

The next chapter—on Rādhā, Krishna's milkmaid consort—is intended to shed a more intense light on the *Sūr Sāgar*'s origin and development by examining one of the major characters in it. In addition, by providing a first taste of the suffering and dislocation that are caused in the lives of those who fall in love with Krishna, the figure of Rādhā introduces us to what I believe to be the dominant theme in Sūr's piety: *viraha. Viraha* is the condition of being separated from the object of one's affections, whether amorous or religious, and the deep sense of longing that underscores such a separation. For Sūr the experience of separation from God is, if not the essence, certainly the primary manifestation of the religious life, and it is at once the most compelling impetus of his poetic creativity: more poems in the early *Sūr Sāgar* concern *viraha* than any other object. Sūr's ironic, affectionate poems of the child Krishna are also justly famous, but Kenneth E. Bryant's *Poems to the Child-God* and my own *Krishna, the Butter Thief* have treated them at length. This book will explore another, somewhat darker obsession in Sūr's religious life.

Chapter four deals explicitly with *viraha,* as experienced not only by Rādhā but by all the herder women (*gopī*s) of Krishna's Braj homeland. In particular, it shows how Sūr portrays these women as models of true religion by comparing them to yogis, with the yogis coming off decidedly second best. Implicit in this comparison, and explicit in the way it is presented in the *Sūr Sāgar,* is the contrast between two fundamental strands of Hindu piety—that which worships the divine in its manifest form (*saguṇa:* the worship of images is one expression of this), and that which insists that God is essentially formless (*nirguṇa*) and should be worshipped as such. The former position is the simpler, the less rarefied, the more suited to the human senses; this is what the *gopī*s archetypally represent. The spokesman for the other side—the *nirguṇa* position—is Ūdho, the messenger Krishna sends to convince the *gopī*s that, though physically absent, he is with them still in some interior, spiritual way. The exchange between the *gopī*s and Ūdho, then, becomes a debate between *saguṇa* and *nirguṇa* piety. It seems obvious that Sūr casts his lot with the former.

There is, however, another genre of *viraha* poetry in the *Sūr Sāgar,* in which the poet speaks apart from any voice in Krishna's cowherd world and gives expression to his own sense of separation from God. As we see in chapter five, the radical nature of Sūr's devotion to Krishna puts him quite definitely in the company of the *sant*s, "saints" whose religious perspective is usually taken to fall on the *nirguṇa* rather than the *saguṇa* side of the great theological divide. This leads us to ask whether such a distinction is really so clear for Sūr as it seems in his dramatic, narrative poetry. If both *saguṇa* and *nirguṇa* dimensions can be seen in Sūr's poetic output, what is the basis of his faith? In the final chapter I argue that it is the very act of singing, singing to God. This not only forms the substance of Sūr's literary life but supports his understanding of the life of faith as well. By translating from the *Sūr Sāgar* as we proceed, I hope even in the absence of musical accompaniment to give some hint of what singing meant to Sūr, and how he sang.

Scarcely one of the translations presented here is wholly my own. Many belong at least as much to Mark Juergensmeyer, who has spent days and weeks subjecting them to the scrutiny of a poet's eye. We have worked as a team, in which I bore responsibility for making sure that our translation did not stray too far from the original Hindi, and we jointly shaped the final outcome in English verse. For his unfailing confidence that these poems were worth translating, and that it could be done, I am deeply grateful. He has also made helpful comments about many of the arguments.

As for the prose, I have been blessed with two of the finest editors in the business. One is my wife, Laura Shapiro, who continues to provide me with the highest standards of writing that I know, and has helped me to try to approximate them. For her clarity of thought and warmth of support I am, as ever, thankful. The other is Linda Hess, who has offered editorial insights about both prose and poetry and has made critical observations based on a finely tuned knowledge of the subject matter itself.

B. N. Choudhury and Shrivatsa Goswami have saved me from a number of crucial errors in translation, and my colleague in the Pacific Northwest, Kenneth E. Bryant, has confronted the book with his rigorous sense of both scholarship and aesthetics. My debt to him extends as well to the imaginative and meticulous work he has done in the cause of producing a critical edition of the *Sūr Sāgar,* a task in which we are both engaged.

I am also indebted to colleagues at the University of Washington in various ways: to Michael C. Shapiro for his confidence and savvy, and for a number of insightful observations; to Thomas B. Ridgeway for his expert help in evaluating manuscripts of the *Sūr Sāgar;* to Naseem Karmali for an enthusiastic check of the accuracy of the translations; to Margery Lang for guiding the book toward publication; and to members of the South Asia Program for approving financial assistance in that cause. Additional thanks are due to the American Council of Learned Societies and the American Institute of Indian Studies for grants of time and travel that made it possible to complete the book; and to the National Endowment for the Humanities, the University of Washington, the Social Science Research Council, and Harvard University for financial support offered at various points in the work of collecting, collocating, and editing the manuscripts of the *Sūr Sāgar* without which this study could not have been made. There is a certain risk involved in abstracting conclusions from that work, which is still in progress. I trust that when the full critical edition is available in print the reader will be able to amplify what I have said with further examples, but it seems inevitable that some qualifications will be necessary too.

Sections of the book have been published in preliminary form in various books and journals, and the editors' permission to rework material already in print is gratefully acknowledged. Portions of chapters two through four, in altered form, have appeared in the following: the *Journal of the American Oriental Society* (99, no. 1 [1979]: 64–72); *The Divine Consort: Rādhā and the Goddesses of India,* edited by J. S. Hawley and Donna Marie Wulff (Berkeley: Berkeley Religious Studies Series, 1982, pp. 42–56); and the *Harvard Theological Review* (74, no. 1 [1981]: 1–20). A version of chapter five will form a part of *The Sants: Studies in a Devotional*

Tradition of India, edited by Karine Schomer and W. H. McLeod (Berkeley: Berkeley Religious Studies Series and Delhi: Motilal Banarsidass, forthcoming). Some of the material considered in chapter one was presented to the Second Conference on Early Devotional Literature in New Indo-Aryan Languages, held under the auspices of the Indological Seminar of the University of Bonn at Sankt Augustin, West Germany, on March 19–21, 1982. The paper has recently been published as "The Sectarian Logic of the *Sūr dās kī vārtā*" in the conference proceedings, *Bhakti in Current Research, 1979–1982,* under the editorship of Monika Thiel-Horstmann (Berlin: Dietrich Reimer Verlag, 1983), pp. 157–69. Numerous changes and corrections have been made since these earlier publications appeared; where discrepancies occur, the option presented in the present work is the more trustworthy.

Manuscripts, Editions, and Verse Citation

POEMS FROM THE *Sūr Sāgar* that are translated or discussed in the text are identified by means of the number assigned to them in the edition published by the Kāśī Nāgarīpracāriṇī Sabhā, for which the abbreviation 'S' is used. Citations refer to the 1972 edition of volume 1 and the 1976 edition of volume 2.

This does not mean, however, that the texts being translated are exactly those that appear in the Sabhā edition. Unless otherwise indicated, I am translating on the basis of what appears in the old manuscripts of the *Sūr Sāgar.* It is not within the scope of the present work to offer a full justification for manuscript readings that have been preferred in translating poems from the *Sūr Sāgar.* A detailed discussion of issues involved in critically evaluating manuscripts of the *Sūr Sāgar* must await the publication of the forthcoming critical edition, which is being prepared by Kenneth E. Bryant and myself, with help from Thomas B. Ridgeway, Mandakranta Bose, and Vidyut Aklujkar. Since scarcely a poem presented here is truly the same as its counterpart in the Sabhā edition, however, I have supplemented each with notes intended to clarify points that might seem puzzling to anyone whose only access is to the standard printed text. In the case of poems fully translated, these are collected at the back of the book in the section entitled "Notes on the Translations," where the reader will also find information relating to points of possible unclarity in the content of these poems. Explanations relating to poems that are only partially translated will be found in the footnotes. Poems translated in their entirety are indexed by Hindi and English first lines at the back of the book.

Since there is often a distance between the old manuscripts on which this book is primarily based and the Sabhā text, it has not been easy to adopt a system of verse citation. Given that the Sabhā edition is currently the standard reference text, I have seen no handy alternative to locating a verse by means of its equivalent or analogous line in the Sabhā *Sūr Sāgar*. This sometimes distorts a reader's impression of the size or order of a poem as it appears in manuscripts, but to insert corrective notes in every case would have burdened the text unduly. If the reference is to a poem translated completely in this book, the Notes on the Translations can be used to ascertain the true shape of the relevant manuscripts. If no manuscript information is given in connection with a particular citation, the reader may assume that the manuscripts containing the phrase or line under discussion are in at least rough agreement with each other. If they differ significantly, the manuscript whose reading is being discussed will be listed. A single line of text as printed in the Sabhā edition—normally the unit of rhyme—is almost always translated here as two lines of English verse, the second being indented to indicate that it continues the first. Such a two-line unit is cited as a single verse.

The poems in the *Sūr Sāgar* begin with a line called the *ṭek* (prop), which serves as the poem's title and refrain. I present it here in italics, and refer to it as verse 1 when discussing a poem. Normally the *ṭek* is only about half as long as an ordinary verse: it corresponds in length to that portion of each of the remaining verses that falls before the caesura. Sometimes it is supplemented by a second phrase that makes it equal in length to the other verses, yet even when this happens it is typical that only the first section is quoted as a refrain; for that reason it alone is italicized in translation. Readers wishing to learn further details about the use of the *ṭek* in performance may consult Rupert Snell, "Metrical Forms in Braj Bhāṣā Verse: The *Caurāsī Pada* in Performance," in *Bhakti in Current Research, 1979–1982,* ed. Monika Thiel-Horstmann, pp. 355–83.

Basic information about the manuscripts referred to in this book is presented in the list that follows. It includes a brief description of each manuscript, together with the abbreviation by means of which it is designated, both here and in the critical edition to follow. Where possible, the abbreviation assigned to a manuscript in the edition of Mātāprasād Gupta (*Sūrsāgar,* Agra: Agra University, 1979) is also given.

(1) J1. MS no. 49 in the Hindi collection of the Maharaja of Jaipur. *Vikram* 1639 (1582 A.D.); written at Fatehpūr; 48 folios and 411 *pads*, of which, once 27 repetitions are subtracted, 241 belong to Sūr; untitled. This manuscript has been published in a facsimile edition edited by Gopal Narayan Bahura and Kenneth E. Bryant:

Pad Sūrdās kā/The Padas of Sūrdās (Jaipur: Maharaja Sawai Singh II Museum, 1984).

(2) B1. Hindi MS no. 156, Anup Sanskrit Library, Bikaner. No date (ca. *vikram* 1655–1685) or other colophon information. 150 folios, 423 *pads*, untitled. Resembles Mātāprasād Gupta's "Bi. 4."

(3) B2. Hindi MS no. 157, Anup Sanskrit Library, Bikaner. *Vikram* 1681, copied by a scribe in the entourage of the Maharaja of Bikaner, 161 folios pertaining to Sūr, 492 *pads*, untitled. Gupta's "Bi. 1."

(4) B3. Hindi MS no. 149, Anup Sanskrit Library, Bikaner. *Vikram* 1695, no place given, 132 folios, 480 *pads* of Sūr, untitled.

(5) U1. Hindi MS no. 575/2396, Rajasthan Oriental Research Institute, Udaipur. *Vikram* 1697, at Ghānorā (near Banswara), 202 folios, 793 *pads* of Sūr, entitled "Sūr Sāgar."

(6) B4. Hindi MS no. 158, Anup Sanskrit Library, Bikaner. *Vikram* 1698, Mathura, 109 folios, 615 *pads* of Sūr, untitled but with divisional headings. Gupta's "Bi. 3."

(7) J2. Hindi MS no. 6732(2), "Khās Mohar" collection, Maharaja of Jaipur. Before *vikram* 1718 (the date of its acquisition by the House of Jaipur), 150 folios, 503 *pads* of Sūr, untitled and without divisional headings.

(8) J3. Hindi MS no. 3538, "Khās Mohar" collection, Maharaja of Jaipur. Before A.H. 1059, the date of the first seal it bears (i.e., *vikram* 1706), acquired by the House of Jaipur A.H. 1075 (*vikram* 1722), 188 folios, 681 *pads* of Sūr, untitled but with divisional headings.

(9) J4. Hindi MS no. 1979, "Khās Mohar" collection, Maharaja of Jaipur. *Vikram* 1733, at Cātsu (near Jaipur), by a scribe of Gokul, 305 folios, 1472 *pads* of Sūr, entitled "Sūr Sāgar," divisional headings.

(10) J5. Hindi MS no. 3387 (1), "Khās Mohar" collection, Maharaja of Jaipur. *Vikram* 1734(?) at Ajavgaḍh (Alwar District): 34 folios contain 95 *pads* of Sūr under the general title "śrī sūr dās jī kā pad."

(11) A1. MS no. 76/220, Allahabad Municipal Museum. *Vikram* 1743, no place given, 213 folios, 585 *pads* of Sūr, entitled "Sūr Sāgar," sporadic divisional headings.

(12) K1. Hindi MS no. 3335, Rajasthan Oriental Research Institute, Kota. *Vikram* 1758, at Pachor, originally 64 folios, 209 *pads* of Sūr, entitled "Sūr Sāgar," divisional headings. Gupta's "Pa."

(13) U2. Hindi MS no. 133/1954, Rajasthan Oriental Research Institute, Jaipur. *Vikram* 1763, at Udaipur, 30 folios, 170 *pads* of Sūr, entitled "Sūr Sāgar," divisional headings. Gupta's "Śrī."

Transliteration and Pronunciation

IN RENDERING HINDI into the Latin alphabet I have departed from the standard method of transliterating devanagari script, which was designed to render Sanskrit usage, where it seemed to misrepresent the sounds produced in spoken Hindi. I have omitted the neutral vowel at the ends of words (*nām*) except where it is audible in Hindi speech (*viraha, vinaya, sadasya*). For consistency's sake I have done the same in transliterating poetry, even though such a vowel can sometimes be metrically significant. Since it is always significant within words, however, I have retained it there in poetry (*banamālā*), whereas in speech the interstitial vowel is normally not heard (*banmālā*). The vocalic 'r' is retained as in Sanskrit (*kṛṣṇa*).

The Hindi system for rendering nasalized vowels is considerably simpler than the Sanskrit, and in manuscripts this is particularly so: *anusvāra* is employed almost to the exclusion of conjunct ligatures. I have modified this radically simplified notation in the direction of the traditional transliteration scheme to approximate the sounds for readers unfamiliar with Indic languages: *ñ* indicates the velar nasal (*satsañg*), which can also occur in the vicinity of '*h*' (*siñh*); dental nasals are rendered with *n* (*sant*); retroflexes with *ṇ* (*muṇḍi*); and the remainder are designated with *ṃ* (*bhaṃvargīt*). The nasalization of long vowels within words is indicated with a tilde rather than any of these (*sā̃dhi*), and if the nasalized vowel is a diphthong the tilde is placed over its first element (*nãinini*). Since the vowel sound is already indicated in a complex way in these instances, I have thought it best not to add an independent consonant (*ñ, n, ṃ*) that could possibly be interpreted as separate from the vowel itself. By a similar logic, all nasalized vowels at the ends of words are indicated with a tilde (*padõ*), since no consonant is heard in these cases either and the use of a consonantal transcription might particularly suggest it at the close of a word. I am aware that this system may seem cumbersome to readers attempting to reconstruct the exact devanagari notation from the transliteration employed here. Such readers can be assured, however, that in manuscripts of the *Sūr Sāgar,* almost without exception, nasalization of all types is indicated by simple *anusvāra.*

Words that have come into standard English usage are given in that form (Krishna, Purana). I have taken this to include the names of most cities (Mathura, Dvaraka; but Kurukṣetra). Personal names and names of deities, however, are normally given with diacritical markings, and normally in their most frequently heard vernacular form (Rām). On occasion, however, I have employed the *tatsam* form in translating poetry (Kāma) or in referring to figures whose names have become familiar in that spelling (Śiva, Pāṇḍava, Vallabha). Sanskrit words, or terms drawn into Hindi usage directly from a Sanskrit context, are transliterated according to the system that is standard for Sanskrit (*nirodha, mahābhāva, guṇa*).

In general I have retained diacritical marks to guide pronunciation. The long vowels *ā, ī, ū, e,* and *o* are pronounced approximately like the corresponding vowels in the English words f*a*ther, mar*i*ne, r*u*le, pr*e*y, and m*o*w. The diphthongs *ai* and *au,* though sometimes given the length of the vowels in English str*i*de and tr*ou*t, are more usually shortened, yielding the vowel sounds contained in m*a*d and cr*aw*l. The vowels *a, i,* and *u* are short and are pronounced like the vowels in the words b*u*t, f*i*ll, and b*u*ll. Vocalic *ṛ* is also short; in modern speech it is rendered as if it were *ri,* as in *ri*b.

The consonant *c* sounds like *ch* in the English word *ch*arm, except that it has less aspiration; the consonant transliterated as *ch* has correspondingly greater aspiration. The aspirated consonants *th* and *ph* should be pronounced like the clusters in goa*th*erd and she*ph*erd rather than their counterparts in *th*ing and mor*ph*ium. The distinction between the sibilants *ś* and *ṣ* is not usually made in modern Hindi usage; both sound like *sh* in English *sh*ort. For the retroflex consonants, produced by curling the tip of the tongue toward the roof of the mouth (*ṭ, ṭh, ḍ, ḍh, ṇ*), there are no genuine English equivalents. To some, they sound as if the corresponding English consonants had been preceded by an American *r* (ha*rd,* hea*rt*), though the placement is slightly farther back in the mouth.

SŪR DĀS

Poet, Singer, Saint

Sūr Dās plucking a drone instrument (*tambūrā*). Chromolithograph created by "Vallabha" in 1979 to honor the five-hundredth anniversary of the traditionally observed birth of Sūr Dās. The poet has a blind man's walking stick at his side, sits before a manuscript of the *Bhāgavata Purāṇa,* and wears a necklace that suggests his initiation by Vallabhācārya. The icon of Krishna as Śrī Nāth Jī in the background reinforces the Vallabhite theme.

CHAPTER 1

The Blind Poet

A PHYSICAL DEFORMITY is nowhere a blessing, but in India it can be a positive curse. Indian children are often allowed to ridicule the crippled and palsied and to taunt the deaf and blind, and adults are sometimes scarcely less callous. In a sort of reverse sacramentalism the outward condition of these unfortunates is taken to mirror a state of inner disgrace; it is explained that their current adversity follows as a simple reflex from misdeeds perpetrated in past lives. Under such conditions, anyone who wishes to communicate politely with a handicapped person will hardly refer to the deformity directly. It is too intrinsically damning. In most cases one searches uneasily for a term of address, but for the numerous blind there is a time-honored formula that avoids embarrassment altogether: one may call the blind person Sūr Dās.

Sūr Dās, a poet-singer who lived sometime during the sixteenth century and has come to be revered as one of the two greatest literary figures in the Hindi language family, was blind from birth, so blind that beneath his eyebrows lay only the empty eyesockets—or so tradition affirms. And yet, like Homer, he was endowed with a vision acute enough to exceed by far the capacities of ordinary eyes. His descriptions of Krishna and his world are so sensitive and detailed that they have for generations been able to make the god of beauty and love and play visible to those who otherwise could not see—the blind leading the sighted. Even in the land where, as nowhere else, seeing is believing, where icons are everywhere and the cinematic is instantly perceived as real, the finest vision is held to have belonged to a blind man.

The Traditional Life of Sūr Dās

The story—or rather, the principal story—goes as follows. In the village of Sihi a little south of Delhi and not far from the Braj region where Krishna himself had passed his youth and adolescence, lived a poor Sārasvat Brahmin family. The wife was pregnant, and when she gave birth there was general horror at the discovery that the child was blind. The father despaired, openly wondering why God had sent him an affliction that would further deepen his poverty, and throughout the years of early childhood, often the happiest years of a lifetime in India, no one would speak to Sūr.

When he was six years old, it happened that Sūr's father was given two gold coins by a local grandee, enough to buy food for several months. He hid them away overnight, but a rat made off with them and stashed them in a hole in the thatch; in the morning they were nowhere to be seen. Sūr, hearing the lamentations of his parents, proffered the advice that they had only to sing and pray to God and all would be well, and received for his pains a torrent of abuse. "Ever since the moment you were born, we have known nothing but ill." To this he replied that he would reveal where the coins had been taken if his parents would allow him one boon: to leave home. He did, and they did (with sudden and manifold misgivings, considering their son's newly discovered gifts), and thus Sūr's wanderings began.

He had made his way only eight miles down the road, when his unusual powers of perception were called upon again. A landowner who had lost ten cows chanced by, recognized Sūr, and told the boy that two of the cows would be his if he could determine where the group had gone. Sūr identified the henchmen of a nearby landowner as the thieves, but refused his reward. Nevertheless the grateful landowner insisted on building him a hut on that very spot and providing for his food and care. Soon many others came for advice and the child became a local celebrity, to the point that he began initiating disciples. But one night as he slept, Sūr understood that to spend his miraculous talents in such a way was to miss the mark, and the next morning he escaped the net of illusion and pushed farther south to Mathura. Mathura was the city Krishna himself had ruled, at the center of the Braj country where Sūr had determined to spend his days singing the Lord's praises. In the magical realm of Braj his own powers would no longer seem worthy of special attention.

He trusted himself on the point, but experience had made him suspicious of others, so he took the precaution of moving south of Mathura to a quiet landing on the River Jumna called Gaughāṭ. If he stayed in town there was always the danger of attracting crowds, and he had no intention of drawing people away from the religious authority of the Caube Brahmins who ruled it. Even at Gaughāṭ, however, he attracted a sizeable following. People flocked to benefit from the miracles his gift for divination could work and to hear the heart-rending songs he sang, songs that bespoke his abject sense of separation from God.

At this point Sūr's life took a momentous turn; and this is a good moment to pause briefly and consider the source and context for this history, since these will become increasingly important as the story develops. We have been following the account of Sūr's youth that is provided in the earliest document that records it, Harirāy's commentary on the *Caurāsī Vaiṣṇavan kī Vārtā* (*Conversations with eighty-four Vaiṣṇavas*).[1] Harirāy was one of the great figures in the literary history of the Vallabha Sampradāy, the community that looks to the sixteenth-century theologian Vallabhācārya, or more simply Vallabha, as its founder. Vallabha, who is traditionally considered Sūr's guru, was a philosopher born into a South Indian Brahmin family that had transported itself to the north. He is remembered as having stunned into silence the pundits of Advaita Vedānta as he circled the subcontinent on a great debating tour. His point of view, as preserved in several independent treatises and in commentaries on the *Brahma Sūtra*s and *Bhāgavata Purāṇa,* was that the world is not fundamentally illusory but rather a partial manifestation of the divine plenitude. This, he proclaimed, was the only truly nondual way in which to perceive the universe (*śuddhādvaita*). And it implied a religious life that diverged markedly from the ascetic mode that had been taken as exemplary by those who claimed the eighth-century philosopher Śaṅkara as their preceptor. One ought not to retreat from the world, but instead to live gratefully within it as an active participant, a householder. Through constant prayer to Krishna, the full manifestation of divinity, and by his mercy, one might peel away the scales that prevent one from actualizing that presence in oneself and recognizing it in the world. This approach Vallabha called

1. I shall cite from the edition of Dvārkādās Parīkh. Also useful, for the *vārtā* on Sūr Dās, is Premnārāyaṇ Ṭaṇḍan, ed., *Sūrdās kī Vārtā*. In what follows the abbreviation *Vārtā* will refer specifically to the *Caurāsī Vaiṣṇavan kī Vārtā*; and *vārtā* will designate the term in its generic sense. The *vārtā* on Sūr Dās, including the commentary of Harirāy but lacking the verse, which is often crucial to the sense of the narrative, has been translated in Richard Barz, *The Bhakti Sect of Vallabhācārya*, pp. 105–39.

the way of grace and fulfillment, the *puṣṭimārga.*[2]

In the generations that followed Vallabha, this teaching took institutional form. Vallabha's second son, Viṭṭhalnāth, became his successor as the leader of the circle of disciples that had formed around the great philosopher. It was almost certainly he who gave the community most of its organizational and ritual structure, setting out daily and yearly schedules of worship that continue to this day to be among the most elaborate in the Hindu spectrum. The images in the care of Vallabha's descendants, who settled in various places in Braj and later in Rajasthan, came to be the focus of particular adoration in the community, but since this was to be a householder's religion, the primary display of devotion was to be undertaken by individual believers in their own homes. Although initiation was still in the hands of Vallabha's own line, who were Brahmins, there was no theological basis for caste discrimination, and the sect became particularly attractive—probably very early on—to mobile, merchant groups from Braj westward to Gujarat.[3]

At least by the time of Gokulnāth (1551–1640 A.D., *vikram* 1608–1697), Viṭṭhalnāth's successor, the worship of the community had come to involve the meticulous decoration and service of images of Krishna in the possession of individual families, and the singing of songs principally provided by the compositions of eight celebrated poets of Sūr's era. In the Vallabhite community these came to be called the *aṣṭachāp,* "eight seals," since the final phrases of each of their poems almost invariably bore the name of the poet himself—his seal or signature, as was customary in the *pad* genre in which they were composed. Partly to draw the life stories of these eight seals into a sectarian framework, relating them directly to the actions and teachings of Vallabha and Viṭṭhalnāth, there developed a literary genre called the *vārtā,* literally a "conversation" between the saints and one of the sect's gurus. These *vārtās,*

2. For a helpful summary of Vallabha's teaching, see Barz, *Vallabhācārya,* pp. 56–93. Other European language sources include Helmuth von Glasenapp, "Die Lehre Vallabhâcāryas," *Zeitschrift für Indologie und Iranistik* 9 (1933–34): 322–30; Peter Johanns, S. J., *Vers le Christ par le Vedanta*; R. D. Karmakar, "Comparison of the Bhāṣyas of Śaṅkara, Rāmānuja, Keśavakaśmirin and Vallabha on Some Crucial Sūtras," *Annals of the Bhandarkar Oriental Research Institute* 1, no. 2 (1920): 105–27; Mrudula I. Marfatia, *The Philosophy of Vallabhācārya*; Bhai Manilal Parekh, *Sri Vallabhāchārya*; and J. G. Shah, *Shri Vallabhacharya: His Philosophy and Religion.*

3. In particular, members of the Lohānā, Bhāṭiyā, Baniyā, and Kanbi castes. See Richard J. Cohen, "Sectarian Vaishnavism: The Vallabha *Sampradaya,*" *Proceedings of the South Asia Seminar, University of Pennsylvania, 1981–1982,* pp. 65–72, and N. A. Thoothi, *The Vaishṇavas of Gujarat,* pp. 92–93.

however, reported not only verbal exchanges but significant events in the lives of the saints, some of which did not concern the scions of the Sampradāy at all, and the word *vārtā* carries as well a broader meaning of story or narrative.

The earliest extant collection of *vārtā*s is the *Caurāsī Vaiṣṇavan kī Vārtā* and one of its eighty-four chapters concerns Sūr, unquestionably the most famous of the eight seals. Harirāy, a fourth-generation descendant of Vallabha who is traditionally ascribed an impressive lifespan extending from 1590 to 1715 (*vikram* 1647–1772),[4] is credited with having arranged the eighty-four *vārtā*s in their present order while yet a boy, but he acted under the supervision of his aging uncle, Gokulnāth. His original contributions, in the form of commentary, are assumed to have been added later, at a date that is usually placed sometime before the end of the seventeenth century.[5] If one trusts this chronology, one must date the *Vārtā* (without commentary) to the first half of the seventeenth century, and one manuscript supports such a dating, since its colophon bears the date *vikram* 1697 (1640 A.D.).[6] That date has been challenged, however, as both too early and too late. On the one hand it has been observed that the colophon gives only the year, not the more precise dating that was customary in manuscripts of the period, suggesting that the colophon is a forgery.[7] On the other hand sectarian historians sometimes urge that credence be given to references in the poetry of Alīkhān Paṭhān and the *Vallabh Digvijaya* of Yadunāth, which state that the *Vārtā* had been given its present order by 1601 A.D. (*vikram* 1658).[8] In short, the date is still in question.

The *vārtā* on Sūr Dās, in its unembellished form, begins and

4. Prabhudayāl Mītal, *Gosvāmī Harirāy jī kā Pad-Sāhitya*, pp. 5, 9.

5. Ṭaṇḍan, *Sūrdās kī Vārtā*, pp. 7–8. Barz's assertion that Harirāy completed ordering the *Vārtā* toward the end of his life is perhaps based on a misreading of Ṭaṇḍan, ibid., p. 7 (Barz, *Vallabhācārya*, p. 102). The *terminus ad quem* for the composition of Harirāy's commentary (*bhāvprakāś*) is normally held to be fixed by a manuscript containing it that dates, according to its colophon, to *vikram* 1752 (1695 A.D.) See Dīndayāl Gupta, *Aṣṭachāp aur Vallabh-Sampradāy*, 1: 130. It is found in the sectarian library at Kankarauli.

6. Gupta, *Aṣṭachāp*, pp. 129–30. The manuscript is preserved in the Sarasvatī Bhaṇḍār at Kankarauli.

7. Vrajeśvar Varmā, *Sūr-Mīmāṃsā*, pp. 30–31. Another reason for doubting the manuscript's authenticity is that its date coincides exactly with the year of Gokulnāth's death. If one had been searching for a date that would fit this document into sectarian history precisely where it ought to belong, *vikram* 1697 would have been the obvious candidate.

8. Hariharnāth Ṭaṇḍan, *Vārtā-Sāhitya*, p. 128.

ends by describing the intimate contact that the poet had with the two great leaders of the sect, Vallabha and Viṭṭhalnāth. To this *vārtā* Harirāy added a considerable commentary. Most of it was intended to answer questions that might occur to members of the Sampradāy who were accustomed to a more developed theology than was available at the time the *vārtā* itself was written. Harirāy injected these brief clarifications into the *vārtā* wherever such puzzles might arise. At the beginning, however, he was more expansive, supplying a lengthy description of the childhood of the blind poet, since the *vārtā* itself had said nothing on the subject. These are the stories—evidently current in his day—that we have summarized above. As Harirāy tells them, they prepare the way for a dramatic confrontation between Sūr and Vallabha, his guru-to-be, and with that the *vārtā* proper begins. Rejoining the story at this point, then, we follow the *vārtā* itself.

At an unspecified time after Sūr had ensconced himself at Gaughāṭ, Vallabha and his entourage arrived on the scene. The *vārtā* supplies no motive for Vallabha's visit to such an uncelebrated place; it merely states that he arrived from his home at the sacred confluence of the Rivers Ganges and Jumna at Allahabad, or to be precise Aḍel. On hearing that Vallabha had come, Sūr charged his disciples to find out when the best time for a meeting would be, and once Vallabha had bathed and eaten, Sūr and his coterie approached.

The encounter altered the course of Sūr's life. The poet prostrated himself before the philosopher and Vallabha bade him sing for the assembly. When Sūr obeyed, intoning two songs of humble petition to the Lord, the master was strangely unimpressed. In some of the most famous sentences in the *vārtā,* he confronted the poet with a rebuff and a challenge: "Sūr, what's the point in simpering like that? You should describe God's playful story [*bhagavadlīlā*] instead."[9] Sūr was so overwhelmed by this directive that he simply confessed he did not know what Vallabha was talking about. Vallabha answered the request implicit in Sūr's words by sending him off to bathe and welcoming him back with a rite of initiation, making the poet his pupil and a member of the Sampradāy. Then he explained to Sūr the whole of the *Subodhinī,* his Sanskrit commentary on the *Bhāgavata Purāṇa,* until the divine *līlā* was manifest in his heart.

Thus transformed, the new Sūr Dās was ready to sing again,

9. *Vārtā*, p. 405.

and after a poem giving expression to the joy he felt at his metamorphosis, he responded to Vallabha's request by singing of Krishna's childhood. He began with the very day Krishna was born, describing the happiness throughout Braj that day, and as one turns the pages of the *vārtā* many of the most beloved incidents in Krishna's childhood are related in song, until finally Sūr celebrates the love between Krishna and Rādhā in the full flowering of adolescence. The biography is arranged in part so as to make Sūr's life a backdrop for his description of Krishna's life. The poet's own history and his poetry to the god are interspersed. Once Sūr has sung his songs of Krishna's birth, for instance, the *Vārtā* transports him to Gokul, the site of Krishna's infancy. It was in Gokul, according to the *Vārtā*, that Sūr described in song how the Lord appeared as a tiny child, and Vallabha was responsible for taking him there. He wanted to show Sūr the image of Navanītapriyajī, the child Krishna who was so fond of newly churned butter. After that they went on to the great temple of Braj, situated atop Mount Govardhan and dedicated to Krishna as the lord of the mountain, Govardhannāthjī. The *Vārtā* says that Vallabha had been arranging for the refurbishment of the temple.[10] (One deduces that it had recently come into the hands of his community).[11] He instructed Sūr to join the musical staff there and the poet complied. It is at this point in the *Vārtā* that mention is made of the thousands of poems Sūr began to compose. The implication is that the impetus for his creativity was his encounter with Vallabha, and that the form in which it is preserved is the liturgy of the Sampradāy.

Once this basic statement has been made about the conditions under which Sūr's poetry was generated, the narrative can proceed episodically. The second chapter is didactic. It provides a legendary context for a poem of Sūr in which life is compared to a game of *caupaḍ,* a board game like parcheesi that sometimes involves gambling. Sūr encounters a group of men playing the game,

10. The term is *samarāyo* (*Vārtā,* p. 409), which apparently refers to the decoration of the temple rather than its construction (cf. Barz, *Vallabhācārya,* p. 116).

11. Formerly it had been in the hands of Bengalis. See Kṛṣṇadās Kavirāj, *Caitanya-caritāmṛta, madhya-līlā,* chap. 4, and the Vallabhite account transparently intended to undercut an earlier Gauḍīya claim to the shrine, in *Śrī Govardhannāth jī ke Prākaṭya kī Vārtā,* secs. 8 and 30–31. Cf. Charlotte Vaudeville, "The Govardhan Myth in Northern India," *Indo-Iranian Journal* 22 (1980): 22, 31, 40, 43–45; and, for a relevant passage in the *Caurāsī Vaiṣṇavan kī Vārtā* itself, see Barz, *Vallabhācārya,* pp. 212–13.

recites the poem to his disciples, and is provided with an occasion to expound its symbolic import when his followers do not grasp it immediately. In the course of his doing so the reader is also instructed about details of inner meaning that would not have been clear from a simple hearing of the poem.

The third and fourth chapters concern the Moghul emperor Akbar, patron of the arts (1542–1605 A.D.), who is said to have been so entranced by the poetry of Sūr that he demanded to meet the author. On a journey through Mathura he sent for Sūr, who happened to be in the city. He treated him with great respect, but tested his fealty to Krishna by requesting that he compose a poem for Akbar himself, as would have been expected at court. Sūr responded with a poem whose refrain declared that he had no room in his heart for anyone but Krishna, and with that he passed the test. But Akbar raised another matter. How could a blind man say—as Sūr had done in the final line, the one bearing his own oral signature—that his eyes were dying with thirst for the sight of Syām (Krishna)? To this Sūr answers that the sort of eye of which he is speaking is not the normal kind but rather an eye that is in God's possession. Such an eye has a special property: though constantly flooded with the sight of God, it always thirsts for more. No more succinct defense of his blindness could have been possible, and the boon it earns is the same as the one he was able to obtain from his parents years before when they too, suddenly, became his patrons. All Sūr wants is to be free of anything that would distract him from his singular loyalty to Krishna: he begs Akbar to let him go, once and for all.

Akbar swallows his imperial pride and complies, but continues as a great connoisseur of Sūr's poetry. Indeed he bids everyone in the empire to send in poems of Sūr for the royal collection, promising substantial remuneration, but he notes that not all of the harvest this reaps seems genuine and devises a test to separate authentic compositions from imitations. When a certain Pundit Kavīśvar (whose artificial-sounding name means "lord among poets") submits a poem of his own on the claim that it is Sūr's and awaits reimbursement, Akbar commands that a genuine poem be brought as a standard of measure. Both the authentic poem and Kavīśvar's forgery are submerged in water; the one survives undampened, and the other is ruined.

The next two chapters underscore Sūr's special fondness for the child Krishna and use that rubric to touch again on the theme of blindness and true vision. In chapter five we learn that Sūr slipped off to Gokul whenever he could be relieved of his duties at the temple of Govardhannāth, to catch a glimpse of Navanītapriyajī and to sing hymns of Krishna's early infancy. His cradle songs were particularly stimulated by a Sanskrit verse that Viṭṭhalnāth, Vallabha's son and the guardian of Navanītapriyajī, had composed on the subject and explained to Sūr. It was also in Gokul, as chapter six relates, that the sons of Viṭṭhalnāth, including the man who is supposed to have compiled the *Vārtā* itself, determined to test Sūr's divine eye. They had noted that Sūr always seemed able to describe the image of Navanītapriyajī just as they dressed him every day, so one day they clothed him in such an unusual manner that they doubted Sūr's inner eye would be able to follow. They failed to clothe the image of Krishna at all, merely draping him with pearl garlands and a few other ornaments. But Sūr was blind to their mischief. Undisturbed, he described the exact regalia of the day in song, only pausing to remark that it was an especially wonderful display.

In the next three chapters we find Sūr back at Mount Govardhan, and there, too, great attention is paid to the miracles his blindness can work. In one episode his eyes stimulate a sort of reflexive magic. It is midday, time to eat, and the boy who cares for Sūr and smoothes his way in the material world—one Gopāl, a name that is also a title of Krishna—has gone off to fill his master's little water pot, when a chunk of food gets caught in the poet's throat. He gasps and gags and reaches for water to wash it down, but the boy has tarried on the way, stopping to chat with some devotees. In an instant, nonetheless, Sūr's want is supplied. Seeing that the earthly Gopāl has wandered off, the divine Gopāl steps in—Govardhannāthjī himself—substituting his own golden water pot for Sūr's poor ordinary one. Such an extremity could not have befallen a man with sight, so there would have been no occasion for the loan of the holy vessel. It is only Sūr's blindness that makes such a remarkable reward possible, and there is much amazement when the golden pot is found in his possession.

In a second episode the poet's blindness plays a more direct role: he is blind to the worldly shows that captivate others, and he sees the truth that others do not. The story concerns a merchant who owns a store at the base of Mount Govardhan and caters to the pilgrim trade, but himself only masquerades as a genuine Vaiṣṇava devotee. Although he is always careful to find out how Govardhannāthjī is clothed each day from the first worshippers who return from the temple, he never has time to climb the mountain himself. One cannot serve both God and Mammon, and his busiest hours are just those in which the temple is open. It takes someone with Sūr's special acuity to perceive the fraud, and he threatens to broadcast his discovery to the world unless the storekeeper will begin to see the Lord for himself. The greedy merchant balks and procrastinates in a series of episodes narrated with an expansive, self-confessing humor that betrays just how close the merchant classes are to the lifeblood of the Sampradāy. Ultimately, of course, Sūr wins, bringing the merchant to Vallabhite justice—a vision of Govardhannāthjī and a consequent euphoria that make him seek immediate initiation at the hands of none other than Viṭṭhalnāth himself, who has now become head of the community. Thus a blind man is responsible for giving sight to the sighted.

In the ninth chapter the *Vārtā* explicitly recognizes Sūr's preeminence among the poets of Braj by reporting how the other favorites of the Sampradāy would gather around him to be instructed in their art by attending to his compositions. Often the poems he is said to have recited on such occasions have to do with the life of devotion and religious community: they are not just examples but precepts. One time the gathering is especially intent, for Sūr's death is in the wings and there is not much time left. In chapter ten we see the despair this causes the poet himself, for he had wanted to compose 125,000 poems to Krishna and has succeeded in generating only 100,000. There ensues the story of how he goes to sleep one night weighed down with this thought and wakes the next morning to find the remainder supplied. Krishna has appeared to him in a dream during the night and declared that he will write the rest himself. And so it happens: Sūr receives 25,000 poems whose last lines contain as their signature not merely his own name but the specific designation "Sūr Syām," that is, Sūr's Syām, Krishna himself.

In the eleventh and final chapter Sūr withdraws from the world that he set out to join. He leaves Mount Govardhan for the nearby village of Parāsolī, which the *Vārtā* says is the spot where Krishna performed the incomparable *rās līlā,* his circle dance with the milkmaids (*gopī*s) of Braj and especially Rādhā. Harirāy adds that each of the *aṣṭachāp* was associated especially with one of the eight directional points surrounding Mount Govardhan—a physical expression of their encompassing role in the liturgy—and Parāsolī was Sūr's. This extra association, however, dilutes the effect of the *Vārtā*'s original reference to Parāsolī. Not until Sūr's last days, according to the *Vārtā,* did he sing of the wondrously beautiful union of Rādhā and Krishna, which was consummated in the *rās līlā.* And that was the state of eternal harmony into which he was incorporated at death. The union of Rādhā and Krishna was to become his as well, for it is said that he died beholding them as a pair entwined (*jugal svarūp*). This was the culmination of the spiritual service (*mānasī sevā*) in which, the *Vārtā* reminds us, Sūr was always absorbed.[12] Because he was blind, he could not tend and pamper an image of Krishna as normal devotees—all of them householders—are expected to do. But his service of song was a full compensation.

Nevertheless, the *Vārtā* does not leave its reader with the sense that Sūr's devoted service to God is on a higher plane than what the rest of the well-structured Vallabhite community and its leaders perform. Vallabha and now Viṭṭhalnāth, examplary householders, serve their image-deities with the greatest care, making sure that they exhibit a visual brilliance commensurate with the splendor that Krishna radiates eternally and supernally. When the merchant is saved, he does not become a disciple of Sūr's. Though it is Sūr who rescues him from his errant ways, he does so not by teaching him "spiritual service" but by anchoring him in a tradition of worship that definitely involves the senses, though it transforms them. He takes him to the scion of the Sampradāy and to the temple of Govardhannāth, where the finest attention is given to the physical details of serving God. Sūr's own salvation came by contact with the same tradition, at the hands of the founder himself.

Now the time has come to complete the circle, and the *Vārtā* grants Sūr a last audience with his guru's successor. Sūr has already drifted into a sort of premortuary sleep when Viṭṭhalnāth arrives, and Viṭṭhalnāth must address him before he stirs. Once called, Sūr starts awake and prostrates himself before the master. Poignantly, considering all that he has "seen," the old poet observes that he has been watching for Viṭṭhalnāth (but has not seen him approach), and thanks him for coming to grant his devotee one last chance to see him (*darśan*). Once that is accomplished, Sūr's concentration is ready to shift to absolute truths, to Rādhā and Krishna, but Viṭṭhalnāth's disciples detain the poet with one last question.

It is a crucial one, for it returns the story to where it began, to

12. *Vārtā,* pp. 440–41.

Vallabha, whom the Sampradāy understands to have been himself a complete avatar of Krishna, and who was Sūr's personal guru. Why, they ask, in a body of poetry that measures in the hundred thousands (*lakṣāvidhi*),[13] did Sūr never address a single poem to his own teacher? Such would have been more than customary. Sūr responds in two ways. First he invents just such a poem, one in which he prostrates himself at the feet of Vallabha. It is in no way out of character because Vallabha, meaning "beloved," is also one of Krishna's titles, and the double-entendre makes it fit. But Sūr makes another response as well, more immediate and more telling. He replies that *all* of his poems were dedicated to his guru, since Vallabha is as close to Krishna as is Rādhā herself. That is, they are one and the same. And with that, according to the *Vārtā,* Sūr turned to the divine pair in song and "went off and grasped their play,"[14] leaving Viṭṭhalnāth to commit the poet's empty body to the fire.

THE LOGIC OF THE *VĀRTĀ*

At the heart of the *Vārtā*'s account of Sūr's life is the poet's blindness. It provides the principal metaphor for his sanctity and was obviously the core of the folk tradition regarding him. Harirāy had ample access to stories of Sūr's infirmity in composing his introduction, and additional accounts have been preserved by other authors. Among these, two of the best known share a common purpose: to present Sūr's blindness not as an accident of fate but as a condition of grace that he deliberately chose. Neither account judges Sūr to have been blind from birth. According to one, he plucked out his own eyes when he saw what devastation was being wrought on him by their attachment to a particularly beautiful woman. With the eyes gone, he knew he would be able to concentrate his gaze on the beauties that faith reveals.[15] According to the other, preserved in Miyā̃sinh's *Bhaktavinod,* Sūr once had the misfortune to stumble into a deep well and was not rescued until

13. Ibid., p. 438.
14. Ibid., p. 440.
15. Vrajeśvar Varmā explains that this legend originally was told in connection with a certain Vilvamañgal Sūrdās, son of a Devśarmā Brahmin of Krishnabenā village, and was only later transferred to the great Sūr Dās. It has also been associated with Sūrdās Madanmohan (*Sūr-Mīmāṃsā*, p. 23). And the type is common; a famous version is used to explain why Tulsī Dās left his wife.

Krishna himself took the matter in hand, pulling the poet out of the hole. Sūr was so dazzled by the living spectacle of his Lord that he begged him to remove his visual faculties, so that they would never behold anything less; and Krishna complied.[16]

Originally this story supplied the poet with a rather different background than the one Harirāy reports. The *Bhaktavinod* states simply that Sūr, who had been a friend of Krishna in a former life, was born into a Brahmin family in the Mathura region and became famous as a poet in his youth. In more recent times, however, this story has been conflated with Harirāy's account so as to reinforce natural blindness with an element of volition. One hears that Sūr was indeed blind from birth—why else would he have fallen into a well? The story goes on to say that when Krishna rescued him, he restored him not only to earth but to sight, and it was at that point that Sūr elected blindness, not wishing ever to see anything other than his Lord.[17] This account of Sūr's blindness not only preserves the purity of vision upon which so much hinges in the *Vārtā* but strengthens it: even when Sūr sees, he sees nothing but Krishna.

Such hagiography has a telling effect. It enriches precept with practice, providing the many millions of people who have heard Sūr's poems, and been delighted and instructed by them, with a background against which the verse takes on additional life. Other lives of poet-saints did the same, and an early collection, the *Bhaktamāl* of Nābhājī (ca. 1600 A.D.), with its commentary by Priyā Dās (1712 A.D.), contains hundreds of entries. Many of these, including Sūr's, are very brief—mere panegyric citations. Others, like that of the poetess Mīrā Bāī, all but overshadow the poetry they

16. Charlotte Vaudeville, *Pastorales par Soûr-Dâs*, p. 31; Varmā, *Sūr-Mīmāṃsā*, p. 25. The *Bhaktavinod* is a late commentary on the *Bhaktamāl*, on which see below. A variant of this story is recorded in Mahipati's *Bhaktavijaya*. According to that account, Sūr was born blind because in a past life as Akrūr, the messenger sent from Mathura to summon Krishna away from Braj, he caused the *gopīs* great grief. His misfortune in his current life was to repay the hardship he caused them when Krishna was alive on earth. Becoming aware of this fact, Sūr tearfully bewails his fault, and in response the merciful Krishna restores his sight. At that point the tale turns to what the *Bhaktavinod* reports: Sūr, on seeing the divine form, asks that he be blinded again so that he will not have to endure lesser sights. See Justin E. Abbott and N. R. Godbole, trans., *Stories of Indian Saints: English Translation of Mahipatti's Marathi Bhaktavijaya*, 2: 16–18.

17. See, for instance, Pushpa Bharati, *Soordas, the Blind Bard Who Sang about Lord Krishna*, pp. 13–14.

are intended to accompany, and in Rajasthan today one can as easily hear songs about Mīrā as songs attributed to her.[18] Sūr's blindness is not quite so celebrated as Mīrā's struggle against husband and family for the sake of her devotion to Krishna; but just as the story of the noblewoman's costly indifference to the world deepens the stubborn, intense effect of her poetry, so the legend of Sūr's blindness sets just the needed perspective for his own poetic achievement.

Sūr is celebrated, more than anything else, for his "naturalness" (*svābhāviktā*), for the ease and spontaneity with which he is able to introduce vignettes, proverbs, even clichés from the common life into Krishna's divine realm. His portraits of Krishna's childhood in particular are filled with carefully observed details—the way a child will wince and whimper when he encounters a pepper in his food, the clever prevarications of which he is capable when caught in a little act of thievery, the exact motions and emotions that come to play in a game of ball or hide-and-seek—and they account for much of the esteem in which the *Sūr Sāgar,* "Sūr's Ocean" of poetry, is held.[19] To the eyes of faith, of course, this is not just poetic artifice. It is not that Sūr has observed the world around him and immortalized it by using it to clothe Krishna. Rather, he has detected the correspondences between the divine childhood and what we know in the profane realm. Sūr's blindness, moreover, eliminates any possibility that this wealth of familiar, earthly detail—far beyond what earlier, more classical documents about Krishna had contained—might be peripheral or even illegitimate additions. There is only one way Sūr could have gathered his impressions of the world: if he saw it at all, he saw it in Krishna himself.

To this basic rationale for recounting Sūr's saintly life, the *Vārtā* adds another: it is concerned to present Sūr in a Vallabhite context. Indeed, from the perspective of the Vallabhite community, the only true guarantee of Sūr's holiness is his contact with the master; that is what permits his canonization. And to that end, with considerable artistry, the *Vārtā* recasts stories of the blind poet that must have been current in Braj at the time of its composition. There may be a few isolated clues about the poet's life in the *Bhak-*

18. E.g., *Inde. Rajasthan. Musiciens professionels populaires,* vol. 1, recorded by Geneviève Dournon-Taurelle.

19. On this aspect of Sūr's creativity, see Hargulāl, *Sūrsāgar mẽ Lok Jīvan,* especially pp. 145–49.

tamāl and Muslim sources, as we shall see presently, but as for the stories about him, all we know must be deduced from the *Vārtā* itself.[20] Such deductions, however, are not impossible. One can sometimes see traces of earlier, nonsectarian tales beneath what the *Vārtā* has so carefully redesigned.

Two examples of this process concern *vārtā*s strictly speaking—"conversations" that Sūr is reported to have had, one with the temporal ruler, the other with the spiritual. In both cases there is an element of convolution that makes one wonder whether the *Vārtā*'s account does not mask an earlier, simpler story. As regards Akbar, it is understandable that popular tradition, which remembered the poet and the emperor as contemporaries, should hold that they actually met. Perhaps they did—who can say? In the absence of firm dates for Sūr Dās, it is impossible even to judge whether the possibility existed. But the important fact, some generations after Sūr's lifetime, was that if the two did not meet, they certainly should have, since Akbar, though a Muslim, was famed for his ecumenical world view and ought to have been interested in the devotional raptures of the great Braj poet. Later inhabitants of Braj, consolidating their own sense of history, provided the occasion for such a meeting if it did not already exist.[21]

In so doing they became contributors to a process that continues today: recent popular biographies present meetings between Sūr and other approximately contemporary figures whose work or stance was later seen as relevant to his own. Nowadays one reads, for example, that Sūr also encountered Tulsī Dās, the other founding father of Hindi literature, even though Tulsī was very much his junior and lived, according to most traditions, far away.[22] They discussed their similarities and differences, with Sūr persuading Tulsī to devote some of his poetry to Krishna (as he did in his *Śrīkṛṣṇagītāvalī*) and Tulsī convincing Sūr to sing, on occa-

20. The furthest one can go is to suggest that they were included by Gokulnāth in the collection he called *Vacanāmṛt*, referring to the "ambrosial words" of Viṭṭhalnāth. Hariharnāth Ṭaṇḍan believes that this collection was the basis for the *Caurāsī Vaiṣṇavan kī Vārtā*, but does not review the manuscript evidence that would be necessary to show that this is so. See Ṭaṇḍan, *Vārtā-Sāhitya*, pp. 105, 151–52. He bases his information on the Gujarati edition and translation of the *Caurāsī Vaiṣṇavan kī Vārtā* made by Mahādev Rāmcandra Jajuṣṭhe and Lallūbhāī Chaganlāl in 1974.

21. The same thing happened with Mīrā Bāī, the story of whose encounter with Akbar is recorded in Priyā Dās's commentary on the *Bhaktamāl*. Nābhājī, *Śrī Bhaktamāl*, p. 721.

22. Bharati, *Soordas*, p. 29.

sion, of Rām (which he also did, and for which the Vallabhite legends provide no easy explanation).

The much earlier story of Sūr's meeting with Akbar, however, has as its moral a certain sort of victory rather than a rapprochement. Its simple point is that the emperor, for all his worldly wherewithal, had to come to Sūr, rather than the other way around; and Sūr further reveals his defiance of every rule but Krishna's by refusing to compose a poem in adulation of temporal authority. This must have been the story as it was remembered traditionally, for the *Vārtā* builds on it with an additional remark that does not quite fit. Akbar was remembered as having been especially munificent with the Sampradāy[23]—Harirāy's commentary makes it plain that the emperor's Muslim birth was only the consequence of an involuntary error in a past existence as a pious Hindu[24]—so there was an urge to rescue him from any possibly adversary relation to the great poet. Therefore the *Vārtā* reports, in a detail that vitiates the inherent drama of the encounter, that Akbar knew he was testing Sūr when he asked for a personal encomium, and rejoiced when it was not forthcoming.[25]

A similar and even more telling complication is embedded in the story of Sūr's meeting with Vallabha. As the *Vārtā* relates it, Sūr was the one to go to Vallabha; anything else would have been an offense to sectarian eyes. But considerable refinement was required to make the story come out that way.[26] It is plain even in the *Vārtā*'s rendering that if one sees the encounter in its larger dimensions, it was Vallabha who came to Sūr, not the other way around. It was he who traveled to Gaughāṭ, and the need of Vallabha and his party to bathe seems a thin rationalization for their appearance on the threshold of Sūr's durbar. For bathing and prayer, any spot on the Jumna would have sufficed. Furthermore, no attempt is made to cover up the fact that Sūr had a considerable following. Perhaps the *Vārtā* could afford to retain this historical fact (or, at least, earlier tradition) because once Sūr's disciples were converted they simply enhanced the glory of the Sampradāy. But it seems very likely that the earlier, nonsectarian tradition had Vallabha coming to hear the most famous poet in the land soon after he arrived in Braj.

23. Indeed, the records of the Muslim court show that Akbar honored Viṭṭhalnāth with donations attested in two *farmāns*. See D. Gupta, *Aṣṭachāp*, 1: 32.

24. *Vārtā*, p. 418.

25. Ibid., p. 417.

26. Ibid., pp. 404–5.

Other facets of the narrative show equally clearly the pains the author of the *Vārtā* had to take to incorporate Sūr in the Sampradāy. We know from an independent source that in some circles Sūr's collected poetry had come to be called the *Sūr Sāgar* by 1640,[27] and the manuscript that reveals it betrays no obvious debt to the Sampradāy. Evidently this, reflecting the poet's greatness, had become the common designation for Sūr's work—perhaps only recently at the time the *Vārtā* was written—and the *Vārtā* was anxious to claim it as its own. According to the *Vārtā,* Vallabha himself was responsible for coining the term, but the circumstances are rather awkward. The master refers not to Sūr's poetry but to the author himself as "Sūr's Ocean."[28] In a phrasing that would be more apt if not more felicitous (it includes an Urdu word), both Vallabha and Viṭṭhalnāth call Sūr "the ship [*jahāz*] of the *puṣṭimārga,*"[29] the latter term being the official label for the Sampradāy and its theology: "the path of grace."[30] But that is to put the general concept, "Sūr Sāgar," in the obvious service of sectarian parlance. And as the *Vārtā* concludes, Sūr himself is made, as it were, to bequeath his oceanic mantle to the sect itself. In his final meeting with Viṭṭhalnāth, before he is to depart this world, he bestows upon the leader of the Sampradāy what, coming from him, is a special dignity. He calls him an "ocean of mercy" (*kṛpāsindhu*).[31]

Similar shifts of interpretation are effected in regard to individual poems from the *Sūr Sāgar,* as quoted in the *Vārtā.* Sometimes the *Vārtā*'s attempts to provide etiologies for Sūr's poems are not specifically aimed at consolidating his ties with the Sampradāy (as for example the poem concerning the game of *caupaḍ*) but often enough they are. An instance calculated to show that Sūr's compositions were inspired by what Vallabha taught him about the *Bhāgavata Purāṇa* is particularly glaring because it is so carefully introduced. It concerns the invocatory verse in the *Subodhinī,* Vallabha's commentary on the *Purāṇa,* which the *Vārtā* quotes. In this verse Vallabha offers his veneration to Viṣṇu, recumbent upon the Milk Ocean at the beginning of time and accompanied by his consort Lakṣmī, who serves him with a thousand blandishments

27. The colophon of manuscript U1, dated *vikram* 1697, so designates it. On this and other early manuscripts of the *Sūr Sāgar,* see chap. 2, below.

28. *Vārtā,* p. 414. This usage is justified much later in the *Vārtā,* on p. 439.

29. Ibid., pp. 422, 436, 437.

30. For a brief explanation, see Barz, *Vallabhācārya,* pp. 80–93.

31. *Vārtā,* p. 436.

(*lakṣmīsahasralīlābhiḥ*). The *Vārtā* declares that this passage provided the inspiration for a poem of Sūr's that has a rather different spirit and makes no direct reference either to Viṣṇu or to his reclining pose. The *Vārtā* makes the connection solely because the word *sahasra* (thousand) in Sūr's poem follows directly after the word *śrī,* an alternate designation of Lakṣmī, as if to imitate the Sanskrit compound beginning *lakṣmīsahasra.* But this is a slender thread. Not only does one of the words actually used differ, but the syntax and meaning are entirely divergent.[32]

Other poems that are used to demonstrate a connection with the sect's founder reveal a different kind of gymnastic, of which the poem about Vallabha himself is an example.[33] Whatever one may think about the likelihood that the term *vallabh* refers to the scion of the Sampradāy rather than to Krishna, there can be no disputing that the poem in which it occurs is found in none of the early manuscript collections of Sūr's poems, and the same can be said for the great majority of poems quoted in the *Vārtā.* This leads one to suspect that the *vallabh* poem was composed only after the doctrine of Sūr's dependence on the *Bhāgavata* and its revered expositor had been formulated. Another poem, in which explicit mention is made of the *Bhāgavata,* is similarly absent from these early collections.[34]

Furthermore, very few of the early manuscripts are arranged in such a way as to suggest that Sūr's poems of humble petition, the *vinaya* poems, were composed at the beginning of Sūr's career, before he met Vallabha. They are far more often placed at the end than at the beginning,[35] and in some cases they are simply interspersed with the rest as if the editors saw no distinction in principle between narrative and petitionary verse.[36] This, however, would have been unthinkable for the *puṣṭimārga,* whose liturgical theology dictates that in the presence of Krishna there should be no hint of separation from God or the anguish it causes, and therefore no need for petition. Its solution was to insist that Sūr had composed these poems of yearning (*viraha*) and pleading

32. Ibid., pp. 406–7. The poem of Sūr in question is S 337. At another point (pp. 419–20) the *Vārtā* claims that a Sanskrit composition of Viṭṭhalnāth inspired some of Sūr's verse.

33. Ibid., p. 438.

34. Ibid., pp. 430–32, verse 59. At least one passage in the *Sūr Sāgar,* as known in modern editions, clearly did have the *Bhāgavata Purāṇa* as its model (S 1626.7–8), but it too is missing in early manuscripts. Further on this problem, see chap. 2.

35. As in U1, U2, and A1.

36. As in B2 and J2, manuscripts organized by raga.

(*vinaya*) before he met Vallabha; afterward, when he joined the saved and became a sectarian poet, there would have been no occasion.[37]

Finally there is the matter of Sūr's blindness itself. Even that is made to tell a sectarian story, for in the *Vārtā* the ultimate seal of Sūr's sightless perspicacity is that he sees no distinction between Vallabha and Krishna. Others find it necessary to have him spell out this connection—which he does, to serve their needs, with the poem containing the word *vallabh*. But the main point, as the *Vārtā* tells it, is that until Sūr was queried he never saw the possibility of recognizing a cleavage between his Lord and his master at all. He states simply that all his poems to Krishna were by the same token addressed to his guru.[38]

Just in case anyone had missed the point, the commentator Harirāy drives it home in his exegesis of the poem that Sūr does offer to satisfy his questions. Without sectarian embellishment the poem might be translated as follows:

> *With firmness of faith I cling to these feet.*
>
> But for the brilliance that shines from the moonlike
> toes of the Beloved, all the world would be dark.
> Those feet bring salvation; there is no other vessel
> in this worst of all ages that is separate from him.
> Any diverging, any doubleness, is darkness—
> so says Sūr, a worthless disciple.[39]

37. *Viraha* is the term Harirāy uses to designate these poems (p. 403), in contrast to *vinaya*, the term that subsequently became standard. In early manuscripts of the *Sūr Sāgar* a variety of labels are used. The text of the *Vārtā* itself (p. 414) appears to classify this group of poems under the heading *jñān vairāgya*, "wisdom and renunciation." It is telling that the writer of the *Vārtā* does not always remember to devalue these poems in the measure that his own sectarian logic would seem to require. In vaunting the huge size of the *Sūr Sāgar*, he begins with these "wisdom and renunciation" poems and goes on to mention poems recording "all kinds of devotion"—the *bhakti* poems that are often grouped together with *vinaya* compositions. And when he relates Sūr's encounter with Akbar, he makes use of a long poem in the *vinaya* mode (S 325, p. 416).

38. *Vārtā*, p. 438.

39. Ibid; not included in the Sabhā *Sūr Sāgar*. The last line is somewhat problematical. An alternate translation would render *dvividhi ā̃dharō* as "doubly blind," in which case one would probably understand the reference as to the poet's physical blindness on the one hand, suggested by the attention to light in verse 2, and to his spiritual blindness on the other, as implied by the attention to discipline (*sādhan*, translated above as "vessel") in verse 3. The "worthless disciple" (*binā mol ko cero*) is more literally a servant who works without wages.

But Harirāy sees a different meaning. He makes it clear that the doubleness (*dvividhi*) to which Sūr refers is not the failure to give wholehearted fealty to the Beloved (*vallabh*), but the specific failure to recognize that the two possible references of *vallabh*—Vallabha and Krishna—are really one and the same. In paraphrasing, he supplies Sūr a second time with what from a sectarian point of view is the ultimate meaning of his visual incapacity. He has him say, "I am blind to any difference between Govardhannāth [i.e., Krishna] and Vallabha." The implication is that if Sūr, with his ethereal eye, could see no such distinction, there must not be one.

SŪR AND HISTORY

However much one may admire the artistry in the *Vārtā*'s portrait of Sūr, its coherent hagiography, one must also ask what relation it bears to a critically reconstructed picture of the poet. The answer is that the relation is minimal. The *Vārtā* gives several important clues about the legends of Sūr that were current at the time of its composition or shortly before, but it fails to tell us much about the life of the poet himself. On this point even what was evidently the core of the tradition as received by the writer of the *Vārtā*—that Sūr was blind—appears to be fundamentally misleading. To deny Sūr's blindness strikes many Hindus as sheer heresy. It is almost as heinous as the denial of the virgin birth was to many nineteenth-century Christians, for it calls into question the authenticity and purity of a whole tradition, and one should not offer such offense lightly. But after a careful consideration of the sources, comparing the *Vārtā*'s account with information presented in other documents that may shed light on the poet's life, this is indeed the conclusion to which one is forced.

Among these sources, only the *Bhaktamāl* and the *Ā'īn-i-Akbarī* can have been composed before the *Vārtā,* and the material they present is meager. *Chappai* 73 of the *Bhaktamāl* offers general praise of Sūr's poetry—its poetic devices, its wit, its alliteration, and power of description—and asks what poet, on hearing such verse, will not bow his head. *Chappai* 126, in a similarly laudatory vein, connects the name of Sūr Dās to that of Madan Mohan and declares them to be joined like links in a chain.[40] Whether the reference is to two poets, Sūr Dās and another, or to the single figure Sūr

40. Nābhājī, *Śrī Bhaktamāl,* pp. 557, 745–46. In the edition of Narendra Jhā (*Bhaktamāl: Pāṭhānuśīlan evam Vivecan*), these *chappai*s are numbered 72 and 119.

Dās Madanmohan has been debated. The latter option seems more likely, since the pairing of names that is highlighted in the passage on Sūr Dās Madanmohan refers to that of the poet (Sūr Dās) and his chosen deity (Madanmohan, a title of Krishna) rather than to a pairing between the famous Sūr Dās and this other poet of the same name. Certainly this is what was understood by Priyā Dās, who appended his commentary to the *Bhaktamāl* in 1712 A.D.[41] Yet there is room for doubt: the signature of Sūr Dās Madanmohan apparently comes to light for the first time at the end of a manuscript otherwise entirely devoted to poems of Sūr Dās (B2, dated *vikram* 1681, that is, 1624 A.D.). But even then the Sūr Dās Madanmohan poem is treated as a kind of appendix; it is not integrated into the *Sūr Sāgar*.

It is noteworthy that the *Bhaktamāl*'s verse in praise of Sūr Dās says nothing about his blindness, but given that silence, one aspect of what is said becomes particularly tantalizing. The author of the *Bhaktamāl* makes mention of the "divine vision" (*dibi diṣṭi*) by means of which Sūr's heart was able to mirror the playful acts of Krishna. The phrase is enigmatic. Either its author was so familiar with the image of Sūr as a blind poet that he regarded it as something that could be given artful mention only through an oblique reference, or he did not share that image at all. Given his frontal approach to major aspects in the lives of other saints, the possibility that he did not know of Sūr's blindness is a real one. Furthermore, it is striking that Priyā Dās contributed nothing in the way of hagiographical expansion on this *chappai* of Nābhājī. One would have thought that the phrase "divine vision" would have given him a perfect invitation to exposit Sūr's blindness, if indeed he knew of it.

The *Ā'īn-i-Akbarī* takes us into a world quite different from this devotional milieu: it was written in the ambiance of the Moghul court. Composed by Akbar's favorite chronicler, Abu'l Fazl, the *Ā'īn* lists a certain Sūr Dās as nineteenth among the musicians at court.[42] He is identified as the son of one Bābā Rām Dās, who, according to other imperial records, originally came from Gwalior and served at the court of Avadh before coming into Akbar's entourage, where he ranked second in ability only to the emperor's

41. R. D. Gupta, "Priyā Dās, Author of the *Bhaktirasabodhinī*," *Bulletin of the School of Oriental and African Studies* 32, no. 1 (1969): 58–59. See Nabhājī, *Śrī Bhaktamāl*, pp. 746–50.

42. Abū l'Faẓl 'Allāmī, *The Ā'īn-i Akbarī*, trans. H. Blochmann, *ā'īn* 30.60, pp. 681–82.

chief musician, Tānsen.[43] Encouraged by an anonymous couplet preserved in the *Ā'īn,* in which Sūr Dās is said in effect to be the most eminent of Braj poets (the others being Gaṅgā, Balbīr, and Keśav), Charlotte Vaudeville has proposed that Akbar's Sūr Dās is none other than the famed poet whose compositions we know.[44] If true, this would be the only reference to him that has survived from his own lifetime. It would mean that he was at work at court in the closing years of the sixteenth century but, presumably, considering his relatively low ranking among the imperial poets, that his greater fame came somewhat later.

Vaudeville's suggestion is intriguing but not convincing. If Bābā Rām Dās was native to Lucknow or (as one might deduce from Abu'l Fazl) Gwalior, his chief medium of expression might have been Braj Bhāṣā, but the son would have been raised at court and it seems unlikely that his vocabulary would have been as free of Persian terminology as are the poems included in early manuscripts of the *Sūr Sāgar.* I cannot claim to have made an exhaustive list, but in studies of manuscripts predating *vikram* 1764 (1707 A.D.) I have noticed only a dozen or two Persian words.[45] They are much less frequent than in poems attributed to many other poets of the period, and less frequent than in poems later added to the Sūr corpus. It is noteworthy, furthermore, that without exception all manuscripts of the *Sūr Sāgar* preserved from this early period are written in devanagari, not in Persian script, as one might reasonably have expected in a court poet, even one attached to as cosmopolitan a monarch as Akbar.[46]

43. Al Badāonī, *Muntakhabu-t-tawārīkh,* trans., ed. W. H. Lowe, 2: 37.

44. Vaudeville, *Pastorales,* pp. 35–37. An independent consideration of the matter can be found in R. S. McGregor, *Nanddas: The Round Dance of Krishna and Uddhav's Message,* pp. 23–24.

45. Examples are *khūn* (S 198.3 in J4); *dīvāṇ* (235.6, found only in B2); *jori* (for *zor,* 720.4 in B2, B3; other manuscripts lack the verse: B1, U1, B4); *sirdār* (i.e., *sardār,* 834.6, found only in B4); *jān* (2980.4 in all manuscripts, with orthographic variations); and *behāl* (3067.4 in B1, B2, U1, B4, J2, J3, and folio 1 of A1). There are other examples too, but the proportion remains so low as to be remarkable, and often one finds that an Urdu word in the Sabhā version is absent from the relevant manuscripts. This is the case, for instance, with *ṭhāḍhe darbār* in S 1021.5, which reads *gaṭhai hāi dvār* in the only available manuscript, U1. Similarly *khyāl* disappears in S 1441.3; the entire line in which it occurs is absent in B4, the only manuscript to contain the poem. This is also true for the line containing *gumān* (S 2086.3) in B1, B2, U1, and J3. Only B4 has the line, and it reads *gvāl* instead of *gumān.*

46. The first manuscript in nastaliq of which I am aware is that housed in the Bibliothèque Nationale, Paris (Indien no. 824), and dated to 1183 A.H. (1769 A.D., *vikram* 1826).

The *Bhaktamāl* and Muslim sources having been considered, the only early materials to which one can turn for information about Sūr are the compositions attributed to the poet himself. Since there do exist manuscripts from *vikram* 1639 (1582 A.D.) onwards, swelling in size to collections of some fifteen hundred poems by the last quarter of the seventeenth century,[47] they form the only reasonable yardstick against which historical judgments about the poet can be made.[48] And they have the effect of wiping away the most vivid lines—indeed, almost every feature—in traditional portraits of the poet, reducing his personal life to near invisibility.

Take, for instance, the matter of Sūr's ties with Vallabha. An internal analysis of the *Caurāsī Vaiṣṇavan kī Vārtā* has already suggested that many of these were invented after the fact, as part of a tradition that continued to grow until long after the *Vārtā* was complete, until people came to hold such beliefs as that the poet and the philosopher shared the same birth month in the same year.[49] Early manuscripts of the *Sūr Sāgar* fail to supply any further data, hinting nothing about whether the two ever met and casting thorough doubt on whether Sūr was at all indebted to Vallabha's teachings. One looks in vain, in these early poems, for the central terms in Vallabha's theological vocabulary—concepts such as *puṣṭi* (support, nourishment, fulfillment, grace), *nirodha* (restraint, in Vallabha's usage, restricting the focus of one's attention to Krishna), *āvirbhāva* (manifestation), *tirobhāva* (concealment), and *anugraha* (grace). And mention is never made of the general cat-

47. J4, dated *vikram* 1733 (1676 A.D.) contains 1472 *pads* of Sūr Dās.

48. It is well to note that this excludes from consideration a number of works for which Sūr's authorship has been claimed, notably the *Sāhitya Laharī*, the *Sūr Sārāvalī*, and the *Nal Daman*. Vrajeśvar Varmā has advanced telling arguments against the authenticity of the former two (*Sūr-Mīmāṃsā*, pp. 52–72), as claimed by such traditional scholars as Prabhudayāl Mītal in his editions of these works (*Sūrsāgar Sārāvalī*, pp. 18–25, and *Sāhitya Laharī*, pp. 53–60). Varmā's position is given strong support since no manuscripts of any of these works is extant from a period before the nineteenth century. I base this statement on my own searches for manuscripts, and those reported by Javāharlāl Caturvedī and Udayśaṅkar Śāstrī (in reference to his work in collaboration with Mātāprasād Gupta) and in the *Khoj Reports* of the Nāgarīpracāriṇī Sabhā. Caturvedī: *Sūrdās*: *Adhyayan-Sāmagrī*; Śāstrī, interview, Nov. 10, 1975; Nāgarīpracāriṇī Sabhā, *Hastalikhit Hindī Pustakõ kā Saṅkṣipt Vivaraṇ*, and reproduced insofar as they concern the *aṣṭachāp* in D. Gupta, *Aṣṭachāp*, 1: 168–76.

49. Vallabhite tradition holds that Sūr was born ten days after Vallabha, whose birthdate is fixed by the *Vallabh Digvijaya* as the tenth of the waning fortnight of the month of *vaiśākh*, *vikram* 1535 (i.e., in late spring of 1478 A.D.). See Harbanślāl Śarmā, *Sūr aur unkā Sāhitya*, p. 23. For an analysis of the verse in the *Sūr Sārāvalī* that is intended to establish the poet's debt to Vallabha in his own words, see Vaudeville, *Pastorales*, p. 45.

egories under which Vallabha treats the various phases of Krishna's life in Braj: *tāmasa, rājasa,* and *sattva* (rough, passionate, and pure). These terms may appear in Sūr's vocabulary, but never in the sense in which Vallabha uses them. The word *tāmasa,* for example, appears as part of a simple slur made by Krishna's foster mother, Yaśodā, on the quality of the *gopīs*' love for her son, not as the theological category by means of which Vallabha describes the first phase in the *gopīs*', and by extension all devotees', approach to Krishna: the rough, stubborn, self-willed stage. As used by Sūr the term is invective rather than descriptive, and without systematic intent.[50] Only one item could be said vividly to characterize the language of both Sūr and Vallabha: the designation of Krishna as *antaryāmī,* "clairvoyant, perceptive of what is within." But since the term is widely used, Sūr need hardly have borrowed it from Vallabha. Finally, there is the crucial fact that Rādhā, such an important presence in the *Sūr Sāgar,* simply does not figure in the writings of Vallabha. Indeed, if technical terms and stock images are to be taken as indexes of the relation between the poet and his patron philosopher, one is embarrassed to find that Sūr is perhaps as much indebted to Śaṅkara, whom Vallabha seeks time and again to refute, as to Śaṅkara's critic. Recently, in fact, a book that was written with the specific intention of showing the imprint of Vallabha's philosophy on Sūr Dās came reluctantly at several points to this very conclusion.[51]

One may answer, as some modern leaders of the Sampradāy do,[52] that it is the general influence of Vallabha that is pervasive in the *Sūr Sāgar,* not any particular teaching. But there seems little convincing evidence of the influence either of Vallabha or of his successors on early poems attributed to Sūr. Members of the Sampradāy have often pointed to Sūr's great affection for the child Krishna who was especially fond of butter as an indication of his membership in the Vallabhite community, and indeed Sūr's butter-thief poems enjoy an unusual fame.[53] The argument is, as the *Vārtā* itself proclaims, that Sūr's fondness for the butter thief in poetry was a reflection of his devotion in real life to Navanītapriyajī, the image in Viṭṭhalnāth's charge at Gokul. The *Vārtā* says

50. Similarly there is nothing technical in Sūr's use of such common words as *doṣ* (fault, sin) or *maryādā* (*marjād*: propriety, good behavior), terms that bear considerable weight in Vallabha's systematic writings.

51. Nārāyaṇ Prasād Vājpeyī: *Sūr Dās ke Dārśanik Vicār,* e.g., pp. 47–50, 71, 83.

52. E.g., Śyām Gosvāmī, interview, Bombay, Sept. 4, 1975.

53. See John Stratton Hawley, *Krishna, the Butter Thief,* chaps. 3–5.

the poet's attachment was so strong that Sūr would slip away from his duties on Mount Govardhan whenever he had the chance to worship there.[54] Such a line of reasoning collapses, however, in face of the likelihood that images of the butter thief were quite common in the Braj of Sūr's day, and none of the visual features that would have distinguished Navanītapriyajī from similar images is evident in the early poems of the *Sūr Sāgar*.[55]

The case is even more clear-cut in regard to Govardhannāthjī, whom Sūr is supposed to have described at such uncommon length. Nowhere among the many poems describing Krishna's appearance in the early *Sūr Sāgar* are lines that imply a knowledge of the distinctive facial appearance of this image, now installed at Nathdvara, or the distinctive patterns according to which he is customarily clothed. True, Krishna's arm is sometimes said in these early poems to be raised aloft, as is that of Govardhannāthjī, but never in contexts where it would not be otherwise expected. And the epithets that have to do with Krishna's lifting up the mountain are certainly not among Sūr's favorites, though he does on occasion use them. If epithets were to be one's guide, it would make more sense to ascribe to Mīrā Bāī a role at the temple on Mount Govardhan than to Sūr Dās: the mountain-lifter (*giridhar*) is her favorite image of Krishna.

Nor can one find reliable traces of the Vallabhite liturgy, though a recently published book has tried to show that one can, and that the *Sūr Sāgar* took its shape in response to the liturgical needs of the Sampradāy.[56] A look at poems contained in early manuscripts fails to confirm the thesis. Many of the poems of Sūr that now figure prominently in Vallabhite worship are not even present, and if they are, the ragas to which they are assigned often suggest that they cannot always have been sung at the time of day for which they are now prescribed. In fact, even the liturgical orders of the present day, associated with various branches of the community, differ as to when individual poems ought to be sung,[57] so

54. Dharmanārāyaṇ Ojhā has so argued in *Sūr-Sāhitya mẽ Puṣṭimārgīya Sevā Bhāvanā*, pp. 183–86.

55. Hawley, *Butter Thief*, pp. 74–95.

56. Ojhā, *Sūr-Sāhitya*, pp. 358–470. To the contrary, Udayśaṅkar Śāstrī, "Sūrsāgar kī Sāmagrī kā Saṃkalan aur uskā Saṃpādan," *Bhāratīya Sāhitya* 17, no. 1–2 (1972): 93.

57. I am grateful to Śyām Gosvāmī of Bombay, Amṛtlāl Kīrtankār of Nathdvara, Śyām Bhāī of Gokul, Śyāmsundar Kīrtankār of Kota; and Rādhākrishna Kīrtankār of Nathdvara for discussions illuminating this point (interviews, Aug. 24; Sept. 4, 15, and 17; and Nov. 7 and 22, 1975); and to the latter two for permission to

that to argue back from contemporary liturgy to ancient composition is inherently difficult. Even in broad outline it is impossible to discern the Vallabhite liturgical calendar as the pattern according to which Sūr's poems were ordered in any of the old manuscripts. And the many *vinaya* poems are ritually inappropriate in any case.

Similarly discouraging results appear in regard to Sūr's caste origins. As Vrajeśvar Varmā and, subsequently, Charlotte Vaudeville have argued, Sūr's criticisms of religious authorities suggest that it is unlikely he himself was among their number. Implicit denigration of Brahmins, together with other passing slurs, can be found in both earlier and later strata of the *Sūr Sāgar.*[58] Can one, then, show the opposite, as Vaudeville has tried to do, arguing that Sūr was not a Brahmin but rather a member of a lowly minstrel caste called *ḍhāḍhī*s? Vaudeville rests her case on four poems in which Sūr presents himself as such a *ḍhāḍhī,* saying that he has come to sing at the birth-celebrations heralding the arrival of Krishna in Braj.[59] However, only one of these poems bears an early pedigree (S 653). Nor is Sūr the only poet-singer to cast himself in this role for this occasion. Most of the other members of the eight seals do the same.[60] It appears that this is a poetic convention rather than an autobiographical confession. Furthermore, it is doubtful that Sūr's musicianship was strictly dictated on the basis of caste allegiance. After all, the Āḻvārs of South India were all singers, but they are said to have belonged to a wide range of castes. And as we shall see at the end of this study, Sūr's musi-

photograph hymnbooks (*sevā praṇālī*) used in the temples of Mathurādhīś and Viṭṭhalnāth that prove the point. Cf. also Śāstrī, "Sūrsāgar kī Sāmagrī," p. 92. The shape of the earliest dated *sevā praṇālī* that has come to my attention—an anthology in the possession of Nareś Candra Bansal of Kasganj that bears the date *vikram* 1750 (1693 A.D.)—suggests that the Vallabhite liturgy was still being defined at the end of the seventeenth century.

58. Varmā, *Sūr-Mīmāṃsā*, pp. 30–34; Vaudeville, *Pastorales*, pp. 36–37. There is the further point that Harirāy's designation of Sūr as a Sārasvat Brahmin suggests a vagueness about his precise caste standing, and it conflicts with other traditions that take Sūr for a Rāv or Bhāt (Varmā, *Sūr-Mīmāṃsā*, p. 36; Vaudeville, *Pastorales*, pp. 33–34).

59. Vaudeville, *Pastorales*, p. 37. The poems are S 653, 654, 655, and 657; and another one, in which the poet declares that he is of humble caste (S 196) is also relevant. In addition one might bring to bear S 961, in which the poet represents himself as a *ḍhāḍhī* at the birth of Rām, but it too is absent from the early manuscripts.

60. So Varmā, *Sūr-Mīmāṃsā*, p. 38, and Ojhā, *Sūr Sāhitya*, pp. 425–27.

cianship had a meaning for him that extended far beyond the boundaries of caste.

What then remains of the *Vārtā*'s account? We have still to consider two of its most basic assertions: that Sūr was blind and that his output was gargantuan. These also prove unfounded when one sees Sūr in the light of the early manuscripts. True, a relatively large body of verse was collected under his name, but nothing to approach a lakh or a lakh and a quarter; and it seems very doubtful that Sūr himself had these poems committed to writing—making his own collection, as the tenth chapter of the *Vārtā* implies—much less counted them. Manuscripts make it appear instead that in the early years many poems attributed to Sūr circulated orally and independently of one another, until they were collected at different times and places, and in different orders.[61]

As for his blindness, the author or authors of these early poems do not refer to it unambiguously on a single occasion.[62] Passages from three of the poems that appear before about 1700 A.D. have been pointed to as evidence that Sūr was blind, but each of them presents problems of interpretation that make the conclusion untenable, or at least uncertain. In the first instance, both the general and the immediate context make it clear that the blindness the poet bemoans in himself is of a spiritual, not a physical nature (S 198.1–3, found in B4 and J4):

Who could have fallen, Hari, further than I?

Lord, you know with an inward knowing
  all of the deeds I've done,
How blind, how base, how blank I've been,
  yet you've counted my counterfeit as right.[63]

61. See chap. 2 below.

62. The poems in the *Sūr Sāgar* that do make clear reference to the poet's blindness, even blindness from birth, are uniformly late in origin. Such is the case, for instance, in regard to all those cited by Dvārkādās Parīkh and Prabhudayāl Mītal, (*Sūr-Nirṇaya*, pp. 77–79) and Harbanślāl Śarmā (*Sūr Sāhitya*, pp. 27–29), with the exception of S 135, which I shall discuss below. Vrajeśvar Varmā considers five additional poems that seem to bear on Sūr's blindness (*Sūr Mīmāṃsā*, p. 27). On S 198, which falls in the early group, see below. The poems remaining (S 5, 47, 166, and 180) are late.

63. The third line presents slight manuscript variations. B4 has *khoṭenu kahatu khare*, whereas J4 has *khū̃n hū̃ karat khare*, neither of which exactly agrees with the Sabhā's, *khoṭani karat khare*.

The words *adh* (blind), *adham* (base), and *avivekī* (blank) are knit together not only by proximity but by a relentless alliteration that makes it impossible to regard the latter two as moral failings and the former as a physical defect. In fact, their order seems interchangeable: baseness precedes blindness in J4.

A second poem (S 296, found in B4, J2, J4, and J5) displays a similar pattern of associations. The poet bewails his days squandered on attending only to the things of the flesh, never calling upon the Lord. Now, in old age, his senses have betrayed him and it is seemingly too late to ransom a life misspent (S 296.3). In one version (B4, J4) he restricts his attention to defects experienced by the senses lodged in his head:

> The ears do not hear, the eyes do not respond,
> and the voice is sluggish of speech.

In the alternate version (J2, J5) he expands a bit:

> The eyes have turned blind, the ears do not hear,
> and the feet become tired when they walk.

Whichever version one chooses, the reference is not clearly physical, and in neither one is blindness singled out for any particular attention. Even when it is explicitly named and advanced to the head of the list (*andh,* J2, J5), it is merely invoked as one of the infirmities that comes with age. In the other reading the poet's lament about his eyes (*nain nahi sūjhat,* B4, J4) is even more plainly but one in a series of geriatric complaints, and there is no way to know if true blindness is meant or merely failing sight. The whole passage, in fact, has the ring of formula rather than of personal history, and indeed very similar phrasings can be found as far back as the literature of Apabhraṃśa, written more than half a millennium before Sūr.[64]

The third poem (S 135, found in J1, B2, B3, U1, J2, J4, and

64. I am indebted to Michael C. Shapiro for drawing my attention to the following passage (3.3.8–9) in the eighth- or ninth-century Paümariü of Svayambhūdeva: *ṇa suṇaṁti kaṇṇa ṇa ṇiyai ṇayaṇu ṇa calanti calaṇa ṇa karanti kara.* Ram Adhar Singh translates: "The ears do not hear, the eye does not see, the legs don't walk and the hands do not work." R. A. Singh: *Syntax of Apabhraṃśa,* p. 19. A similar reference to failing eyesight as part of a general deterioration is found in S 305.4, but the poem is not found in old manuscripts.

A1) is the only one that bears cogent claim to testify to the poet's blindness, but it too is ambiguous. As normally interpreted, it would translate as follows:

They say you're so giving, so denying of yourself

That you offered Sudāmā the four fruits of life,
  granted your guru a son,
And gave to Vibhīṣan, because of his full
  devotion to you, the whole of Lañkā
Despite his evil brother, whose ten heads you severed
  simply by reaching for your bow.
To poor Prahlād you fulfilled your vow;
  terrible Indra you turned to a sage;
Why then be so harsh with Sūr Dās
  as to leave him without his very eyes?

This may indeed be a reference to physical blindness, or it may be a plea for Krishna to remove a lack of spiritual vision and appear to the poet, as would be more consonant with other poems in this very definite genre. Finally, it may not involve blindness of either sort, for one could also translate the last verse, with its crucial finale (*nāinani hī kī hāni*), as follows:

What then could be the misfortune of Sūr Dās,
  to be such a blight to the eyes?

One further poem ought to be mentioned alongside these three. It has escaped critical attention because it is not included in printed editions of Sūr's works, yet it can be dated almost to the period in which the three previous poems appear. It is found in a manuscript containing an anthology of poetry (*Sarvāñgī*) dear to the Dādū Panth; the manuscript, from the Jodhpur district of Rajasthan, bears the date *vikram* 1793 (1736 A.D.).

This poem seems more explicit than any of the others: it begins with the words *aj hõ andh,* "Now I am blind," and gives special attention to the eyes throughout. Yet context makes it clear once again that the defect is essentially spiritual. The poet's complaints about old age may be regarded similarly as reflexes of spiritual decrepitude, and in the end even death seems to appear on the scene to fill a vacuum that has been created by the absence of faith.

Now I am blind; I have shunned Hari's name.

My hair has turned white with illusions and delusions
  that have wrung me through till nothing makes sense.
Skin shriveled, posture bent, teeth gone;
  my eyes emit a stream of tears;
    my friends, a stream of blame.
Those eyes once ranged as free as a cat's,
  but failed to measure the play of Time
Like a false-eyed scarecrow failing to scatter
  the deer from the field of the mind.
Sūr Dās says, to carry on without a song for God
  is courting Death: his sledge stands poised
    above your waiting head.

Even after hearing this poem, we are not entirely sure about the poet's eyesight. Perhaps he did grow gradually blind, as this and the second poem suggest, and as so many people in India do. Perhaps the legend of Sūr's blindness began with a loss of sight in old age and eventually extended itself over the poet's entire lifetime; we cannot say. But one should remember in any case that such ad hominem extrapolations should be made with care. Poems in this *vinaya* genre are not necessarily to be understood as autobiographical in the literal, as against spiritual, sense. Only one thing is clear after all has been said: if Sūr was blind, he did not make a great point of it before the world.

Is there, then, anything that can be judged about the poet's life? Perhaps the legend that Sūr was a wandering, unmarried singer (*vairāgī*), as the *Vārtā* implies and Harirāy explicitly states,[65] deserves some credence, since such a status is distinctly frowned upon in Vallabhite theology.[66] By the same logic one might be tempted to conclude that Sūr did, on occasion, play the *nisān* drum, since two of the old poems make this claim[67] and subsequent tradition can have had no interest in spreading the idea. It ascribes to Sūr the one stringed *ektār* instead, an instrument to which no reference is made in the old manuscripts. One must be cautious, however. The *nisān,* an unwieldy instrument used to summon people for an important announcement, would have been an unlikely ve-

65. *Vārtā*, p. 403.

66. A succinct attack on asceticism is found in Vallabha's "Saṃnyāsanirṇaya," part of his *Kṛṣṇaṣoḍaśagranthāḥ*.

67. S 233.6 (U1, J4, J5, with orthographic variations) and S 235.3 (B2).

hicle for vocal accompaniment. Furthermore, Sūr is by no means the only medieval poet to speak of sounding the drum to herald his message; his mention of the *nisān* seems more formulaic than autobiographical. A somewhat stronger case could be made, perhaps, for the proposal that Sūr's self-denigrating poems of petition say something about the poet's own circumstances, betraying his humble origins. Tulsī Dās the Brahmin also composed poems in roughly this format, but they were never so extreme. Still one must be cautious: the oldest dated manuscript of the *Sūr Sāgar* seems to downplay this very element.[68]

About the life of the poet, then, one can make only meager, scattered suggestions, all of them tentative. The legends of Sūr are well loved, and they bring to the saintliness implicit in his poetry a story adequate to serve as its background. In doing so, however, they seem to have buried most of the memories that originally served to inspire them. Fortunately the situation is different with the poetry attributed to Sūr. It too has seen changes in the course of time, but we still have access, through manuscripts, to some of the earliest moments in the process. The story of the gradual development of the literature associated with the name of Sūr Dās is an ample and compelling one, and we shall devote the next chapter to telling it. It enables us to form a definite impression of who Sūr Dās was, even in the absence of convincing biographical data to help the process along.

68. Kenneth E. Bryant has drawn this matter to my attention (personal communication, August 1981). Further on the contrast between Sūr's poems of petition and those of Tulsī Dās, see chap. 5 below.

Illustration for a poem from the *Sūr Sāgar,* Mewar, ca. 1700 A.D. Courtesy of George P. Bickford. Sūr Dās is depicted in the lower left-hand corner. The poem that serves as the occasion for this painting (Sabhā addendum 14) describes the *gopīs*' fascination with Krishna's boyhood charms. In one verse these are compared with the allurements that stimulate erotic passion, hence the comparison of two kissing scenes in the painting—one in childhood and one in maturity—seems deliberate.

CHAPTER 2

The Growth of the *Sūr Sāgar*

Finding the Early *Sūr Sāgar*

In its present form the *Sūr Sāgar* is a massive thing, almost as oceanic as its title implies. The Nāgarīpracāriṇī Sabhā edition, which is currently standard, contains upwards of five thousand poems, and even that is not the full extent of the *Sūr Sāgar* as it is popularly known. The Sabhā edition bases itself primarily upon poems that had been committed to writing by the nineteenth century, and the large manuscripts upon which it draws do not contain all the poems that were attributed to Sūr even then.[1] Many of the Sūr Dās verses listed in the *Caurāsī Vaiṣṇavan kī Vārtā*, for instance, do not find their way into the manuscripts that the Sabhā editors have used. In addition there are vast numbers of poems sung in the name of Sūr around the countryside today—in the Krishna plays of Braj, for example—that are not to be found on any page.

1. It is a considerable task to determine just how the Sabhā editors made use of the manuscripts and printed editions upon which they based their edition. Both the explanatory note at the beginning of the first edition of the Sabhā *Sūr Sāgar*, the only one that includes critical apparatus, and the apparatus itself are minimal. Initially a volume was projected as part of the first edition that would have been devoted in part to questions of a critical nature, but it never appeared. The Sabhā editors make mention of a number of dated manuscripts that are said to exist in the collection of the Sabhā itself (nos. 2, 3, and 8, dating to *vikram* 1880, 1916, and 1909), but I can find reference to none of them in the relevant catalogues. Two other manuscripts belonging to the Sabhā collection are also listed (nos. 13 and 19); these, however are undated. These numbers seem to correspond to MSS 771 (1149/764) and 240 (357/255) in the Sabhā collection; they show the strongest general resemblances to the Sabhā edition. The manuscripts singled out by the editors as being especially valuable (nos. 11 and 17) came from private collections and were undated. The only dated manuscript of any antiquity that was consulted by the Sabhā editors is no. 9, dated *vikram* 1753 (1696 A.D.), from the collection of one Keśavdās Śāh. Kenneth Bryant undertook a special search for this manuscript in 1977 and found it unlocatable. The full roster of manuscripts and printed texts upon which the Sabhā edition was based is given in *Sūrsāgar*, ed. Jagannāthdās 'Ratnākar' et al., 1st ed., vol. 2 (vol. 1 never appeared), 1934, pp. 1–2.

If one were to compile all these with the intention of producing a truly comprehensive *Sūr Sāgar*, its size would doubtless swell to seven or eight thousand poems. And in fact, one huge manuscript of the *Sūr Sāgar* exists in out-of-the-way Datia that well exceeds this number. Its physical magnitude practically matches that of the Gutenberg Bible, and its enumeration of the poems it contains pushes above the ten thousand mark, though only by virtue of slight mathematical miscalculations along the way.[2] One would think that such a vast collection would awe people, but instead it merely adds to the widespread conviction that in reality Sūr composed many more poems than this—a lakh and a quarter, all told. The problem, people say, is that so many have been lost.

If one studies the manuscript tradition that has gone into the making of the present-day *Sūr Sāgar*, however, the process seems to have been the reverse. "Sūr's Ocean" is not some primeval sea of verse that has dried up over the years, but rather a body that has grown steadily, drop after drop, over the centuries. The earliest collections of Sūr's verse are some of the smallest—the oldest manuscript of all (J1, dated 1582 A.D.) contains only 268 poems with his signature[3]—and they grew regularly with the passage of time. Half a century after the first manuscript one finds collections that contain about twice as many entries,[4] and in another half-century a manuscript had appeared that contained double again that number.[5] Not every subsequent manuscript was larger than the ones that had gone before. Some may have been selections from earlier collections; others were doubtless compiled in places where the full extent of the growing corpus was not known; still others focused on specific themes. But on the whole one saw a

2. The manuscript is no. 951, undated, in the collection of the erstwhile Datia State Library, now housed at the Government Degree College, Datia. It consists of 1028 folios and credits itself with 10,038 poems. Owing to misnumberings, however, 219 should be subtracted from that total, and very occasionally the compositions of other poets than Sūr Dās are included in the sum.

3. Of these 268, however, 27 *pads* are repetitions or close variants of others in the list, bringing the effective total to 241. Other poets are also included in J1, for a total of 411 *pads* (Kenneth Bryant, personal communication, April, 1984). Earlier analyses of J1 yielded slightly different figures: see G. N. Bahura, "*Sūrdās kā pada*: The Fatehpur Manuscript of 1639 V.S. (1582 A.D.)," in *Bhakti in Current Research, 1979–1982*, ed. Monika Thiel-Horstmann, p. 21, and K. E. Bryant, "The Fatehpur Manuscript and the *Sūrsāgar* Critical Edition Project," ibid., p. 38. The manuscript is published as *Pad Sūrdās kā/The Padas of Sūrdās*, ed. Bahura and Bryant.

4. B2 (1624 A.D.) has 492 *pads*; B3 (1638 A.D.) has 480; B4 (1641 A.D.) has 625; and U1 (1650 A.D.) has 793 *pads* of Sūr out of a total of 795.

5. J4 (1676 A.D.) contains 1472 *pads*.

gradual increase over the years: by the last quarter of the eighteenth century large collections had grown to the size of 2,000 poems,[6] and by the time the great Newal Kishore edition was published in the nineteenth century one was dealing with a corpus that took more than 700 folio-sized pages to print.[7]

Though not every manuscript recorded its full extent, the size of the *Sūr Sāgar* tended to increase by measured, almost regular intervals over the years. Yet at a certain point its shape altered dramatically, yielding a final product, as it were, whose design is plain to see. If one opens to the table of contents of the modern Sabhā edition, one finds a work divided into twelve books (*skandhas*) corresponding to the twelve books of the *Bhāgavata Purāṇa.* The problem comes when one looks more closely. Each of the books contains a number of headings referring to episodes familiar from the *Bhāgavata,* but the poems are distributed very unevenly beneath them. While it is true that the tenth book of the *Bhāgavata,* the section describing Krishna, is the most extensive, it can hardly approximate the weight that the corresponding book carries in the Sabhā *Sūr Sāgar*: over four-fifths of the total. The rest is uneven, too. Book one, the introduction, accounts for almost half of the remainder, and book nine, concerning Rām, takes up over half of what is left after that. The other parts of the *Bhāgavata* limp along with almost no content at all.

Something is odd here; one has the feeling that this is a book not to be judged by its cover. When one examines individual poems, the feeling intensifies, for it often takes an act of considerable imagination to make any of the poems of the *Sūr Sāgar* comment upon substantial portions of the *Bhāgavata*'s narrative. A passing reference to the story of Prahlād, for instance, in the course of illustrating the Lord's faithfulness to those who call upon him, is enough to place a poem (S 422) in the seventh book, even though it more logically belongs with the rest of the poems of petition and praise (*vinaya* poems) which are themselves rather arbitrarily assigned to the first book. True, one finds the occasional programmatic poem (e.g., S 421) that provides a link between the *Sūr Sāgar* and other parts of the *Bhāgavata Purāṇa* than its tenth book, but such poems are absent from the older manuscripts. None of the early manuscripts of the *Sūr Sāgar,* in fact, is organized in such a way as to approximate the *Bhāgavata.* The first that is said to dis-

6. An example is Hindi MS no. 10/2 in the collection of the Tilakāyat Mahārāj Śrī of Nathdvara, dating to *vikram* 1830.

7. Sūr Dās, *Sūr Sāgar,* 5th ed.

play such an order is dated *vikram* 1753 (1696 A.D.), well over a century after the earliest extant collection of Sūr's poems, and even it is mysterious. After persistent search in 1977, Kenneth Bryant concluded that it was unlocatable.[8]

Earlier manuscripts reveal a variety of editorial schemes. The greatest number (B1, B3, U1, J3, J5, A1, K1, U2) follow Krishna's life from childhood to maturity and then append various other materials, such as poems about Rām or petitionary poems. There are also manuscripts organized by aesthetic mood (*ras*, B4) or raga (B2, J2) or even in loose alphabetical groupings (parts of U1). But none of them follows the order set down in the *Bhāgavata Purāṇa.* As one would expect from the *Bhāgavata*, poems addressed to Rām certainly appear in these early manuscripts (though not in all: they are lacking in K1 and J4); yet nowhere are they prefaced to those concerning Krishna, as the *Bhāgavata*'s order would demand. Quite the opposite, they are usually placed near the end. And the *vinaya* poems, which are treated in the Sabhā edition as pertaining to the first book of the *Bhāgavata*, are typically placed near them, usually directly at the end; in one case (J5) they comprise the entire manuscript.

These early manuscripts match ill with the Vallabhite conception of Sūr's poetic vocation. In the first place, it would make little sense from a Vallabhite point of view to collect Sūr's petitionary verse—his "simperings," as the *Vārtā* says Vallabha called them—and preserve them in a separate volume. Even to have a good sampling of such poetry included along with the rest of the *Sūr Sāgar*, as in almost all manuscripts (B1 and the two related manuscripts J3 and J4 are the only exceptions), would seem an embarrassment. A second difficulty in the picture of Sūr held by the Sampradāy is the absence of early manuscripts organized according to the plan of the *Bhāgavata Purāṇa*. In the Sampradāy's view such an organization would have been appropriate, since Sūr is

8. This is the *Sūr Sāgar* said by 'Ratnākar' to have been lent him by its owner, Śāh Keśavdās Rāis (*Sūrsāgar*, 1st ed., p. 2). 'Ratnākar' makes no comment about the manuscript's organization; it was Javāharlāl Caturvedī who first asserted that it was arranged by *skandha*, and one wonders whether he had seen the manuscript itself or inferred its nature from the *skandhātmak* format of the Sabhā edition (*Sūrdās: Adhyayan-Sāmagrī*, p. 7). A similar uncertainty pertains to a manuscript reportedly dated *vikram* 1740 (1683 A.D.) that was in the collection of Naṭvarlāl Caturvedī of Mathura. Harbanślāl Śarmā, basing his information on that supplied by Javāharlāl Caturvedī, asserts that it is *saṅgrahātmak*, but Caturvedī then later lists it as *skandhātmak*. Śarmā, *Sūr aur unkā Sāhitya*, p. 51; Caturvedī, "Sūrsāgar kā Vikās aur uskā Rūp," p. 128; Caturvedī, *Sūrdās: Adhyayan-Sāmagrī*, p. 14. Attempts by myself (in 1976 and 1981) and Bryant (in 1977) to find this manuscript were unsuccessful.

said in the *Vārtā* to have derived his genuine inspiration from hearing Vallabha's *Subodhinī*, his commentary on the *Bhāgavata Purāṇa*. If one looks carefully, however, one sees that the *Vārtā* is not unequivocal on this point. It does claim that Vallabha taught Sūr the whole of the *Subodhinī*, but in the course of making this point it states that the philosopher's entire meaning sank indelibly into the poet's heart on the basis of his merely hearing his mentor recite the introductory verse. The verse in question is not the preface to the whole *Subodhinī* but only to that portion of it serving as a comment on the *Bhāgavata*'s tenth book.[9] It seems, therefore, that when the author of the *Vārtā* spoke of the *Subodhinī* he had the tenth book principally in mind.

In the course of time it became common practice to take more literally the claim that Sūr derived his poetic inspiration from the *Bhāgavata*. Manuscripts organized in this way begin to appear around the turn of the nineteenth century, adopting roughly the format that has imprinted itself on current thinking about the *Sūr Sāgar* through the Sabhā edition. The two oldest dated manuscripts of this type are to be found in the collection of the Sabhā itself.[10] These, like other undated manuscripts of the same type,[11]

9. *Vārtā*, p. 406.

10. Sabhā Hindi MSS 496 (726/526), dated *vikram* 1847 (1790 A.D.), and 4469 (269/26), dated *vikram* 1850 (1793 A.D.). Considerably earlier manuscripts of the *Sūr Sāgar* have been reported to bear the *skandha* (book) format of the *Bhāgavata Purāṇa*. Unfortunately, it has thus far been impossible to verify this claim. The oldest of the manuscripts to be so identified (*vikram* 1740, 1683 A.D.) comes from the collection of the late Naṭvarlāl Caturvedī of Mathura, and was first introduced into the scholarly discussion of Sūr manuscripts by Javāharlāl Caturvedī. In his *Sūrdās: Adhyayan-Sāmagrī* (p. 14) he reported that it was a *skandhātmak* manuscript, a claim that he did not repeat in his subsequent "Sūrsāgar kā Vikās" (p. 128). The manuscript in question is said now to be in Javāharlāl Caturvedī's own library but has at least so far proved inaccessible to outside examination. Other relatively old manuscripts (*vikram* 1745, 1753, 1792, and 1798; 1688–1741 A.D.) listed by Javāharlāl Caturvedī as being *skandhātmak* (*Sūrdās: Adhyayan-Sāmagrī*, p. 7) have also proved unlocatable in manuscript searches undertaken by Bryant in 1977 and myself in 1976 and 1981. With the exception of the one dated *vikram* 1753 (1696 A.D., see n. 8, above), all are ascribed to the Nāgarīpracāriṇī Sabhā, but none appears in Sabhā records and none was used by 'Ratnākar' and company in editing the Sabhā *Sūr Sāgar*. Udayśaṅkar Śāstrī, in compiling a table of early dated *saṃgrahātmak* and *skandhātmak* manuscripts, appears to have taken over information given by Caturvedī without further question. See "Sūrsāgar kī Sāmagrī kā Saṃkalan aur uskā Saṃpādan," *Bhāratīya Sāhitya* 17, no. 1–2 (1972): p. 88.

11. E.g., Hindi MSS 12/2 and 12/14 in the collection of the Tilakāyat Mahārāj Śrī of Nathdvara and Hindi MS 12,009 in the collection of the Vrindaban Research Institute, a manuscript recently donated to the institute by Rādhe Śyām Dvivedī of Mathura. Hindi MS 951 at Datia is of the same general mold, though its section headings only approximate those found in manuscripts of the *Bhāgavata* type.

are large, carefully inscribed books, impressive enough in appearance that it seems they were intended to function as vernacular *Bhāgavata*s, scriptures of the first order. It was in just this period, indeed, that works genuinely intended to be vernacular renditions of the *Bhāgavata* began to proliferate, and in these *Bhāgavata*-type *Sūr Sāgar*s, not surprisingly, one first encounters poems specifically contrived with the purpose of showing that Sūr too was "translating" the *Bhāgavata*.[12] These poems, entirely foreign to earlier manuscripts of the *Sūr Sāgar*, are rather a dismal lot, of which the following may serve as an example (S 225):

Viṣṇu, from his sacred mouth,

explained four *śloka*s to Brahmā;
Brahmā told them to Nārad,
and Nārad to Vyās in turn;
Vyās told them to Śukdev,
expanding them to twelve volumes,
And these Sūr Dās told as songs,
sung in the common tongue.

Literary scholars writing in the present day have continued to hold high the torch, claiming the Sanskrit purana as the model for everything Sūr ever wrote—at least after meeting Vallabha—and thus anchoring him, though a vernacular poet, in India's high tradition. Whole books have been written to defend the point, but their arguments collapse when their predecessors in verse, later additions to the *Sūr Sāgar* such as we have just quoted, are disqualified as inadmissible evidence.[13] One does find a passage or

12. In the Sabhā edition these are collected as S 225–231. The implication that Sūr was translating the *Bhāgavata* is also present in poems such as S 342–345, 376–380, and in all of the poems used to introduce the twelve *skandha*s that demarcate the Sabhā's *Sūr Sāgar*. None of these is found in the early *Sūr Sāgar* except for S 345, and that only in one manuscript, J4. The tradition of the vernacular *Bhāgavata* has roots extending all the way back to the sixteenth-century *Haricarita* of Lālac Dās, but had become influential enough to the turn of the nineteenth century that Lallūjī Lāl chose such a work in Braj Bhāṣā for adaptation into Hindi, creating his very popular *Prem Sāgar*. On the tradition of Braj Bhāṣā *Bhāgavata*s, see Grahame Niemann, "Bhūpati's *Bhāgavat* and the Hindī *Bhāgavat* Genre," in *Bhakti in Current Research, 1979–1982*, ed. Monika Thiel-Horstmann, pp. 257–67; also Niemann, "The Bhāgavat Daśam Skandh of Bhūpati," *I A V R I Bulletin* 8 (1980): 3–8.

13. Examples of books in this genre are Ved Prakāś Śāstrī, *Śrīmadbhāgavat aur Sūrsāgar kā Varṇya Viṣay kā Tulnātmak Adhyayan*, and Viśvanāth Śukla, *Hindī*

two in earlier poems that show a knowledge of the *Bhāgavata Purāṇa,* but they fall far short of demonstrating that Sūr took the *Bhāgavata* as his chief inspiration. When the *Purāṇa* is mentioned, in fact, it is apt to be cited as one of several scriptural authorities, not as a lone beacon of truth:

In the *Gītā,* the Veda, and the *Bhāgavata*
it says that the Lord of the world
Stays closer than close to his people, listening,
and always remains at their side.[14]

Or if the poet mentions it alone among sacred texts, he does so in such a way as to bemoan his ignorance of it rather than to establish his fealty:

I've squandered this life in useless pursuits.

I have not sung of Hari, have not served my guru,
did not go to live in Madhuban,
And to give ear to the *Bhāgavata*
was a taste I never could cultivate.[15]

Kṛṣṇa Bhakti Kāvya par Śrīmadbhāgavat kā Prabhāv, pp. 196–216. An example of the sort of passage that is said to be patterned on the *Bhāgavata Purāṇa* is the following (S 1626.7–8):

kām krodh neh suhṛdatā kahū bidhi kari koi
dhare dhyān hari ko je dṛḍh kari sūr so hari sam hoi

Its putative antetype in the *Bhāgavata Purāṇa* is the following passage:

kāmaṃ krodhaṃ bhayaṃ sneham aikyaṃ sauhṛdam eva ca
nityaṃ harau vidadhato yānti tanmayatāṃ hi te

The correspondence is convincing. The difficulty is that S 1626 is not among the early compositions in the *Sūr Sāgar.*

14. S 196.11–12. Among the old manuscripts, the passage is attested only in B4 and J4.

15. S 155.1–2, 7. In J2, B3, and both instances recorded in A1, however, these lines are sequential; in J4, the remaining manuscript, the first two are separated from the third by two intervening lines. Madhuban is one of several wooded areas in the Braj country, as the term *ban* implies, and may have been mentioned here because it is the nearest of such forests to Mathura—a distance of only four or five miles. It is traditionally the first stop on the extensive *banyātrā,* a circumambulatory pilgrimage in which devotees visit numerous sacred sites in Braj, including prominently the twelve *bans.* One reaches Madhuban easily on the first day. Like the other "forests" of Braj, Madhuban is associated with Krishna's cowherding, but it alone is remembered as the place in which Dhruv practiced his austerities in hopes of winning the favor of Viṣṇu.

If, then, the *Bhāgavata* was not Sūr's model, what was? The obvious and probably correct answer is that he had none, save for the earlier vernacular poetry to which he would certainly have been heir, though none of it remains today.[16] For Sūr was surely an oral poet. Everything about the early *Sūr Sāgar*—by which I shall mean the poems collected under his name before *vikram* 1764, that is, by about the end of the seventeenth century—suggests as much.[17] The early *Sūr Sāgar* is made up of short, discrete poems, rarely more than twelve verses in length, that are almost entirely without serial relation. To the extent that they depend for their effect upon anything external to their own content, it is not the preceding poem in any written collection, but rather the general store of information that the poet could assume in aural repertory.[18] For the most part these are artful poems, often terse and ironic, but as their scribes remembered them they also contain a substantial proportion of verse that was generated by constructing variations on well-known sequences of ideas and sounds, much as one would expect in an oral poet.

The disposition of the early manuscripts further confirms the point. Thirteen manuscripts are available from this early period, and in only one case is the editor of a manuscript clearly dependent upon another in the series (J3, J4).[19] In addition there is a strong affinity between B1 and parts of U1, and between parts of B3 and A1.[20] Almost undoubtedly other cases exist in which a scribe

16. A detailed consideration of the tradition to which Sūr was heir in the case of his butter-thief poems may be found in John Stratton Hawley, *Krishna, the Butter Thief*, chap. 2. So far as one can tell, all of these "sources" were indirect.

17. This somewhat arbitrary cutting-off point is late enough to permit the inclusion of manuscripts from a variety of locations without expanding the number of manuscripts under consideration to an unmanageable size.

18. Cf. Kenneth E. Bryant, *Poems to the Child-God: Structures and Strategies in the Poetry of Sūrdās*, pp. 45–48, 60–65, 136–39.

19. The forthcoming critical edition will amplify the number of manuscripts from the period we are designating as "early" by one. This fourteenth manuscript escaped earlier attention because it is composite, containing verse attributed to several other poets beside Sūr. It is Hindi accession no. 1057 in the K. M. Hindi Institute of Agra University, and it contains 534 poems of Sūr on 99 folios. The colophon governing these poems gives no date, but the Nand Dās section that follows it in the same hand is dated to *vikram* 1713.

20. Kenneth Bryant was the first to uncover the latter resemblance, which will become apparent from a perusal of Notes on the Translations, below. It is possible that other instances of close affinity, even dependence, can be demonstrated at a more minute level, but that must wait until work on the critical edition has been completed. Such information will be presented with its publication.

based his work on prior written texts that are now lost. It becomes plausible to imagine such earlier texts when a manuscript appears to have been compiled from more than one source, as when poems covering the same subject are numbered in several sequences rather than in one. This happens rather commonly in later manuscripts from this early group (J5, A1), but the pattern is already evident in the very first among them (J1). Or again, one may discover that an editor has made an effort to place poems in alphabetical groupings but has produced several alphabetical sequences rather than one, suggesting that he was systematizing, or copying from, several independent manuscripts (U1).[21] But such plurality merely suggests that what is true at the broad level also pertains at a level of greater detail. It appears that we are dealing not so much with a single *Urtext* that has been bowdlerized in the copying, but with successively more elaborate collocations of poems that were originally written down from oral memory at different times and places. Indeed, the tradition remained an oral one even after it had begun to be committed to writing. Very often the variants that distinguish one manuscript from another are not the sort that stem from errors in copying. Instead they seem to have arisen because the scribe or the person who dictated to the scribe had in his ear a different version of the poem from what he saw written on the page before him.

The legend that Sūr was blind from birth gives a nice turn to these facts, explaining in its own way why Sūr cannot have been anything but an oral poet. At the same time, however, it assumes that there was only one of him, whereas the diversity of these early manuscripts and the period of time over which they developed make it natural to postulate the existence of more than one contributing poet. Still, if one lacks a single author, one has a tradition with a certain integrity. To look at its broad lines is to see that, for all its diversity, it developed in a generally coherent and in some ways almost predictable fashion over the years. The Sūr tradition[22] has a developing personality whose most distinctive contours can be described even before the exact details of manuscript transmission have been fully ascertained—if ever that should

21. I am indebted to Thomas B. Ridgeway for this observation. It is confirmed by the existence of a certain number of individual poems that appear twice in the manuscript—once in the form given by B1 and once in a form for which there is usually no clear prototype. An example is S 2320, for which critical notes are given in Notes on the Translations.

22. A phrase coined and discussed by Bryant, *Child-God*, pp. xi–xiii.

be—and that is what we shall do in the remainder of this chapter. From now on, when we speak of "Sūr" we will be referring to that tradition as we see it in its early phases. "Sūr" will mean not an historical person or the legendary personage that was projected in the wake of such a person's achievements, but the author or authors of the poems attributed to Sūr that were committed to writing before *vikram* 1764. Obviously to make such a division between the early and the late *Sūr Sāgar*, between "Sūr" and other poets that wrote in his name, is artificial. On the one hand the tradition was more continuous than such a division would suggest; on the other, various manuscripts in the early group have arguably distinct emphases. Still, such a chronological separation helps one recognize the major differences between the tradition in its earlier and its later stages; and, as it happens, the differences are marked.

THE SHAPE OF THE EARLY *SŪR SĀGAR*

In the earliest form we know it, the *Sūr Sāgar* is no *Bhāgavata*. Not only does it lack twelve divisions, it lacks any divisions at all. The oldest Sūr manuscripts in the royal libraries of Jaipur and Bikaner (J1, B1),[23] the earliest we have, are untitled listings of poems that contain no section headings. J1, in fact, is a composite manuscript that includes poems attributed to other poets as well, resembling several other anthologies preserved from an almost equally early period except that it devotes extensive attention to Sūr. The second oldest Sūr manuscripts in both the Jaipuri and Bikaneri col-

23. B1 has lost its colophon page but can be reliably dated in the vicinity of *vikram* 1655–1685 (1598–1628 A.D.) because it seems to have been written in the hand of one of the favorite scribes of Maharaja Sūrya Siñh of Bikaner. Sanskrit manuscript 209 in the same collection, dated *vikram* 1668, is very similar in appearance (cf. also B2, dated *vikram* 1681), and the condition of the paper in B1 suggested to the former curator of the Bikaner collection, Dinanath Khatri, that B1 is the oldest of these three. Further evidence for the great age of B1 is provided by a technique recently developed by Kenneth Bryant. Bryant has shown that a definite progression exists among dated manuscripts of the *Sūr Sāgar*, according to which the oldest contain the smallest percentage of poems not found in any other manuscript and the most recent, the greatest. B1 contains an even lower percentage of poems shared by other manuscripts than does the oldest dated manuscript, J1 (Bryant, personal communication, August, 1981; see also Bahura and Bryant, eds., *Pad Sūrdās kā*).

lections do show a definite scheme of organization, but again it has nothing to do with the *Bhāgavata*. B2 and J2—the latter considerably more recent than former—are arranged by raga, adopting a practice that is still current in many of the hymnbooks (*sevā praṇālī*) of the Vallabha Sampradāy and may or may not have had a specifically liturgical impetus. These two manuscripts, however, are entirely distinct with regard to the order of ragas and the poems grouped beneath them, and both of them stand at a distance from the method of organization that was to become dominant in shaping the early *Sūr Sāgar*.

That pattern had already been suggested in B1, which, though it lacked subject headings, did give its poems a loose arrangement that followed the rhythms of Krishna's life story. The next Bikaneri manuscript (B3) is of the same type, but at some point an editor formalized the system by adding a table of contents with topical headings. This may have happened rather early, for in three other manuscripts that are almost contemporary (U1, B4, and J3), such headings are interspersed in the text itself. B3 is dated to *vikram* 1695 and the others are, respectively, *vikram* 1697, 1698, and sometime before 1706—all falling within the decade that extends from the late 1630s into the 1640s A.D. This is significant, for none of these latter three is dependent on any other—indeed, it may be that they represent three separate branches of a manuscript stemma[24]—and no two, so far as one can tell, were written in the same place.[25] Once established, this pattern became very influential. All subsequent manuscripts in this early group (J4, A1, K1, U2)—but for one exception, the Jaipur manuscript devoted entirely to the petitionary *vinaya* poetry (J5)—follow the same general format; and all of them adopt the title first announced in U1: *Sūr Sāgar*. When the writer of J5 declined to use that title, preferring instead to call his *vinaya* collection "poems of Sūr Dās" (*śrī sūr dās jī kā pad*), he was apparently distinguishing it from a well-known entity.

This more or less "standard" *Sūr Sāgar*, however, was not identical from place to place. B4, written in either Mathura or its environs, is structured as follows:

24. Kenneth E. Bryant, "Toward a Critical Edition of the *Sūrsāgar*," in *Early Hindī Devotional Literature in Current Research*, ed. W. M. Callewaert, p. 10. Cf. Bahura and Bryant, *Pad Sūrdās kā*.

25. In the case of J3 and B3 no place is mentioned in the colophon.

bāl caritra	118 poems	
govardhan samai	15	
muralī	32	
dhyān	34	
siṅgār	280	
karunā ras	112	
pramodh (i.e., *pramod*)	23	
TOTAL	614 poems[26]	

The *bāl caritra* are the childhood adventures of Krishna, and the *govardhan samai* refers to the most heroic of Krishna's childhood feats, the episode in which he lifted up Mount Govardhan to protect the people and cattle of Braj from the angry, rainy ravages of Indra. The *muralī* poems comprise not only those devoted to describing the beguiling effects of Krishna's flute Muralī, but a number of poems that other manuscripts characterize under the heading of *anurāg*; they concern the *gopī*s' newly awakened love for Krishna. The *dhyān* poems detail these women's infatuation with his beauty—their "concentration" on him, as the term indicates. When we come to poems that deal with the full extent of the amorous attachment between Krishna and the *gopī*s—whether it be Rādhā, his favorite, or another—the editor chooses a category taken from classical aesthetic theory to designate the mood: *śṛṅgār ras.*[27] The *vinaya* poems receive a similar designation. The editor regards them from the point of view not of the poet's emotion but of what the poet hopes the Lord's response will be, since that too can be described in one of the classical categories, as compassion: *karuṇā ras*. The final category, *pramod* (joy), refers to expressions of gratitude and praise, and they, like the last group, are directed to Krishna apart from any dramatic context. Later this sort of poem was typically to be combined with poems of the

26. As to the provenance of B4, the scribe uses the term *mathurākṣetre* in a way that is ambiguous enough that it could conceivably even refer to his own place of origin rather than to the place in which he was writing. As to the number of poems, note that the final entry in the *karunā ras* section bears the seal of "Tursī Dās," not Sūr, bringing the total of Sūr pads to 613.

27. A number of *pad*s are included in this section, however, do not refer specifically either to the love of Rādhā and Krishna or to the amorous sentiment at all, for instance S 371 and 791. Hence although the number of poems grouped here is impressive, it is rather exaggerated. The other categories more exactly approximate a single theme or phase in the *kṛṣṇacaritra*. Furthermore it is worth noting that by far the majority of poems collected in this section record not love's fulfillment but, in some measure, love's pain.

karuṇā variety under the heading of *vinaya*, perhaps due to the influence of Tulsī Dās's *Vinaya Patrikā.*

U1 presents us with what ostensibly is quite a different set of headings. There are twice as many as in B4, to begin with, and of those about half are devoted to aspects of the Krishna story that are not highlighted at all in B4's scheme. Six of fourteen groupings are devoted to events that take one beyond Krishna's life in Braj, and beyond the familiar *vinaya* mood as well. They point up episodes concerning Balarām, Krishna's brother; incidents involving the other Rām, Krishna's prior avatar; and stories about Krishna's full maturity as ruler of Dvaraka and participant in the struggles of the *Mahābhārata.* But if one looks carefully, one sees that only one of these categories embraces more than ten poems and that collectively they hold only ninety, less than an eighth of the total manuscript. The others, though they are differently named, correspond quite well to what we had in B4. There are childhood poems, though the heading has been omitted for some reason; poems of new love (here called *anurāg* and corresponding to B4's *muralī* poems); poems of infatuation (*khaṇḍitā,* B4's *dhyān*); and poems that describe love in its most mature form. B4 had labeled these *śṛṅgār,* following the classical model, but U1 provides terms that are closer to their actual content: *viraha*, the yearning lovers feel when separated from one another, and *bhamargīt,* the "songs of—or more accurately to—the bee."

This black bee is Ūdho, the messenger whom dark Krishna (his name literally means "black") sends to his erstwhile lovers in Braj after taking up his new, royal career in Mathura. Ūdho is to comfort the women of Braj with a message of yoga, convincing them that they need not pine since the real Krishna is within. But in ironic and heart-rending songs addressed to this messenger bee, the *gopīs* make it clear that they refuse to accept such a palliative. The *bhramargīt*, then, are merely a particular, and particularly famous, form of the songs of *viraha* that comprise the preceding group, for at this point in the development of the *Sūr Sāgar* the pangs of lovers' separation are voiced exclusively by the *gopīs*, not by Krishna. *Viraha* and *bhramargīt* together comprise what B4 had called, rather distantly, *śṛṅgār.* And as we can now clearly see, here as there they are overwhelmingly the most prominent group in the collection. The category remaining, *bhagat* (i.e., *bhakti,* devotion), comprises the *vinaya* poems. Special mention is made of the *sūrpacīsī*, a group of twenty-five couplets (not *pad*s) that makes its first appearance in J1, but it is clear that the *bhagat* section continues after the *sūrpacīsī* has been concluded, since no new heading is introduced.[28]

The following, then, are the contents of U1:

childhood (*bāl līlā*, untitled)	53 poems
the onset of love (*anurāg*)	169
the deserted woman (*khanditā*, i.e., *khaṇḍitā*)	47
separation and longing (*viraha*)	187
songs to the bee (*bhaṃvargit*, i.e., *bhramargīt*)	122
concerning Balarām (*balibhadracaritra*, i.e., *balabhadracaritra*)	6
events in Dvaraka (*dvārikācaritra*)	5
concerning Sudāmā (*sadāmācaritra*, i.e., *sudāmācaritra*)	7
concerning Rukmiṇī (*rukhmiṇīcaritra*, i.e., *rukmiṇīcaritra*)	4
poems in the *kaḍakhā* meter (*karakhā*)	6
events from the *Mahābhārata* (*bhārath*, i.e., *bhārat*)	10
concerning Rām (*raghunāthcaritra*)	42
poems of devotion (*bhagat*, i.e., *bhakti*), including Sūr's twenty-five (*surpacīsī*, i.e., *sūrpacīsī*)	137
TOTAL	795 poems[29]

The editor of J3, the third manuscript in this "standard" series, attempted much finer discriminations, using upwards of sixty headings. The *khaṇḍitā* poems, for instance, concerning the woman who has been temporarily deserted or otherwise wronged by her lover, are divided into several groups. In one, Rādhā tells a friend of her pique; in another she openly displays her anger (*mān*); in a third Krishna tries to pacify her; and in a fourth she gives voice

28. Two independent *sūrpacīsī*s date to this early period, with another coming just after the cut-off point we have adopted. The first forms a part of an anthology dated *vikram* 1751 (1694 A.D.) and is preserved as Hindi MS 6/3/3 in the Sarasvatī Bhaṇḍār, Kankarauli. The second, dated *vikram* 1752 (1695 A.D.), is Hindi MS 70 in the Anup Sanskrit Library in Bikaner. The third, dated *vikram* 1766 (1709 A.D.), is MS 1054 in the collection of the K. M. Hindi Institute at Agra University. Prabhudayāl Mītal took note of the J1 *sūrpacīsī* in "Sūr Kṛt Padõ kī Sabse Prācīn Prati," *Nāgarīpracāriṇī Patrikā* 67, no. 3 (*vikram* 2019, 1962 A.D.): 266.

29. The scribe counts a total of 812 *pads*, but I am unable to find the remaining 17. Of these, two must be discounted since they bear the signatures of Tursī Dās and Caturbhuj (Dās). These occur respectively on fol. 110 verso and fol. 167 verso. Kenneth Bryant was the first to notice them (Spring 1980).

to her response, for the most part unyielding. It is noteworthy that the editor should have felt confident that Rādhā was the subject of these poems, since she is mentioned in so few of them; we shall return to the point in the next chapter. For now it is sufficient to observe that the proportions of the large groupings of poems, such as were established in B4 and U1, remain roughly the same. All that has happened is that they are much more closely discriminated. The poems pertaining to the *gopīs*' sense of dispirited longing (*viraha*) are divided into some seven or ten categories, depending upon how one calculates, and Yaśodā's grief is listed in yet another. More striking still, the bee songs, a subset of the general *viraha* group, are listed in no fewer than fifteen segments.

It is clear, then, that in these typical formulations of the early *Sūr Sāgar* the leading theme was *viraha*; the great text throbbed with poems of anger and despair, irony and complaint. U1 is organized in a manner that makes it particularly plain how the various stages of *viraha* develop from one phase of the *gopīs*' involvement with Krishna to the next. New love (*anurāg*) soon turns to betrayal (*khaṇḍitā*), and betrayal to deep longing (*viraha*), and that issues ultimately, once Krishna has departed from Braj altogether, in the hopeless songs of the bee (*bhramargīt*). Even the *vinaya* poems follow suit, casting the same message in a different form by placing it in the mouth of the poet himself. In J3, approximations of many of whose subject headings were to become widely standard at a later date,[30] this clear logic is somewhat obscured by greater differentiation, but it remains nonetheless, and in B4 one finds the same pattern if one looks behind aesthetic categories that were fashioned primarily to describe other texts than this.

Prabhudayāl Mītal, one of the foremost traditional scholars of Sūr Dās and a member of the Vallabha Sampradāy, was at one point given the rare opportunity of glancing over the earliest extant Sūr manuscript with a dated colophon, J1. He came away convinced that it could not be a very good manuscript since it contained what seemed to him such a small proportion of poems devoted to the antics of Krishna's infancy and adolescence (*bāl* and *kiśor* poems).[31] But the old Jaipur manuscript is no exception in this regard. The relative absence of these genial childhood poems

30. As, for instance, in manuscripts collected in the Vallabhite libraries at Nathdvara and Kankarauli. See Hindi MSS 10/2 and 12/3 in the private collection of the Tilakāyat Mahārāj Śrī, Nathdvara, and MSS 7/5 and 58/3 in the Sarasvatī Bhaṇḍār at Kankarauli.

31. Mītal, "Sūr Kṛt Padō kī Sabse Prācīn Prati," p. 267.

simply reflects the dominant preoccupation with *viraha* in all early expressions of the *Sūr Sāgar*. That, together with the relatively high proportion of *vinaya* poems, goes a long way toward explaining why it would have seemed so natural in these early days to group the poems of Sūr in a single anthology with other poets of the period who were devoted to a view of the religious life that later generations came to see as distinctly more sober: *nirguṇa* poets such as Kabīr who insisted that God could not properly be worshipped through any definite attributes, through legend or image. Sūr was not, of course, a *nirguṇa* poet in this sense, but his emphasis on the *gopīs*' separation from Krishna and his from his Lord relates him not only to other Krishna poets such as Mīrā Bāī but to these *nirguṇa* voices as well.[32] What was later conceived as Sūr's chief "specialty," his poetry describing the child Krishna, is certainly represented in these earlier poems; early compositions on this theme, in fact, are often considerably more artful than what was to be added later.[33] But the major voice is *viraha*.

To observe that this is so, of course, is to cast further doubt on the accuracy of the Vallabhite picture of Sūr's career; hence Mītal's discomfiture. It suggests that even the regenerate Sūr, if there ever was such a being, was never quite separated from the anguish that he expressed in the *vinaya* poems that Vallabha tried to discourage him from singing. All that has happened is that the voice has changed: the women of Braj share the agonies of estrangement with him. The preponderance of *viraha* also means that a great deal of the early *Sūr Sāgar* would have been inappropriate for liturgical usage in the Sampradāy. It is no surprise, then, that the tripartite liturgical scheme that has become standard in the Vallabhite community, according to which poems sung in daily worship are distinguished from those appropriate to calendrical festivals and the cycle in use at Holī time, is altogether absent in the organization of these early manuscripts. Although at certain points in the year the Vallabhite ritual calendar closely parallels the sequential story of Krishna's childhood adventures that is followed in most of these early *Sūr Sāgar*s, it must deviate occasionally to accommodate particular festivals. The festival celebrating the *dān līlā*, for instance, when Krishna demanded a tax in milk products from the *gopīs* on their way to market, is commemorated by the Sampradāy on *bhādrapad śukla* 11, little more than a fort-

32. Further on this point, see chap. 5.
33. See Hawley, *Butter Thief*, chaps. 3–5.

night after Krishna's birth. For such liturgical alterations the various manuscripts of the "standard" early *Sūr Sāgar* make no allowance. Indeed, in a striking contrast to the importance of this particular festival, at least in the current Vallabhite calender, the early *Sūr Sāgar* contains only a few *dān līlā* poems.[34] The oldest Sūr manuscript that I have been able to find that bears even the slightest possible trace of Vallabhite liturgical usage dates only to the late seventeenth century.[35] One can perhaps argue that early manuscripts designed for liturgical use would have been in such constant service that they would have disintegrated long ago, leaving no trace today. But it is well to remember that the princely families who preserved the oldest surviving Sūr manuscripts were themselves in close contact with the Sampradāy, and that even so these manuscripts show no trace of sectarian influence.[35] I know of only one indication that the Vallabha Sampradāy was involved in the production of these early *Sūr Sāgar*s, and it is indirect: the scribe who wrote J4 states that he comes from Gokul, the tiny town that is one of the sect's major seats. But the manuscript itself betrays no obvious signs either of liturgical usage or of sectarian theology, and it is possible the scribe is speaking of Gokul in a more general sense, as a region. The scribe of a slightly earlier manu-

34. These are discussed in ibid., pp. 125–27; cf. 144–50.

35. This is MS no. 10/2 in the private collection of the Tilakāyat Mahārāj Śrī of Nathdvara, dating to *vikram* 1830 (1773 A.D.). One only infers a possible liturgical association from its lack of *vinaya* poems; its order is not that of the liturgical year. Another manuscript in the same collection, although it bears no date, can be shown to be a predecessor of 10/2. Its divisional headings correspond exactly to those in 10/2, though they are sometimes simpler, and scribal errors in 10/2 can usually be clarified by reference to 12/3. Like 10/2, it omits *vinaya* poems, so one can, if one chooses, infer on the basis of Vallabhite collections of the *Sūr Sāgar* that the Sampradāy entertained a theological or liturgical disdain for these compositions somewhat earlier than 1773 A.D. I repeat, however, that the evidence is faint.

36. The involvement of the rulers of Mewar with the Sampradāy is abundantly clear and dates back to the middle of the seventeenth century, and there are good indications that a connection with the House of Bundi was established in the same period. In regard to Bikaner the evidence is scantier, suggesting perhaps that a strong connection was in force by the middle of the eighteenth century. See Edwin Allen Richardson, "Mughul and Rajput Patronage of the Bhakti Sect of the Maharajas, the Vallabha Sampradaya, 1640–1760 A.D." (Ph.D. diss., University of Arizona, 1979), pp. 58–110. Richardson's judgment that a definite relation between the Vallabha Sampradāy and the House of Jaipur dates back to the mid-seventeenth century (p. 106) seems to be based on his dubious assumption that the *gosvāmī*s of the temple of Govind Dev were Vallabhites, not Caitanyites.

script—similarly composite and equally nonsectarian—seems to take the name in that sense.[37]

THE LATER *SŪR SĀGAR* AS COMMENTARY

The earliest collections of Sūr's poetry must have been amassed from aural memory, and it seems likely that this process continued to greater or lesser extent throughout the years spanned by the manuscripts we have designated collectively as "the early *Sūr Sāgar*." Poems known only to the ear continued to be added to this diffuse "corpus." As time passed, however, such new additions to the Sūr corpus tended to be less and less independent of what had gone before. Instead, many served functions that would have been assumed by commentators in the case of fixed, written texts. We find poems that elaborate on hints dropped in earlier compositions;[38] poems that explain points that would have posed logical and theological puzzles to later, more systematic minds;[39] poems that rectify what were later seen as narrative lacunae;[40] even poems

37. MS no. 1057 in the Hindi collection of the K. M. Hindi Institute, University of Agra, bearing the date *vikram* 1713 (1656 A.D.) In a brief colophon the scribe seemingly identifies himself by caste and name and then adds "*gokal medapāṭ madhye*" as if to indicate a specific locale, Medapāṭ, within the Gokul region. If this manuscript has any sectarian leaning, it would seem to be toward the Rādhāvallabha Sampradāy rather that toward the Vallabha Sampradāy, since it begins by recording the *Hit Caurāsī* of Hit Harivaṃś.

38. E.g., the expression *das bīs man*, literally "ten or twenty hearts," occurs in the refrain of S 4344, in which the *gopī*s explain to Ūdho that they have only one heart apiece and it has been led into captivity by Krishna. Hence they have nothing left with which to worship the yogic god of whose virtues Ūdho is trying to persuade them (see my translation in *Butter Thief*, pp. 151–52). The same idiom is employed in a very similar context in S 4320.3, a later poem. As in the earlier poem the expression is poetically inverted to *man das bīs* and again the last word is used for rhyme. All this suggests that the poet of S 4320 may have had S 4344 in his ear as he composed.

39. E.g., it became a mystery why Krishna sent Ūdho out to confront the *gopī*s once the advaitan aspect of the *Bhāgavata Purāṇa*'s teaching was no longer theologically acceptable. Ūdho's message lost its validity. It was necessary, therefore, to invent a motive, which was supplied in poems describing how Krishna had sent Ūdho to the *gopī*s precisely so that he be defeated, to convert his friend to true religion (S 4031, 4032).

40. E.g., the story of Krishna's confrontation with the crow-demon, reported in the *Bhāgavata Pūraṇa*, is added to the *Sūr Sāgar* in its later phases (S 677, 678), and reference is made to a thread-investiture ceremony that would by rights have been necessary before Krishna and Balarām could assume their regal responsibilities in Mathura (S 3711).

that introduce whole new episodes.[41] The poetic medium in which Sūr composed, the *pad*, was so elastic that these later contributions, even if they were much longer than the poems that were standard in early *Sūr Sāgar*, could be made in the form of the "original" itself. Since there was little tradition of commenting in a formal way on a vernacular, as against a Sanskrit, text, it must have seemed appropriate for such additions to be freely interleaved with earlier poems. After all, as we have seen, the very fact that the *Sūr Sāgar* was a vernacular creation suggested that it itself was sort of commentary, an elaborate footnote to the *Bhāgavata Purāṇa*. And since the "text" in this case was porous, consisting of a large number of separate entries that originally bore no direct relation to one another, such interpolating was easy to do.

In fact, it was possible to insert additional lines within the confines of individual poems to amplify, clarify, or even defuse the original intent. These may have been the earliest "interpolations" into the *Sūr Sāgar*, and in some cases it is plausible to argue that they simply represent variations in the poem that were heard from one performance to another.[42] At the same time, however, whole poems were being added to the corpus—poems whose spirit was rather different from those that had gone before. In such verse the editorial or commentarial hand is plainer to see, and the position that such poems were accorded when first they appeared in the Sūr manuscripts often gives the matter away. These longer, more didactic poems tend to be placed at the beginning or end of a group of poems that an editor/commentator interpreted as pertaining to a particular theme. Like bookends, they are usually more strictly substantive and more wooden than the poems that

41. E.g., the cycles concerning the *gāruḍī* and the pearl necklace, discussed in chap. 3. The *gāruḍī* poems are S 1362–1364 and 1368–1382. S 1366 and 1367, older poems with less specific subject matter, have been interleaved by the Sabhā editors. S 1365, another old poem, has been adapted to the *gāruḍī* theme at some point. The phrase that ties this poem specifically to the *gāruḍī* cycle in the form given by the Sabhā (*syām gāruḍī*, S 1365.6), is absent in all manuscript versions of the poem. The necklace poems are S 2584–2634. As in the *gāruḍī* cycle, several old poems (S 2605, 2609, 2617) have been interleaved with these necklace poems. Though their present position in the Sabhā edition makes them appear as if they belong in the cycle, a closer look reveals that they make no reference to the necklace in question.

42. S 709 and 909, for instance, are both poems that are commonly found in six-line versions. In both instances, however, A1 interleaves an additional pair of verses, as does J3 in the case of S 909, and the Sabhā edition includes still two more.

come in between. Whether these poems were composed by the scribes who set these manuscripts in their final form or whether they owe their origins to some other, perhaps earlier hand is impossible to say and doubtless varies from case to case.

One of the earliest examples of such extended, narrative poems (it is found in the very oldest Jaipuri manuscript) and one of the most pleasant, is one that currently appears as number 642 in the Nāgarīpracāriṇī Sabhā edition. It describes in great detail the celebrations that attend the birth of Krishna in Braj, and as one encounters it in the Sabhā edition it stands out from those that surround it because of its length. It contains some sixty lines,[43] whereas its neighbors only occasionally extend to twelve or sixteen. In the old manuscripts the contrast is even more stark; there a norm of six or eight lines is rarely exceeded. The tone of S 642, methodical and chronological, also contrasts to that of its neighbors. Though it contains pleasant alliterations, there are no metrical surprises; and there is never a hint of irony, no intrusion of the unexpected. Here is a segment in translation (S 642.1–12):

"Braj has been blessed with a headman's son"—

this news traveled to everyone
And how they were filled with joy.
The worthy astrologers of Gokul,
Knowing that the merits of the family's past
had established a pillar that time would not shake,
Searched out the moment ordained in the skies
and chanted the sounds of the Vedas.
When the Braj women heard, they all came running,
dressed, as always, in a simple way,
But they decked themselves with their newest clothes
and applied mascara to their eyes.
Their forehead marks all set in place,
new blouses on their bosoms, necklaces on their breasts,
With braceleted hands they sat about
to decorate a golden offering plate.
They raised their blessings beneath dangling earrings
and hair that haste had left half-braided,

43. Sixty verses are given in the Sabhā edition. In manuscript, however, the poem varies in length; a couplet is lacking in U1, for instance, giving a total of 58 verses, and J1 stops at verse 41 (Sabhā v. 44), well short of the signature line.

As sweat rained down from their hard-working brows
  like droplets sprinkling from clouds.
Their faces flushed a rosy red,
  vermilion was daubed in the parts of their hair,
And the breeze began to loosen their colorful,
  brilliant saris—but then, what did they care?[44]

As one can see, the poem is told from a straightforwardly narrative perspective, as if simply to review the details in a well-known picture. In this it is very unlike most of the early poems that allude to the same moment in time, of which the following is a simple example (S 639):

I've hurried on over, for the news has come:

Yaśodā's a mother, given birth to a son.
  The courtyard throbs with songs of acclaim,
And what am I to say at the sight of such a scene?
  Jewels strewn thick cover the earth;
Everyone's dancing, from aged to infants;
  the air is stirred in a swirl of dirt and curds;
Cowherds and herdswomen crowd at the door
  with even more praises—what am I to say?
Sūr Dās's Lord is the one who knows each mood
  and gives the world its joy—as Nanda's little boy.

Obviously this poem is shorter than S 642, but it also displays a different sort of art. It achieves its effect by taking the hearer immediately within the Braj setting. One of the women of the region speaks to another, and the audience is propelled into the scene

44. The poem is found in J1, B2, U1, B4, J3, and J4. The manuscripts show some flexibility in the ordering of verses, but all but one agree in the order assigned to the first eight lines. The exception is B4, which reverses lines 3 and 4. The last four verses translated here are presented in their Sabhā order, but if one were following the sequence adopted in the old manuscripts, five or six lines that the Sabhā understands to come later would be interposed. Readers familiar with the Sabhā edition may occasionally notice turns of phrase that suggest other vocabulary than one finds in the printed text. Among these are *rūpī kul* for *ropī* in verse 3, as in all manuscripts except B2; *bal* for *pal* in verse 4, on which the manuscripts are unanimous; and *śram jal mukh prasved* (J1, B2, U1) in beginning line 10. B4 and J3 approximate the Sabhā reading at this point with the seemingly more genteel variant *sir baraṣat kusum sudes*: "as blossoms rained on [from?] their shapely [?] heads."

by overhearing their conversation. It conveys its sense of wonder by thrusting the hearer into a scene in which the voice of the spokesperson is not the only one that is heard. Others too shout their congratulations, and the sight of it all leaves the woman with whom we have come into this crowd at a loss to know how to add her praises to the rest. She is dumfounded, poor thing, and every time she mentions others' songs she falters herself (verses 3a and 5b). Indeed, these two little confessions of verbal inadequacy frame the body of the poem; when the second is heard, we know that our guide has come to an end. Then it is time for the concluding line, the poet's signature line, which, as so often, shifts the ground a little. Though the cowherd spokeswoman could have uttered everything in it except the signature itself (one need only substitute for "Sūr Dās's" a neutral term such as "the" or "my" to see that this is so), the poet's presence in the line suggests a broadening of perspective that fittingly comes at the end. A small surprise, however, is still in store. The audience may too quickly be lulled to generality by the almost formulaic affirmation that the Lord is omniscient (*antarjāmī*: "the one who knows each mood"[45]), only to find that the joy he dispenses with equally general ease (*sukh dāi*) derives in this case from just the moment that the poem has described. God is not only Lord of the world; he is Nanda's little boy.

Compositions resembling this in their brevity and in their use of perspective and surprise—many more carefully wrought and more widely represented in the manuscripts than this one—are so frequent in the early *Sūr Sāgar* that one may wonder how such a poem as "Braj has been blessed" (S 642) found its way into their midst. A glance at one of the first manuscripts in which it appears (U1) may help to explain how it made its entrance, for it is listed as the first poem in the entire manuscript. Inserted even before the table of contents, it introduces the childhood poems with a programmatic completeness that someone evidently thought was called for—in this case apparently after the original collection had been made. It was used for the same purpose in B4, written a year later, but in that case still another poem of the same type (S 622) was prefaced to it, and that one is longer still: in the Sabhā edition it runs to more than eighty lines.[46] In B4 it is plain that long,

45. The meaning of this term in the Upaniṣads is "inner controller," but in Braj Bhāṣā it is regularly used to mean "the one who knows what is within."

46. Since the beginning of the manuscript has been lost, it is impossible to tell exactly how much of it was quoted in B4, but from the portion that appears—

narrative poems are being employed by the scribe with this summary or introductory intent. Not only the section of the manuscript describing Krishna's childhood, but all other portions as well, save one, begin with extended compositions of the same type.[47] Of course, not every manuscript fits this mold. In J3, for instance, one encounters two shorter poems before coming to S 642, and J1 simply includes S 642 among other poems in a section near the end of the manuscript that is devoted exclusively to poems of Sūr (earlier, other poets are also represented). But the general pattern is widespread, as one can see in other usages of S 642: even after many years—in Al, for instance—it was still quoted as the introductory poem in the series describing Krishna's childhood. The *Caurāsī Vaiṣṇavan kī Vārtā* carries this commentarial logic to its extreme by asserting that this poem was in fact the first that Sūr ever composed on the subject of Krishna's infancy or, indeed, any aspect of his life.[48] The *Vārtā* often chooses just such pale, encyclopedic poems for quotation, since they make the poet seem as straight and unambiguous as the writer of the *Vārtā* himself must have been.

In more recent strata of the *Sūr Sāgar*, poems designed with such a systematic intent are much more frequent than in the early *Sūr Sāgar*, where they are exceptions to the rule. They grow to proportions that exceed even what we have seen already. S 1009, for instance, is a poem of almost a hundred lines that is nowhere to be found in early manuscripts of the *Sūr Sāgar*. Its scope matches its size, for it goes beyond any particular event in Krishna's childhood and gives a running account of the whole—all in the most strictly narrative of styles. Whereas earlier poems might present a dispute between, say, Yaśodā and the *gopīs* by making the listener follow sudden, unannounced changes of perspective as the argument lurches from one side to the other, this poem makes it easy to follow the dialogue.[49] It inserts the equivalent of paragraphs and quotation marks, supplying phrases such as "the *gopīs*

---

amounting to more than half of the Sabhā version—it seems the B4 version approximated that of the Sabhā.

47. These include S 1245 and 1690, the *sūrpacīsī* (S 325), and a poem whose corresponding Sabhā version I have not yet been able to locate: *muralī adhar dharī mere sāvare*. The exception is S 9, a short poem introducing the section labeled *karunā ras*.

48. *Vārtā*, pp. 407–8.

49. An example of the earlier type (S 908) is translated in Hawley, *Butter Thief*, pp. 125–26.

complain" and "Krishna says" so that the reader can pass quickly and without confusion from one speech or episode to the next. Such poems are to the majority of entries in the early *Sūr Sāgar* what muzak is to music; they regularize the beat and predigest the melody. Their heirs are works that carry the same tendency further and are overly commentarial. The most notable of these is the *Braj Vilās* of Brajbāsī Dās, a full-length work of the mid-eighteenth century that is separate from the *Sūr Sāgar* but explicitly intended as a digest of it. Its purpose is to convey a single, connected narrative rather than so many vivid little parts.

Unlike the poems we have just been examining, many of the poems of the later *Sūr Sāgar* are neither unusually long nor specifically didactic; they more closely resemble the compositions contained in the early *Sūr Sāgar*. But even in them one often detects this commentarial perspective as the voice of an all-knowing narrator intrudes into dramatic situations described in the poems themselves. In the poems describing Krishna as a thief of butter and, consequently, of love, this commentarial tone is so widespread as to alter fundamentally the tone of the whole group. Whereas in earlier poems the hearer never knows whether the *gopīs*' charges against Krishna are justified or whether the cowherd girls themselves have lured him into their homes, later poems collapse the drama so that the reader is assured that no scandal is involved.[50] These more recent contributers to the *Sūr Sāgar* were unwilling to forget for a moment that Krishna was God rather than some thoughtless marauder, and they were anxious to make sure that their audiences understood the point as clearly as they did. In such poems, everything Krishna does on earth appears as part of a providential design that he himself, in a lapse of dramatic exigency, is allowed to announce. He describes himself as the ineffable one, the one who pervades everything, and above all as *bhaktavatsal*, that divinity whose quality it is to incarnate himself on earth from time to time for the sake of his devotees (*bhakta*s).[51] Often this heavenly overview has the effect of whitewashing the *gopīs*' reactions to Krishna: they become his ever-willing hosts. But it is also possible to comprehend even adverse emotions *sub specie aeternitatis*, as theologians had long since shown, for Krishna is a divinity drawn to emotion per se. Indeed it is a measure of his irreducible supremacy that he can be dependent on the emotions

50. Ibid., pp. 122–29, 167–74.

51. *avigat avināsī [brahmā]* (S 2138.6), *brahmā kīṭ ādi lāu vyāpak* (S 2140.4), *bhakt hit het avatāri līlā karat* (S 3445.5), and to the *gopīs*, *tum kāran baikuṇṭh tajat hāu, janam let braj āi* (S 2232.3). Such phrases occur numerous times.

of those who love him.[52] So complete is his control that he can afford to generate a game in which he himself is a participant.

Remarks about the nature of Krishna's divinity, injected here and there, have the effect of aligning the poems in which they occur with larger, providential perspectives that make sense of the narrative as a whole. Many of them, in fact, are little more than theological clichés that belong equally everywhere and nowhere.[53] Another facet of the commentarial impetus that colors the later *Sūr Sāgar*, however, moves in just the other direction. Instead of bringing the overall picture constantly to bear on its parts by means of some predictable phrase, it leads to the amplification of the whole with altogether new material. In this mood episodes described or allegations made in the earlier *Sūr Sāgar* are amplified until their full implications have been spelled out, for commentators abhor an open ending as much as an interstitial vacuum.

In a number of early poems, for instance, the *gopīs*' complaints about their absent lover lead them to indulge in a barrage of slander directed against their newfound rival, a certain Kubjā of Mathura. The name is generic, "Hunchback," and she has become their rival only because Krishna has taken pity on her and removed her deformity, turning her into a stunning beauty. The *gopīs*, however, have no intention of forgetting her cursed history and scorn her mercilessly, depicting her as the worst sort of *parvenue*. There is no way for us to know whether their charges about Krishna's current liaison are justified, for we only hear one side of the story, and there is no reason to find out. The *gopīs*' charges are intended not to inform us about what Krishna is doing but about what they are feeling. A later poet, however, like a humorless commentator, was unsatisfied with this state of affairs—perhaps he objected to such intentionally provocative language—and resolved to set the record straight. He invented (or possibly reported) a vignette in which Kubjā dispatches a letter to the women of Braj, using Ūdho as a messenger (S 4061). In this epistle she exonerates Krishna of any wrongdoing. The whole episode, she explains, redounds to her master's grace, not his disgrace. And with that the story is not only completed but sterilized.[54]

52. *bhāv adhīn rahāu sabahī kāi, aur na kāhū nāiku ḍarāu* (S 2140.3).

53. Examples include variants of those cited in n. 51 in addition to such titles as *tribhuvan-rāi* (S 1593.1), *jag-svāmī* (2330.2), and the very common epithets *antarjāmī* and, in a different vein, *cit-cor*.

54. Similar revisions in puranic accounts having to do with Kubjā have been studied by Noel Sheth, "The Justification for Kṛishṇa's Affair with the Hunchbacked Woman," *Purāṇa* 25, no. 2 (1983): 225–36.

The device of a letter (*pātī*) sent with Ūdho, an appealing one to such later "commentators," may suggest that they were composing for the page as well as for the ear. It may also indicate that they were influenced by the important *Vinaya Patrikā* of Tulsī Dās, a series of petitionary letters to Rām; and Tulsī himself was certainly literate. Another poem added to the *Sūr Sāgar* in its later years (S 4060) concerns a letter that Devakī and Vasudev, Krishna's biological parents, who also lived in Mathura, sent to Braj with Ūdho. What must they have felt, these commentator-poets evidently asked, to be separated from Krishna and Balarām all those years? This poem provides the answer: they are grateful for the way in which Yaśodā and her husband Nanda have raised their sons to be such fine boys, but they cannot help being a little envious that they themselves could not have tasted the joys that such a charmed childhood must have brought. It would seem that this poem casts a shadow of regret across the sky of unremitting bliss that similar commentators saw in Krishna's youth, but in fact the hint of lament in the message of Devakī and Vasudev is probably merely an answer to the lament that Yaśodā expresses in earlier poems. These too involve "letters"—in this case oral messages dispatched in the reverse direction, from Braj to Mathura—and the plaintive tone is much more pronounced. Yaśodā begs to see her boys again (S 3796, 3797), and she cannot bring herself to believe that her little Krishna will ever outgrow his childish fondness for butter, though he may be too embarrassed to ask for it (S 3793, 3797). Thus she suffers in his absence, but in the later poem we are reminded, ever so gently, that the suffering has not been hers alone: Devakī and Vasudev have missed the most precious years. By supplying this perspective, missing from the early *Sūr Sāgar*, the commentator sets the record straight: everything proves just.

This rectification of grief is carried out on a much grander scale by involving the emotions of Krishna himself. The suffering, even the bitterness, expressed in the early *Sūr Sāgar* falls almost entirely on the side of the women who love him. Typical of such anguish is a poem such as this (S 3809), addressed by the *gopīs* to Ūdho:

Wayfarer, see how the dark Jumna's blackened.

Carry to that Hari of yours the word
  that she's blackened, scorched in a feverous longing
As if from her couch she had fainted to the earth—
  her weight too great for her wave-washed bed—

Hoping a poultice of sand from her banks
  could salve her riven body, rivered with sweat.
Her hair is a tangle of grasses and reeds;
  her sari's flowered pattern is fouled and black with mud;
She flails about like aimless, restless bees
  through a thousand tortured courses, horrid and forlorn,
Subsisting on foam, babbling night and day
  like the pitiful bird who calls when its mate is away.
Sūr Dās says, Lord, the sad state of the Jumna
  is not hers alone: it's also our own.

Later contributors to the *Sūr Sāgar* once again stepped in to right the record, ironing out the inequality if the situation itself could not be altered. In the final phases of the early *Sūr Sāgar* we find Krishna explaining to his wife in Dvaraka that for all its blandishments his new life of royalty can never compare with what he knew in Braj (S 4890, introduced in J4 and K1). And in the later *Sūr Sāgar* Krishna is made to experience at least a measure of the *viraha* that is borne by those he has left behind (S 4774):

"Ūdho, the memory of Braj never fades:

Brindavan, Gokul, the glades and jungles,
  the shade of thick-grown groves,
The mornings when mother Yaśodā and Nanda
  would come in to see me and smile;
They'd ply me with butter and bread and fine curd
  as if feeding me was their highest reward.
The milkmaids, the cowherds, the children at play—
  daily they'd dally, gay and laughing—
Sūr Dās says, thanks to the folk from Braj,
  who are ever beloved by their Yādav lord.

In a final stroke, such later poets of the *Sūr Sāgar* even altered the facts of the case. Krishna had promised on leaving Braj that he would return before long. In earlier poems, when this parting scene is reenacted, the audience overhears Krishna's words and, knowing that they are never to be fulfilled, experiences a poignancy that would be impossible if Yaśodā and Nanda and the *gopī*s were also aware of the dismal extent of the separation that is in store for them. Their pointless struggle with hope and fate is deeply pathetic. But Indian literary tradition, especially the high, Sanskrit tradition, decrees that no unhappy ending can be final; such pathos cannot remain the last word. Therefore one finds a little group of poems in the more recent levels of the *Sūr Sāgar*[55] that tell how Krishna did in fact fulfill his vow, achieving a reunion with his family and lovers on the field of Kurukṣetra many years later. High theology, and perhaps popular legendry as well, had already supplied this episode; the poets of the later *Sūr Sāgar* did not have to invent it out of whole cloth.[56] But they made sure that it was included in what came increasingly to be seen as the definitive vernacular statement of the Krishna legend, giving assurance that *viraha*, though a necessary concomitant of the religious life, is not its culmination.[57]

One of the most telling transformations of all in the growth of the *Sūr Sāgar* from its earlier to its later form concerns the group of poems that constitutes the very epitome of *viraha* in the early *Sūr Sāgar*. These are the "poems of the bee," the *bhramargīt*, but in the early *Sūr Sāgar* they should rightly be called poems *to* the bee since Ūdho never inserts a word.[58] The intensity of the *gopīs*' *viraha*, whether in a yearning or in a sarcastic mood, stifles any potential debate. Anyone who hears these poems is presented constantly with the possibility that the *gopīs* are right: perhaps Krishna really has sent Ūdho in his stead because he lacks the courage to present himself before them and face up to his past. When Ūdho returns to Krishna after a merciless verbal lashing from these rustic women, he is exhausted. All he has to say is that in the face of love like theirs, knowledge counts for little. If Krishna does not believe him, he can go and see for himself (S 4747.1–6, 4762.8). What he reports to Krishna merely underlines the anguish his friend and master has unleashed in Braj (e.g., S 4762).

Certain later poems tell a different story. Krishna's mischievous, seemingly irresponsible role is less apparent. It survives only in the sense that he has dispatched Ūdho on a mission whose true purpose he has not revealed to him. Krishna's real aim in sending

55. S 4900–4902. The earliest of this group, S 4901, goes only as far back as J4, the only manuscript in the early group to include it.

56. One finds it in Jīva Gosvāmī, *Gopālacampū*, 2: 489–513.

57. In one of these later poems Krishna observes, apropos of the *gopīs*, that "where the pain of separation is not felt, love [*prem*] cannot grow up" (S 4031.3).

58. The poems in the Sabhā edition in which Ūdho is given a chance to speak are universally late: S 4102, 4103, 4157, 4224, 4303, 4484, 4666, 4670, 4671, 4711, 4712, 4742. Ūdho does speak in S 4696 (B3, A1), but this is to record his conversion to the *gopīs*' point of view rather than to argue with them.

Ūdho to the *gopīs* was, we learn, to win him away from *nirguṇa* religion in general and from the insipid obsessions of yogic concentration in particular (precisely what he had told Ūdho to preach) by bringing him into confrontation with the world's most eloquent spokespersons for the opposite position (S 4031). The whole venture was designed to teach the glories and depths of the simple religion of love—not only to Ūdho, of course, but to any in the audience who might be straying toward the *nirguṇa* path. What once had seemed scandal, therefore, is now comprehended as a part of Krishna's providential plan. When Ūdho returns to his liege he is no longer the frustrated personage we see in the earlier poems but a bubbling convert. He reports a momentous change of heart in himself rather than urging such a thing on Krishna. Instead of pitying the women of Braj for their intractable condition, he praises them in extravagant terms (S 4670, 4671).

Later contributors to the *Sūr Sāgar* could not remove the pithy ironies, the artful shifts of perspective, or the striking expressions that were the hallmark of the *Sūr Sāgar* in its earlier form. But they could surround them with more discursive, placid verse intended to bring out the happy, overarching logic that no reader should forget in encountering compositions that often seemed so provocative at first. Sometimes, of course, the poems added to later strata of the *Sūr Sāgar* were fine creations; many have been regarded as some of Sūr's best poetry. In fact, the most famous of all (S 952), "I didn't eat the butter, Ma," is not found in the early manuscripts. But as a group they do not stand up to what came earlier, and their number is so substantial that they have altered the tone of the corpus as a whole.

It would be folly to think that by paring away later accretions to the *Sūr Sāgar* one could find the real Sūr Dās, but the rewards of such an undertaking are great nonetheless. When one attends to these early poems, one finds a focus and depth, as well as a measure of humor, that is all too often lost as the *Sūr Sāgar* expands and becomes embedded in ever more elaborate commentary on itself. In the chapters remaining we shall devote by far the greater part of our attention to these early poems. But before we forget the later *Sūr Sāgar* altogether, it is well to give some thought to the figure who, next to Krishna, plays the major role there: Rādhā. In studying how she emerges and flowers as the corpus develops, one gains a particularly clear understanding of what was gained as the *Sūr Sāgar* grew, and what was lost.

Rādhā dancing. Ink on paper, Jaipur, late eighteenth century. Courtesy of the Museum of Fine Arts, Boston (Ross-Coomaraswamy Collection, 17.3082).

CHAPTER 3

Sūr's Rādhā: A Case Study

MODERN-DAY CRITICS have praised Sūr's portrayal of Rādhā chiefly for its comprehensiveness. They point out that whereas Sūr's Maithili and Bengali predecessors, Vidyāpati and Caṇḍīdās, dwelt exclusively on the intense adolescent amours that bind Rādhā to Krishna, Sūr takes a longer view. He explores every stage and vicissitude of Rādhā's emotions, from the first time Krishna chanced upon her as a young girl playing in her yard, to the long aching years after he had left her behind, gone off to the city of Mathura to defeat wicked King Kaṃsa.[1]

How casually, how mischievously it all begins in the dialogue poem critics invariably cite (S 1291):

"Who are you, my fair one?" the Dark One asks,

"And where is your family, your house?
You've never been seen in Braj lanes."
"Never you mind—I stay in my yard
and play behind my gate, never venture out
Where, I've heard, Nanda's boy is bound
to steal our butter and curd."
"Now what of yours would I possibly steal?
Come on, let's both of us play."
That gourmet of love, Sūr's Lord, with his words
disarms poor Rādhā, simple girl.

1. Hazārīprasād Dvivedī, "Sūrdās kī Rādhā," in *Sūrdās*, ed. Harbanślāl Śarmā, pp. 193, 196, 198; Dvārkāprasād Mītal, *Hindī Sāhitya mẽ Rādhā*, p. 300; Omprakāś, *Madhyayugīn Kāvya*, pp. 83, 88ff. Although the contrast with Caṇḍīdās and Vidyāpati is not explicitly drawn out in the recent article by B. B. L. Sharmā, he surveys the same range of material in the *Sūr Sāgar*. See Sharmā, "Rādhā of Sûradāsa," in *Suradasa, A Reevaluation*, ed. Nagendra, pp. 110–17.

How naturally we see the love of childhood sweethearts grow as we turn the pages of the *Sūr Sāgar*. How inevitably it turns to the solemnity, even the tragedy, of a woman's devotion to her man. The critics observe that Rādhā is gradually transformed from a charming girl to an archetypal wife,[2] suffering all and refusing to share her difficulties with the family and acquaintances of her chosen one.[3] Nobility itself, she endures the mockery broadcast by a world in which we cannot have what our hearts demand. To the end she remains steadfast in love's perilous path.[4]

The appeal of this extended, detailed portrait of Rādhā is easy to understand. In the first place it befits the exalted position that she occupies in modern Indian piety. Evidently a minor presence in the first millennium A.D., Rādhā has come since the sixteenth century to dominate the devotional and theological attention of such communities as the Rādhāvallabha and Nimbārk Sampradāys and to be regarded as of equal importance to Krishna elsewhere: in hymn-singing groups as far away as Madras, for example, and in the Caitanya or Gauḍīya Sampradāy that exerts such an important influence in east and north India.[5] In Braj itself she exercises a remarkable sway, particularly in the town of Brindavan, which more than any other place has come to be regarded as the spiritual center of the region. In Brindavan the standard Vallabhite greeting, "Jai Śrī Krishna" (Hail Krishna), is scarcely heard.

2. D. Mītal, *Rādhā*, p. 301.
3. Dvivedī, "Sūrdās kī Rādhā," p. 200.
4. Omprakāś, *Madhyayugīn Kāvya*, pp. 92–93.
5. On Rādhā in general, and for further bibliography, see John Stratton Hawley and Donna M. Wulff, eds., *The Divine Consort: Rādhā and the Goddesses of India*, pp. 1–128. On the Rādhāite theology of the Rādhāvallabha Sampradāy, see Charles S. J. White, *The "Caurāsī Pad" of Śrī Hit Harivaṁś*, pp. 28–31; Vijayendra Snātak, *Rādhāvallabh Sampradāy: Siddhānt aur Sāhitya*, pp. 199–205; Rupert Snell, "Scriptural Literature in the Rādhāvallabha Sampradāya," *I A V R I Bulletin* 4 (1978): 22–30; and Lalitācaran Gosvāmī, *Śrī Hit Harivaṃś Gosvāmī: Sampradāy aur Sāhitya*, pp. 201–23. On the earlier history of Rādhā, see articles by Charlotte Vaudeville, Dennis Hudson, and C. Mackenzie Brown in *Divine Consort*, ed. Hawley and Wulff, pp. 1–12, 57–71, 238–61; also Barbara Stoler Miller, "Rādhā: Consort of Kṛṣṇa's Vernal Passion," *Journal of the American Oriental Society* 95, no. 4 (1975): 655–71. On Caitanyite theology in regard to Rādhā, see Shrivatsa Goswami, "Rādhā: The Play and Perfection of *Rasa*," in *Divine Consort*, ed. Hawley and Wulff, pp. 72–88. Concerning the role of Rādhā in popular religion in modern South India, see Milton Singer, "The Rādhā-Krishna *Bhajanas* of Madras City" and T. K. Venkateswaran, "Rādhā-Krishna *Bhajanas* of South India: A Phenomenological, Theological, and Philosophical Study" in *Krishna: Myths, Rites, and Attitudes,* ed. M. Singer, pp. 139–99.

Krishna shares his eminence with his consort in the greeting that is common all over Braj: "Rādhe-Syām," a vocative compound addressed to both partners in the divine couple. Or, perhaps even more prevalent, the salutation to Krishna is dropped altogether and people greet each other in the name of Rādhā alone: "Rādhe!"

This is no accident, for by and large the people of Brindavan feel that Rādhā is their queen, even more than Krishna is their king. True, in many ways the two stand equal: her birthday celebrations balance his, and the town in which he grew up is venerated alongside her natal village.[6] But as the Rādhā-Krishna plays (*rās līlās*) of Brindavan are performed, it is at the mention of her name that hands are raised in adulation all over the audience: "Jai Śrī Rādhe" (Hail Rādhā!). Simple men and women submit the vagaries of their lives to Queen Rādhā's will. Letters from Brindavan offer assurances that although much else in the world may have gone awry, there, where Rādhā rules, all remains peaceful and loving. And in the plays of Brindavan her ascendancy is explicitly celebrated, a supremacy she wields not only over all of Braj, but over Krishna himself. The moments when he comes to her with the humility of one who would place his head in the dust at her feet or wash those feet and even drink the water left over as a substance of grace (*prasād*) are greeted by their spectators first with hushed awe and then with shouts of excitement.[7]

One reason, then, for the critics' acclaim of the generous description of Rādhā that one finds in current editions of the *Sūr Sāgar* is that it answers to and provides background for one of the dominant aspects of modern Vaiṣṇava piety. But there is another reason as well. Today's critics—both academic and devotional, and often a combination of both—are in large measure the bearers of the commentator's mantle, and their tastes reflect the same commentarial tradition that has had such a significant impact on the later strata of the *Sūr Sāgar*. One of the most important concerns of that tradition, as we have seen, is completeness, and it is in

6. The pairing is explicit in both cases. In regard to sacred time it seems that Rādhā's birth festival (Rādhāṣṭamī) grew up to match the more venerable Kṛṣṇajanmāṣṭamī, of which the *Bhaviṣyottara Purāṇa* takes considerable note; it follows exactly a fortnight later. In regard to sacred place, however, Rādhā's town Barsānā has a preeminence that Krishna's nearby Nandagāõ only somewhat palely matches.

7. Such scenes are witnessed in the *rādhācaransparś* (cf. also *naukā*) and *kākmāl līlās*. On the genre as a whole, and for further bibliography, see John Stratton Hawley, *At Play with Krishna: Pilgrimage Dramas from Brindavan*.

those terms that Sūr is especially praised. Yet the "Sūr" whose comprehensive vision of Rādhā these critics laud is in reality the *Sūr Sāgar* itself, in its current, massive form. When one examines the earlier portions of the *Sūr Sāgar*, one finds that Rādhā does not preside over every stage of the Krishna's life to the extent that she does in later, larger editions. Of particular importance, she does not accompany him in his childhood, the span of time that Sūr has described with such an unrivaled flare.[8] Whereas, for instance, there are a number of poems in the current Sabhā edition that describe the first meeting of these two special personages, only two of them are attested in the old manuscripts (S 1305, 1307). Of these, only the first appears to mention Rādhā specifically, calling her Syāmā (S 1305.8). And if one consults the manuscripts one finds that this identification has been made only in relatively recent times. In the earlier versions this alluring girl is called simply *taraṅgiṇī*, a supple young woman; she may or may not be Rādhā.

This is no isolated instance. Sūr—using the term now to designate the collective authorship of poems included in the early *Sūr Sāgar*—has no interest at all in chronicling Rādhā's youth. Evidently it is only her encounter with Krishna that he finds compelling, with all it entails. In the single old poem describing their first meeting there is nothing to suggest that it happens when they are children, whereas in later poems, such as the one translated above, the childhood romance is depicted vividly. We do hear, in the early *Sūr Sāgar*, how Krishna used to grab Rādhā's clothes and steal them away (S 2298.1, 4387.5), but all this is only recalled by a more seasoned Rādhā.[9] We also hear how ever since Krishna first heard her name it has been his constant mantra: *hā rādhā hā rādhā* (S 3399.1-2). But that too is refracted through a later vision: it comes from the mouth of one of Rādhā's friends, who is trying to draw her out of her disconsolate sulking. Aside from that, Sūr is silent: Rādhā's innocent childhood does not appear per se. In this respect Sūr's Rādhā is much closer to the involved and suffering lover portrayed by Caṇḍīdās and Vidyāpati than critics who surveyed a later cross section of the *Sūr Sāgar* had thought.

The case is similar at the other end of the story. Critics are apt

8. Generous samples of such poetry may be found in Kenneth E. Bryant, *Poems to the Child-God*, pp. 152–80, some from earlier poems in the *Sūr Sāgar*, some from later.

9. In the modern plays of Brindavan, significantly, it is the other *gopīs* whose clothes are stolen, for Rādhā has risen too high to be the victim of such trickery on Krishna's part.

to make a good deal of the reunion Rādhā has with Krishna long after he has left Braj, when both of them journey to holy Kurukṣetra on the occasion of a solar eclipse. Hazārīprasād Dvivedī, for instance, draws the culminating flourishes of his portrait of Sūr's Rādhā from S 4911.[10] She reports her own experience to a friend:

Nothing, today there was nothing I could do.

When Hari appeared I was stunned
  as if beholding a precious work of art.
I held back my heart, though it flushed at the thought
  he might make it his throne, his lotus home.
My breast bowed low, but my eyes refused
  to release the torrential oblation they held,
And though my breasts, round pitchers,
          heaved against my sari,
  never did my bodice-string snap at the strain.
Now shame has burst through the caverns of my mind
  when I measure my acts, sense what I have done;
At the sight of his face how strange I have become—
  how senseless and mindless, my friend.
Even so, says Sūr, this numbness, this dumbness—
  I reckon it as nothing but my luck.

Persuasive as this poem is in recording the noble restraint of a woman who has had to endure much for the sake of love that has been denied her, there is nothing in what it says that explicitly ties it to Kurukṣetra. Indeed, one cannot be absolutely sure that it is Rādhā who gives it voice, since her name does not appear. Only its general mood and a tradition either created or solidified by the editors of the Sabhā *Sūr Sāgar* make it obvious that this poem describes the emotions of a mature Rādhā encountering the love of her life for the last time.

Indeed, the tradition of associating this poem with the incident at Kurukṣetra goes no further back than the eighteenth century. The poem from which this one was fashioned is a very old one, but it had to be entirely transformed to fit its current position near the end of the Sabhā *Sūr Sāgar*. Its original form is much closer

10. Dvivedī, "Sūrdās kī Rādhā," p. 203. Dvivedī quotes the Nāgarīpracāriṇī Sabhā version, which is translated immediately below.

to the very similar poem preserved in the Sabhā edition as S 2498, a poem introduced considerably earlier in the text under the heading of *grīṣmalīlā*, "the joys of summer." And joys they are. In this version the poem is stripped of the negative particles that principally make it possible for its Kurukṣetra cousin to convey a sense of Rādhā's great restraint, and one is left with a poem whose message is utterly different. The speaker's words now testify not to her inner emotion and outer decorum, but to the ease with which infatuation breaks through any barriers that modesty might erect. It translates from manuscript as follows:

Nothing, nothing, there was nothing I could do

When Hari appeared; I could only stare
  as if beholding a precious work of art
And flush with joy that my heart's lotus home
  should be offered as a flower, as his throne.
An oblation was made with the water from my eyes,
  the garment at my shoulders bowed deep,
And shame burst forth in the caverns of my mind
  when I sensed what my soul had done;
But my sari bore fruit, baring the pitcher of my breast,
  and my bodice-string snapped with the strain.
My mind, my friend, refused to give credit
  to any discretion my elders ever urged.
This stunning dumbness, this numbness, says Sūr—
  my Lord has reckoned it my luck.

Other poems considered by the Sabhā editors as bearing on the episode at Kurukṣetra fall away less dramatically but as surely—they simply are not found in the old manuscripts—and one discovers that there is just one poem in the early *Sūr Sāgar* (S 4904) that could fairly be construed as referring to the reunion between Rādhā and Krishna. Even that, however, is only an oblique possibility, and if it were true, furthermore, one would gain no sense of Rādhā's deportment under the circumstances, for she plays no active role. Instead Rukmiṇī is featured, Krishna's royal bride from the western city of Dvaraka over which he reigns after leaving Mathura. She surveys a group of *gopīs* and begs to know which of them is her erstwhile rival. It is not clear whether her query is prompted by an actual meeting, for which the Kurukṣetra story would have provided a rationale, or by a picture of Krishna's Braj acquaintances that she has chanced to see in Dvaraka. Perhaps the latter explanation is more likely, since such an incident was given considerable prominence in the writings of Sūr's younger contemporary at Brindavan, Jīva Gosvāmī.[11] If that is the case, the narrative span over which Sūr's portrait of Rādhā could be said to range is considerably diminished, for Rādhā's presence at Kurukṣetra is no longer required. The poem reads as follows in its earliest version, that recorded in B1:

Rukmiṇī asks, "Which maid, my dear,

is Bṛṣabhānu's child?
Come, let me know which one she is,
your childhood sweetheart from long ago,
Who taught you to be so cleverly wise,
and that at such a tender age:
She taught you the art of being a thief,
stealing even your peace of mind.
Her virtues you number and string like beads
that never abandon your breast.
You meditate, you memorize
that beauty with a gaze that will not stray . . .
Look there—that girl!—standing out from the others,
outstandingly fair and clad all in blue:
My mind has been caught by her," Sūr Dās says,
"tied and tethered with the rope of the eye."

This poem, as it happens, bears not only on the concluding episode in Krishna's involvement with Rādhā but on its genesis as well. It provides the one unambiguous statement in the early *Sūr Sāgar* that Krishna's childhood was closely intertwined with Rādhā's—a fact of considerable importance, especially from the point of view of the critics to whom we have referred. Yet even this one reference is less in the nature of chronicle than of perspective. Rukmiṇī, after all, has never been to Braj. For her it is all a matter of legend, a world in which she did not participate, a mysterious earlier affair. No wonder she tends to exaggerate, imagining Rādhā not only as the cause of all Krishna's mischief but also as his constant companion since infancy. When Rukmiṇī envisions Braj, she sees Rādhā behind every tree. All this

11. Jīva Gosvāmī, *Gopālacampū*, 2, chaps. 23–24: 489–529.

prepares the way for the unexpected shift that concludes the poem. There is more than a hint of jealousy as Rukmiṇī describes Krishna's preoccupation with Rādhā, likening it to that of an ascetic who, wearing the beaded necklace with which his guru would have initiated him, directs his attention totally to the object of his disciplines. In the course of this characterization, however, her own eye falls on a golden-complexioned, blue-clad girl whose identity she does not know, but we, from her description, do. Then suddenly Rukmiṇī too—like the poet himself—is absorbed in the contemplation of the very one she was just disparaging.

Rādhā in Perspective

One of the hallmarks of this poem, and of other early poems depicting Rādhā, is that nothing is seen point-blank. Rukmiṇī's thoughts hardly comprise a neutral historical account: they provide no clear narration of the circumstances in which the episode occurred, or of Krishna's youth, the time to which it indirectly refers. If anything is chronicled here, it is a shift in perspective. Another poem, one that seems to proceed as a straightforward description of Rādhā's very unstraightforward beauty (the poet emphasizes the curvature of her eyebrows, her sidelong glances, and the disorienting perfume she exudes, like that of elephants in rut), must be understood not only as the poet's description but one also offered, implicitly, by one of Rādhā's friends (S 2320). Like other poems in the early *Sūr Sāgar*, this poem can be read as having been spoken within its own dramatic context, not merely as the removed diction of the poet. We imagine that one of Rādhā's friends has encountered her after a tryst with Krishna:

Rādhā, how brilliant your shining face:

When side to side you flutter your glance,
  the Lord of the Night, the moon, seems pale.
Beneath the calm of your sandalwood brow
  you train your arrow-sharp eyes across bows
That are eyebrows, as if Kāma, Passion's Lord,
  should shelter himself behind garment and veil
And tender his hunter's aim, sequestered
  in the presence of that most dangerous prey:
An elephant in rut—I swear that's what you are,
  exuding the maddening perfume of love.
You've ravished in varied and manifold ways
  the heart of your lover, of Hari, Sūr's Lord.

If the poet himself seems to take the reins, as in the following composition (S 2741), he takes other measures to ensure a similar effect. Though he does not actually reproduce Rādhā's speech, he draws the listener into an experience of her vantage point in a way that keeps matters of perspective to the fore. There is no simple focus, for Rādhā's vision, as she gazes at Krishna, is hopelessly confused. She is unable to believe her senses and wonders if it is all hallucination:

She's found him, she has, but Rādhā disbelieves

That it's true, what she sees when her eyes behold
  her master's moonlike, heavenly face.
Her gaze is fixed, but her mind is glazed;
  her eyes have forgotten ever to close;
And her intellect wages a raging debate:
  Is it a dream? Or is this her true Lord?
Her eyes fill and fill with beauty's high pleasure,
  then bury their plunder deep in her breast,
But like bees driven wild at any distance from honey
  they dart back and forth from the hoard to the source.
Sometimes she musters her various thoughts; she wonders:
  Who does he love? Who can this Hari be?
For love, says Sūr, is an awkward thing.
  It stirs and ripples the mind with waves.

Rarely does Sūr show us Rādhā and Krishna while they are actually making love, and again for reasons of perspective. Faced with an audience that would have been aware of almost every detail in the amours of the charmed couple before he told them of it, his task was to surprise his listeners with a point of view that would enable them to see it all afresh.[12] One way to encourage this, as in "Rādhā, how brilliant," was to bend their perception of the scene through that of some other observer, perhaps one of Rādhā's friends. If he injects a note of doubt or ambiguity into the telling of the tale, as in "She's found him," so much the better, since it contributes to his aim of maneuvering the audience into a position in which they must reconstruct what really happened themselves, participating more actively than if they had been granted the luxury of seeing the scene point-blank.

Still another technique is to have Rādhā herself play the ancil-

12. Extended investigations of this point are found in Bryant, *Child-God*, especially pp. 43–90.

lary role. She too can be the observer, imagining an unseen, prior love. Often she passes a restless night without her partner only to find him slinking back unkempt in the morning: evidently he has been with another woman. As she decries his unseemly appearance, we imagine the encounter that caused it, and not only that one, but the one that Rādhā wishes had replaced it, her own. The immediate intensity of her language as rejected lover (*māninī*) makes all the more vivid our knowledge of her own battles of love with Krishna. They are refracted only palely, one must assume, in the scars we see after his engagement with another (S 3122):

Away! Go back to where you spent the night!

Manmohan, what clues are you trying to erase?
  Signs of tight embraces are not so quickly hid.
A necklace, now stringless, is etched into your chest:
  who's the clever girl whom you've pressed so to your heart?
Your hair is disheveled, your clothes and jewels askew,
  tangled in a bout with the hardened breasts of lust;
Teethmarks, nailmarks: poor you, what you've endured
  to have your fill of passion in that other woman's lair.
Your honey lips, says Sūr, have lost their taste and sheen
  and your sleepless eyes are heavy with the lethargy of love.

There are times when we are taken to the battleground itself, but again nothing is simply seen. In the following example (S 2742) we begin by experiencing the love match from the heroine's perspective—presumably Rādhā's—and again, as in "She's found him," her vision is clouded. Then we shift to the voice of the poet, which seems at first intended to set us straight about what we see, but soon proves to be much more than the purveyor of neutral description. The poet's remarks reshape our vision by turning the scuffles of Rādhā and Krishna into a match between the Love-god himself and his mate; and they compare the encounter with the epic stand-off between Arjun and Karṇa, a battle over which, ironically, Krishna himself presided in quite another guise. In the concluding line both points of view, Rādhā's and the poet's, are combined in a way that further challenges the audience's comprehension. It is clear as the line begins that she is being quoted, but the inclusion of the poet's mandatory signature implies that he shares her intense observation of Krishna. Since quotation marks are absent from the original and there are no verbs to indicate who is speaking—only the signature "Sūr"—the audience must make its own synthesis, and thus develop its own point of view:

"Seeing the Dark One is like staring in the dark,

Like looking without seeing, it seems. What to do?
My battle-weary eyes have passed the night awake."
His, like Kāma's, is a handsome sight,
and hers is a radiance no measure can trace.
They're intimate rivals, like Arjun and Karṇa,
and neither will ever consider surrender:
She's poised for battle, in finery arrayed,
and he opposed, his limbs like glistening mail.
"My eyes," says Sūr, "are so filled with pride
that only the Dark One can fill their demands."

In other poems, such as the one we have already heard involving Rukmiṇī, remembrance provides the tool that on the one hand protects the scene being described from a frontal assault and on the other draws the audience in as fellow observers. They too, after all, are aware of what has transpired between Rādhā and Krishna—a knowing audience—and vivid recall is just what is being asked of them as they listen. In the following poem it is Ūdho through whom the memory is filtered. He returns to Krishna in Mathura after having encountered the women of Braj and describes Rādhā's desolate state (S 4721):

"Hari has come, at last he's come!"

These were the words that tumbled from Rādhā
as soon as she saw me; she gestured in the dark.
Her body trembled with the tremors of longing
and her heart beat hard in her tortured breast.
She started toward me, she stumbled, she fell,
her body all sheathed in beads of sweat.
She grasped me, unyielding, though her bangles broke
and her elegant bodice severed at the seam.
It seemed love's messenger dove had been downed
by an arrow from the very same love it brought;
She flailed, O Ramāpati, as aimless as a snake
when the guiding gem falls from its cobra crown.
Lord of Sūr Dās, her words are at an end.
She knows no more knowing. She's losing her mind.[13]

13. Cf. S 4721 and 4724. S 4730, which appears to be another poem in which the sufferings of Rādhā are described retrospectively, is not necessarily so. The Sabhā edition, it is true, mentions her name in the title line, but this is an innovation. It occurs nowhere in the manuscript versions of the same poem (J1, B1, U1, J2, J4, A1, K1), which leave the *virahiṇī* in question unnamed.

Discussions between the sulking, withdrawn Rādhā and her friends achieve a similar effect. They provide particularly appropriate occasions on which reference can be made to the trials that Krishna too has had to endure for the sake of love. The following, for instance, is placed in the mouth of one of Rādhā's companions (S 3399):

Ever since your name has entered Hari's ear

It's been "Rādhā, oh Rādhā," an infinite mantra,
  a formula chanted to a secret string of beads.
Off by the Jumna he sits, in a grove
  far from his friends and his happiness and home.
He yearns for you. He has turned into a yogi:
  constantly wakeful, whatever the hour.
Sometimes he spreads himself a bed of tender leaves;
  sometimes he recites your treasurehouse of fames;
Sometimes he pledges silence: he closes his eyes
  and meditates on every feature of your frame—
His eyes the invocation, his heart the oblation,
  and his mutterings the food to feed the priests
    who tend the fire.
In all these ways Syām's body has wasted away.
  Says Sūr, let him see you. Fulfill his desire.[14]

Such use of perspective on the part of the poet permits the hearer a vivid access to the world of Rādhā and Krishna while at the same time shielding its intimacy. And on the rare occasions when that intimacy is not otherwise present, Rādhā is apt to call for it herself, as she does when she asks for a blanket in the following poem. The completed, blanketed scene, in which the divine couple is enclosed in a sheltered space that separates them from all possible viewers, is one that has often been depicted in miniature painting (S 2609):

"Give me, Kānh, a shawl for my shoulders.

Raindrops are starting, a drop here and there:
  the red dye will run from my clothes."
Over and over Rādhikā shows distress:
  "Look at that awesome event in the clouds!"

14. Cf. also S 3217, 3432, 3434, 3435, 3440.

So Rādhā and yellow-clad Krishna take cover
  and cuddle and smile and laugh, just the two.
Śiva and Sanaka, Nārad, the sages,
  and beast-men creatures—all kept at bay.
Sūr Dās says not even a glimpse is revealed,
  and the unknowing cowherds go on with their meal.

FROM INTIMACY TO EXALTATION

Even within the confines of the early *Sūr Sāgar* there was a tendency for this tart, intimate world governed by perspective to become increasingly flat as Rādhā and her relation to Krishna were described; texture turned more and more to filigree. Take, for instance, the poems that describe Rādhā's beauty. In the earliest ones there is invariably some perspectival twist. In one such poem, for instance (S 4690), the poet asks us to envision her immaculate beauty by seeing through her disheveled state. The title describes her, in fact, as "awfully dirty" (*ati malīn*). But if he depicts her loveliness in more obviously favorable terms, there will always be some technique or gesture that will alter the image and anchor the scene firmly in its dramatic context. The poem that follows (S 3067) provides a good example. We hear one of Rādhā's friends try to soften her anger at an absent Krishna by portraying him, not her, as the weaker party:

"Rādhā, a look at your loveliness has him:

He's weakened and shaken, he's sent me to say,
  as if war were waged, Kāma's army engaged.
Your footsteps—a graceful elephant's gait—
  the links of anklets, the slope beneath your navel,
And the sound at your waist of girdle bells
  have visited Mādhav with utter imbalance.
The ornamented bodice you've cinched around your breast
  seems a breastplate worn by a victor in war,
And when the upper edge of your garment flows free,
  it's a pennant of battle to his faltering mind.
When your eyebrows raise their perilous bow
  and aim their arrowhead, the mark on your brow,
Then your unerring eyes pierce him—
  the leader of the Yādavs—shattering his pride.
Your hair is as thick as a royal yak-tail fan
  and your crowning veil shades like a regal parasol.

Now give me the word. Let me take you to his side.
  Stretch forth your merciful arm."
The courier girl, lovely and ever so clever,
  framed these elegant words of love,
Revealing Sūr's Lord's amorous desire—
  then broke into a sweet and telling smile.

This artful composition makes use of two standard poetic conventions: first, a comparison between the battle of love and the battle of war; and second, a descriptive technique known as *nakh-śikh*, according to which the poet provides a systematic statement of the beauty of the figure he is describing by moving "from toe to head," as the phrase literally says, or alternatively from head to toe.[15] As he moves from the soles of Rādhā's feet—whose gentle and rhythmic pace he compares, in a standard simile, to the gait of an elephant—to the veil that covers her head, he intensifies the martial imagery at every step. Near the end (v. 9) he emphasizes the regal dimension of the classical battle: it was always a noble affair. This provides just the right moment for the intermediary between Rādhā and Krishna, into whose speech the whole poem has been committed up to this point, to ask for a signal both royal and warriorlike: a cue at once that an audience is to be granted, and that the battle is to commence. This cue, if given, will satisfy both poetic conventions. First it will move the scene beyond the array of love-battle that has been so carefully set forth, and signal the actual engagement of forces. In addition, it will conclude the toe-to-head succession with a surprise addition. Since Rādhā is almost always pictured as seated and bent over when she sulks, the gesture of a hand raised up and out toward the go-between will probably reach higher than her head. *Nakh-śikh* can reach no farther.

At this point the monologue—the poem within the poem—ends, and we are ready for Rādhā's response. But in the couplet that follows (vv. 11–12), we learn nothing of what that was. Sūr describes for us not what Rādhā did, but what the go-between did, and her actions have the effect not of relieving the suspense but of reinforcing it. When we learn in the very last word of the poem that the messenger girl cannot suppress a smile, we are reminded that all this praise of Rādhā is offered in anything but the spirit of detached objectivity. It is the speech of desire, for the girl is an

15. This genre, as used in poems of the *Sūr Sāgar* describing Krishna, is discussed in Bryant, *Child-God*, pp. 97–98. In regard to later *nakh-śikh* poetry describing Rādhā, see Karine Schomer, "Where Have All the Rādhās Gone?" in *Divine Consort*, ed. Hawley and Wulff, pp. 92–97.

emissary of Krishna. If one has been seduced into believing that her long paean states plain and simple fact (as the messenger hopes Rādhā has been), or if one has been carried away with the force of the obvious accoutrements of Sūr's poetic craft, one is abruptly chastened and returned to the dramatic setting out of which the poetry was generated.

As time passed, this attention to perspective was increasingly relaxed. In fact, this very poem altered significantly, in large part through the changing of one important word. All the old manuscripts begin the penultimate line with the word *dūtikā*, signifying the go-between, but in the later version recorded in the Sabhā edition this *dūtikā* has become *rādhikā*: Rādhā herself. When that change was reinforced by an alternate verb ("to say" rather than "to hear"), and the mention of Krishna was deleted from the last line (the word *prabhu*, "lord," was replaced with *ruci*, "wish,") the result was as follows:

> She listened—the clever, lovely Rādhā—
>   to all these elegant words of love,
> And signaled, says Sūr, her wish and her desire
>   by sweetening her visage with a smile.

With this ending, Rādhā's reaction to the messenger's speech is no longer in doubt. It is evident that the go-between has succeeded in circumventing Rādhā's *mān*, the proud depression she has felt in Krishna's absence. The final smile becomes Rādhā's, not her friend's, and with that transfer a poetic closure has been supplanted by a narrative one.

Even so, the poem retains a dramatic character. It is more than a one-dimensional description of Rādhā's appearance. Other examples of the same genre, however, move perilously close to making Rādhā's beauty per se the sufficient subject of their poetry. As one moves toward the margins of the early *Sūr Sāgar*, the control provided by dramatic perspective is increasingly loosened, and the poetry seems flatter than what went before. Such poems do not go so far as to leave totally behind the Braj context that makes their utterance plausible, but they tend to anchor themselves in poetic convention in a way that earlier poems do not. In the following poem (S 2732), for instance, the *nakh-śikh* prescription becomes more singularly determinative, proceeding systematically from the tip of the head downward and bringing along with it a formulaic alteration of verses. The first describes some facet of Rādhā's beauty and the second provides a simile to round out the picture. So unabashed is the poet's employment of this alternating technique that the second line in each couplet is invariably introduced by some form of the same word: *mānau*, "like, as if, resembling, matching." These successive couplets are less carefully subordinated to a single dramatic perspective than are the poetic figures employed in the example previously translated. Sometimes the need for poetic comparison seems sufficient cause for their existence, and metaphors range where they will:

Listen, let me tell about Bṛṣabhānu's daughter,

About her beauty, beautiful Syām,
 which even the night cannot equal.
First of all, her lovely black braid
 shimmers and shines, I would say,
Like a snake with its face turned toward the moon's,
 hoping to drink the nectar it holds.
How to picture the vermilion powder
 that separates her hair? The thought brings defeat.
It resembles a deep red ray from the sun,
 parting the darkness with light.
Shaded by her hair is a *kumkum* mark
 her friends have affixed to her forehead,
As if to festoon the aura of the moon
 with the liquid of beauty's distillate.
Her eyebrows are fearsome, and near to her eyes
 they glisten on that finest woman
As if world-conquering Kāma had finished his work
 and passed on to her his lowered bow.
Her eyes are sprightly, her nose glistens bright,
 and her lips are rounded and red,
As if between two wagtails a parrot should perch,
 tempted by red-berried *bimba*s below.
Elegant earrings; her nose-ring near her lips;
 a charming, alluring chin;
A collarbone decked with two necklaces—
 no, three—four would evade every metaphor.
A scarlet garland circles her breast;
 to see it humbles the body and mind,
For it matches the practice of Śiva, the yogi—
 his whiteness surrounded by smokeless red flames.
Beguiler of minds, if you find you can accept
 what I've described, I will bring her here to you
And praise you, says Sūr, as a master connoisseur
 if you still can lift the flute to your lips.

This poem does work gracefully, and although it is absorbed in the exigencies of *nakh-śikh*, its conclusion is clever and appropriate. The go-between—and the poet—challenge Krishna to see if he can remain a simple connoisseur of art even when the subject of their portrait herself is brought on the scene. This role of paramount aesthete is one Krishna particularly projects in the triply bent pose he assumes as he plays the flute,[16] but the suggestion is that Rādhā's immediacy may so occupy his lips that other interests and postures will intervene. He will then become a different sort of connoisseur, one also allowed by the term the poet uses (*rasik*): a connoisseur of love.

Other poems like this make their way into the later reaches of the early *Sūr Sāgar*, and in them one sees even more clearly the tendency to dispense with context and focus on the praise of Rādhā per se. Few such poems can be traced back before manuscript B4, and few attain a very wide currency in subsequent manuscripts.[17] They are symptomatic, however, of a definite move to exalt Rādhā that becomes pronounced in later strata of the *Sūr Sāgar*. These poems evince a desire to raise Rādhā to the level of Krishna himself, a status she had attained somewhat earlier in the plays of Rūpa Gosvāmī.[18] Descriptions of Krishna's irresistible charm abound in the earliest levels of the *Sūr Sāgar*: now Rādhā's attractions are brought in line and described almost as frequently. Sometimes this has the effect of making the living Rādhā of the earlier poems an object of veneration, as Krishna often is, and the poet may be so direct as to offer his thanksgiving (*dhanya*) for her apparition.

The equality of Rādhā and Krishna is only hinted at in the earliest poems, typically through the medium of Rādhā's friends, who assure her that she and Krishna are equally refined, equally beautiful (S 3435.5, cf. S 3466.6). Sometimes they merely imply it, saying that Krishna is infatuated with her (S 3399); that he is her guest (S 3440.1). In either case they say what they do to coax Rādhā out of her grim sulking. These utterances have persuasion as their rationale, not accuracy of description, and the audience, overhearing the discourse, must always wonder whether Rādhā's friends have exaggerated the facts to cheer her. It is possible for the poet

16. Hence this pose has become particularly apt as a subject for *nikh-śikh* poetry describing Krishna. A fine example, S 1273, is translated and analyzed in Bryant, *Child-God*, pp. 95–98.

17. Examples are S 2736, found in B4, J3, and A1; S 2802, found in B4, J2, J3, and A1; and S 3230, found only in B4.

18. Donna M. Wulff, "A Sanskrit Portrait: Rādhā in the Plays of Rūpa Gosvāmin," in *Divine Consort*, ed. Hawley and Wulff, pp. 27–41.

to say such things in a more neutral vein, though still upholding the sense of drama, by having one Braj woman speak to another rather than to Rādhā herself. But if he does so, he introduces his characteristic note of indirection by supplying his speaker with images of parity that apply to the blessed couple rather than having her speak outright (S 2522.3–5):

He's the bee, and she the lotus bud;
  a clever lad he, and she no fool.
So have them love one another, my friend,
  have them silently from their mothers steal away;
One a young sapphire, a dark *tamāl* sapling,
  the other a vine—fair, pure, and golden. . . .

If the poet seems to speak more directly, more for himself, we may expect an even more elaborate overlay of images. In the last line of the following poem, for example (S 2379), he speaks of a couple (*dampati*), and the poem is much occupied with words and images whose function is to balance Rādhā with Krishna. Yet these figures are sufficiently involved that by the time we hear the final line we are not sure whether the couple of which Sūr speaks is Rādhā and Krishna, or simply their eyes, now married to one another, or even a single set of eyes, whether his or hers:

When Rādhā turns her mindful gaze
  to the clever one who is wed to Passion,
It's a brilliant spray of eyes and faces—
  two moons, four *cakor* birds—
Or a pair of pairs of honey-thirsty bees
  circling liquid faces that promise to sate
Their greed, but these too are bases for bees,
  and the thirst never goes. The eyelids never close.
They've ridden the chariot of lust by night
  and sped through the flickering light of dawn
    into this everlasting day.
They say Sūr's Lord is the thief of the mind,
  and of wealth as well, but now the title
    belongs to a wedded pair.

Later poems tend to be quite different. They establish the parity between Rādhā and Krishna in more blatant ways. It is no longer a matter to ponder, how the two lovers balance and complement one another, but the stuff of conviction that her status is equal to his. Already in the middle stages of the early *Sūr Sāgar* one hears that:

> You are a beauty, and he's the beautiful jewel of Braj;
> you're a clever girl, and he's the cleverest one of all.
> He's Hari, "The Thief," who steals away all sorrows;
> you're Bṛṣabhānu's daughter, and you steal away The Thief.[19]

Such words, however, are placed in the mouths of Rādhā's friends, who are trying to draw her out of her angry pique; these judgments are still guarded by perspective. Later, this qualification is abandoned and one finds, for example, a direct effort to depict Rādhā as no less ingenious than that renowned rogue, Krishna himself. Whole chains of poems—contrasting in every respect with Sūr's short, isolated compositions—are contrived to bear this out. In one of these cycles (S 1362–1364, 1368–1382) Rādhā pretends to be deathly sick from the bite of a black snake and tells her mother that she can be cured only by the local *gāruḍī,* a physician who cures snakebite through his magical possession of the power of the divine bird Garuḍa, whose enmity for snakes is legendary. We can guess who this *gāruḍī* is, of course: Krishna, whose mythical vehicle is Garuḍa himself. One look at him and the stricken girl experiences an instant cure, which earns for him the indebtedness, at least temporarily, of her mother Kīrat. In another cycle, this one including no less than fifty poems (S 2584–2634), Rādhā invents the story that she has lost her pearl necklace and on that account gains permission from her mother to leave the house to go find it. In fact, of course, she has arranged a tryst with Krishna who, hearing her give a prearranged signal, drops what he is eating at midday with his cowherd friends and goes off to rendezvous with Rādhā.

In the later reaches of the *Sūr Sāgar,* thus, Rādhā's initiative and cleverness are pictured as equal to Krishna's own. At many points this is made explicit (S 2519.2, 2624.1, 3143.6, 3070.7, 3106.6), and in one interesting case this parity is achieved, perhaps unwittingly, by altering a phrase in a poem that had quite early made

19. S 3435.5–6. The order of phrases that appears in manuscript versions of verse 5 (B4, J3, A1, K1) is the reverse of that shown in the Sabhā text, and vocabulary varies slightly. Honorifics are omitted.

its way into the *Sūr Sāgar* (S 3280.7). In the original version (B1, B3, J2, A1) it had read:

> That ever clever Hari, exciting and full of passion:
> what ampler treasure of beauty could there be?

Later it was balanced by a reference to Rādhā's beauty, and is addressed directly to her:

> That ever clever Hari; that clever beauty, you:
> what ampler treasure of beauty could there be?

And all that was required was to substitute the phrase *catur ati kāmini* (that clever beauty, you) for *ātur ati kāmi* (exciting and full of passion).

Other poems in the later *Sūr Sāgar* choose a more direct course in lifting Rādhā to the level of Krishna: they assert that Rādhā and Krishna are one and the same.[20] The two components of the divine pair are said to be as inseparable as wave and water (S 2537.4); as indissoluble, once mixed, as turmeric and lime (S 2527.3). They have the same nature (*subhāu*, i.e., *svabhāv*, S 2683.6; *svarūp*, S 2685.8), it is said, and are as intimately and equitably bound together as *puruṣa* and *prakṛti*, the ancient male and female principles of spirit and matter (S 2306.3).[21] They are a single soul housed in two bodies (S 2303.6, 2309.6). Sometimes this conviction lies in the background even when it is not specifically enunciated, as, for instance, in a number of poems that mention Krishna's donning feminine dress to gain access to Rādhā's presence (e.g., S 2773). Such tales of Krishna's dressing himself as a *gopī* and Rādhā disguising herself as a cowherd have become standard fare in the *rās*

20. This point is made prominently in such poems as S 2232, 2305, 2309, 2515, 2521, 2527, 2684, 2685, 2766, and 3055.

21. There is a mention of *puruṣa* and *prakṛti* in an early poem, S 3434.7, but it is no bald theological assertion. Rather it occurs in the context of an attempt by Rādhā's friend to draw her out of her angry sulking by assuring her of Krishna's faithfulness. Furthermore, it contrasts the sentiment (*ras*) of which the relation between Rādhā and Krishna is made with this more archaic relationship and separates the two by two intervening relationships. In this early poem, then, a direct analogy between Krishna and Rādhā on the one hand and *puruṣa* and *prakṛti* on the other is not even established by Rādhā's friend, let alone by the poet himself.

*līlā*s of present-day Brindavan, where, as in the more recent levels of the *Sūr Sāgar,* they serve to teach that Rādhā and Krishna are not only equal but in a sense interchangeable.[22]

It would be misleading to assume that elements of this view of Rādhā are not present in the earlier layers of the *Sūr Sāgar.* In B4, for instance, about midway in the early development of the *Sūr Sāgar,* we find the following paean (S 1673.23–30):

> Rādhikā, jewel of joy and of form,
>   a treasure, a sum of the finest gems,
> Those who bring to your lotus feet love
>   through love attain Krishna too.
> Beloved of this world's lord and king,
>   mother of the world and its queen,
> Who daily diverts the cowherds' darling,
>   making Brindavan the center of your realm,
> Your feet clear a path through the dead ends of life,
>   Śrī Rādhā, dispenser of all that is blessed.
> Taming life's terrors, a raft to the bereft,
>   you the Puranas and Vedas describe
> Not with one tongue but with hundreds and millions—
>   your limitless, boundless radiance they sing.
> Grant us to share in the worship of Krishna,
>   Śrī Rādhā; Sūr Dās begs for such alms.

Note the final reserve, however. Although Rādhā is summoned with the honorific term that is current today—Śrī Rādhā[23]—the poet stops short of implying that her status is equal to that of Krishna. High as she is, she is ultimately the conduit to an even higher presence: Krishna's. Still, such open panegyric, phrased in the voice of the poet himself, is foreign to what one finds in the earliest segments of the *Sūr Sāgar.* There it is very rare for an extraneous voice to intrude upon the dramatic integrity with which the poet is so careful to protect the intimacy between Rādhā and her love. If Rādhā is praised there—and of course she is—it is in the words of someone on the scene, normally one of her friends, as in the following example (S 2314):

22. A *līlā* in which both cross-dressings occur is the *rājdān līlā.* Cf. Hawley, *At Play with Krishna,* pp. 111–12.

23. S 1690, also attested only in B4, provides another early instance of this usage.

Why this sudden burst to bloom?

Rādhā, I wonder where you have been.
What but Mādhav's tight embrace
could have bared a love so fathomless?
Madan's arrows strain at their bows, your brows,
arching over half your face;
They gaze and pierce, they glance sidelong
and force their own archer, Love, to dance.
The experience craved by Śuk and the sages,
the unattained object of Śiva's regimen,
That's what Sūr's Lord has showered on you—
what even for Śrī was just prayer's charade.

Rādhā does seem to have surpassed Śiva and all the sages in this poem, because she has attained the object of their many years of yogic concentration—a total experience of God, reflected here as an intimate relation with Krishna. And yet the poem only records the rapturous suppositions of her friend. The truth is for the hearer to decide. The hearer is also entrusted with another decision: whether Rādhā has surpassed Śrī, the consort of Viṣṇu (that is, Krishna) in the intimacy she has achieved with their common mate, and therefore in status. The poem reaches no conclusions: it only serves to make such an affirmation possible. Yet it does so in such a brief and clever way that a leap of faith has all the more force, for the prayer that Śrī fails to attain (*śrī na lahati ārādhe*), the prayer that is for her but a charade, contains the very name of Rādhā: *ā-rādhe*. This is the word, in fact, in its Sanskrit form as *ārādhita*, that has traditionally been interpreted as the one reference in the *Bhāgavata Purāṇa* to Rādhā, about whom it is otherwise silent.[24] Sūr repeats this play on words, inviting the hearer to perceive that the prayer Śrī would offer suggests Rādhā herself.

SŪR'S RĀDHĀ AND THE RĀDHĀ of FAITH

It is a considerable journey from poems such as this to the sort of composition one meets so frequently in the later strata of the *Sūr Sāgar*, when theological concerns similar to those found in systematic works like the *Brahmavaivarta Purāṇa* have begun to emerge. In these poems the young lovers have become theological abstractions, the very incarnations of the eternal masculine and feminine polarities that provide the structure of reality, *puruṣa* and *prakṛti*.

24. *Bhāgavata Purāṇa* 10.30.28.

Such concepts—often little more than clichés by the time they make their appearance in the later *Sūr Sāgar*—dominate the discourse of late theological treatises such as the *Brahmavaivarta Purāṇa.*[25] Important among these is the question of the nature of the union between Rādhā and Krishna: is she his mistress or his wife?

The earliest poems in the *Sūr Sāgar* are entirely noncommital on this point; it is only the intimacy of the two that counts, not what people think of it. As we have seen, there is more than a hint of ambiguity when Sūr describes them as a couple (*dampati*, S 2379.6). He speaks of their emotional attachment, as all the attention to their eyes in that poem makes clear, not of their marital status. Sūr's mention of any engagement that might have taken place is similarly enigmatic, for the word that would be so interpreted in modern Braj parlance, *sagāī*, seems to have a greater range—it can mean "betrothal" or simply "liaison"—when he has one of Rādhā's friends assure her that Krishna has established no new *sagāī*. Rādhā is left wondering, as we are, just what her friend means.[26] Other terms that can have marital connotations are similarly vague, like *var* (best, husband) and *nāri* (woman, wife).[27] It is only in later strata of the *Sūr Sāgar* that they clearly mean husband and wife (e.g., *pati nārī*, S 2463.2).

The earliest hints of such a nuptial (*svakīyā*) theology emerge, predictably, in long didactic poems that contrast in every way with the tone of the earliest poems in the *Sūr Sāgar*. For the first time Rādhā and Krishna are *dulaha* and *dulahinī*, bride and groom,[28]

25. See C. Mackenzie Brown, *God as Mother: A Feminine Theology in India*, pp. 115–98.

26. S 3434.1. Cf. the ambiguous use of the word in S 4209.6.

27. S 3073.17 (B4, J3, A1; cf. U1; missing in K1). Cf. *nāgari . . . nāgaravar* in S 3435.5. The phrase *vām aṅg* in S 1673.15 carries a hint of Rādhā's wifely status—a status sometimes noted by B4, the only old manuscript to contain the poem—but is not used with precisely that intent in its present context. Similarly the term *suhāg*, occurring in the Sabhā version of S 3280.8, suggests by its context a reference to Rādhā's good fortune as that of a married woman (*suhāginī*). The oldest manuscripts to contain this poem, however, do not convey this implication so directly. The particle *su-* is separated from *bhāg* in B1 and is deleted in U1. B3, J2, and A1, the remaining manuscripts to display the poem, agree with the Sabhā reading.

28. S 1690.30. In its single occurrence in the old manuscripts (B4), this poem, a series of *caupāī*s and *chand*s, introduces a whole body of poetry describing Krishna's dalliance with Rādhā and the *gopī*s. The manuscript's editor calls this dalliance *sṛṅgār*. It seems likely that the poem was constructed to fulfill just such an introductory function and is not to be attributed to the oral poet Sūr. Cf., however, S 642, discussed in chap. 2, which has a very old pedigree indeed.

as they were so clearly to be understood by later contributors to the *Sūr Sāgar* and, in consequence, by modern critics. Such writers are fond of drawing attention to a passage interpreting the circle dance in which Rādhā and Krishna take part as a marriage rite of the informal (*gāndharva*) variety, a rite that claims some scriptural sanction.[29] Like the "bride and groom" poem, this passage (S 1689.1–2) occurs in the early *Sūr Sāgar* only in manuscript B4. It reads as follows:

> *That which Vyās described, the* rās,
>
> Is really a *gāndharva* marriage, so heed
> and hear of its many luscious moments. . . .

Such niceties meant little to Sūr. He felt no need to attach Rādhā to Krishna as his wife, and was equally uninterested in whether she might have been someone else's (*parakīyā*). Unlike the plays of Rūpa Gosvāmī, the *Sūr Sāgar* nowhere mentions Abhimanyu, the husband whom Rādhā repeatedly abandoned for Krishna according to the Caitanyite tradition. True, there are frequent references to a family life, a world of social propriety (*kul kāni, lok lāj*), that has been left behind. But this is true for all the *gopīs*, not just for Rādhā, and in neither case is anything made of the marital offense involved. Emphasis falls instead on the social dislocation that the *gopīs*' and Rādhā's love for Krishna requires of them and the level of commitment entailed by their attraction to him. If anything, then, Sūr seems rather to relish the ambiguity of Rādhā's position somewhere between wife and mistress. Its lack of definition adds to her fascination and, I would argue, ultimately makes her more worthy of worship.

Rādhā's position in the early *Sūr Sāgar* is unique. She is the only *gopī* who is singled out as the object of our attention; at least, she is the only one given a name.[30] Because of her especially close association with Krishna and her especially heart-rending separation from him, she calls forth our attention. It is in such a role that we have described her thus far, for only then is she sufficiently objectified for Sūr to name her.

There are many more poems, however, that one could conceivably understand as having to do with Rādhā. These are the poems

29. D. Mītal, *Rādhā*, p. 289; Omprakāś, *Madhyayugīn Kāvya*, p. 85.

30. Other names, like Lalitā and Candrāvalī, occur only in later poems in the *Sūr Sāgar*, and very sparingly at that.

she might have spoken herself, whether in the awakening of her love, in joy, in anger, or in the throes of agonizing separation from her loved one. (We shall consider a number of the latter in the following chapter.) Yet these are poems that have Krishna as their point of reference, and so absorbed is the speaker in what has happened to her as a result of *his* presence that her own identity becomes irrelevant. So intense is the subjectivity of these poems, in which the speaker either ruminates to herself or addresses some friend, that Sūr refuses to answer any question we might have as to whether this is Rādhā or some other woman of Braj. In claiming many of these poems for Rādhā specifically, modern critics often take their cues from the groupings adopted by Sabhā editors; but the most ancient manuscripts know of no such divisions, and in any case the poems were composed separately. The poet himself offers no help; he is always silent.

The reason, it seems to me, is that he understands the voice through which he speaks to be potentially that of any *gopī*. Her words express the satisfactions and longings—particularly the longings—of them all. In the subjective mood, this is who Rādhā is: she shares her perspective with that of the other *gopī*s and, by extension, with all who have been touched by Krishna. If she speaks, it is with the voice of all. Only in the objective mood is she distinguished from the others: one sees her beauty, sees her dance, sees her sunk in a particular desperation.

In the ambiguity of this double perspective—the nameless subject and the named object—lies the legitimate basis in the words of Sūr Dās himself for the increasingly unreserved exaltation of Rādhā in the later portions of the *Sūr Sāgar*. As the one *gopī* to whom Sūr gives objective focus, she summarizes the states of all the unnamed women whose utterances of longing and praise for Krishna fill his poems. Hers is a supremacy born not only of a special intimacy with Krishna—that is obvious—but also of the representative role she plays in relation to the rest of the *gopī*s and hence, as Vaiṣṇava theologians have consistently urged, to all of us. This role, it seems, is Sūr's way of expressing the conviction to which the Brindavan *gosvāmī*s gave theological voice by regarding the other *gopī*s as extensions (*vyūha*) of Rādhā.

Perhaps this poetic mode of expressing the connection gives a more pointed insight into Rādhā than theology can do. As the one objective figure who can be the possible subject of all the anonymous poems of love in the *Sūr Sāgar*, she connects the two poles of the religious life: the self and God, the praising subject and the object praised. She is the bridge, and when we find that she was venerated with ever greater intensity as the *Sūr Sāgar* grew and the religion of Braj in general evolved, we may understand that this happened largely because as time passed people focused with increasing specificity upon the relation between ultimate subject (self) and ultimate object (God) and identified it—that is, her—as the stuff of religion itself. The object of worship became, in significant measure, that very relationship.[31]

In worshipping Rādhā, then, one is worshipping love, and the only way to worship love is to love. Rādhā is love objectified—or should we say personified? But as the potential speaker of the anonymous poems that rise to the surface of the ocean of love for Krishna, she is also love subjectified. By refusing at any point to name the one who suffers these outbursts of emotion, Sūr holds her personality open to the access of all. As such she becomes what Vaiṣṇavas have repeatedly said she is: *mahābhāva*, great feeling. This is not greatness in the hierarchical sense that she holds a position mediating between Krishna's divine status and the *gopīs*' (or our) more human one. Indeed, just as the early Christian councils labored against the notion that Jesus was half God and half man, arguing that he was fully both, so Vaiṣṇavas have held that Rādhā is both at one with the *gopīs* and at one with Krishna. The mediation she secures is a mediation of feeling, not of station.

This is what lies behind Sūr's unwillingness to confine Rādhā to the role of either wife or mistress. It is not her position that matters but her feeling, and the ambiguity of her position serves to underscore that fact. It is the same with Sūr's attention to perspective. He uses this tool to draw his hearers into a relationship,

31. The increasingly influential position of Rādhā in Braj religion from the sixteenth century to the present is no simple matter to trace. Historical studies of the Braj *sampradāy*s offer only partial help, since the worship of Rādhā is identified with no one of them exclusively. Although the Rādhāvallabha Sampradāy names itself after her, she is also of integral importance in the Caitanya and Nimbārk Sampradāys and to some extent even among Vallabhites. Studies have been made of individual authors whose compositions reflect the worship of Rādhā, but so far as I am aware no one has yet attempted to gauge the extent of their audience, either in their own time or subsequently, or to chart the growth of more popular literature dedicated to Rādhā or of religious institutions that have her at their core. The following works, in addition to those cited in n. 5 above, serve as starting points for further research: Prabhudayāl Mītal, *Braj ke Dharma-Sampradāyõ kā Itihās*; Vrajvallabhśaraṇ, Govindśaraṇ Śāstrī, and Premnārāyaṇ Śrīvāstav, eds., "Śrīrādhā-Aṅk," *Śrīsarveśvar* 23 (1966): 7–12; Satyendra, *Braj-Sāhitya kā Itihās*; and Frederic Salmon Growse, *Mathurá: A District Memoir.*

refusing to temper their access by any neutral or commentarial voice. Thus the relations that obtain in the world of Krishna and his loves become immediately, dramatically available to the audience.

As the patroness and paradigm of relation per se, Rādhā superintends this effort of Sūr's, and in just that role she superintends the piety of modern-day Brindavan. When the people of Braj bow down to Rādhā in love, declaring her their queen and the captain of their emotions (*raseśvarī*), they acknowledge symbolically that true religion is a matter of relation, of love. And when Krishna bows down to Rādhā in the plays of Brindavan, it signifies that same recognition.

In Brindavan it is considered a failing for Krishna to be worshipped in the absence of Rādhā, or her in his; images that outwardly represent only one personality are understood to imply the other as well. There is every good reason for this. It expresses the conviction that religion, and all life at its deepest, is not a matter of coming before any object, even if it be an object of piety. It is, rather, living in full relationship. That is what Rādhā and Krishna represent. But Rādhā represents it uniquely. Her claim to divinity rests especially there, not on any obviously divine ancestry such as Krishna has; and in this sense she is supreme even over Krishna in the piety of Braj. In this sense too she rules over the creativity of Sūr in a way that even Krishna does not, symbolizing not only the love that is present when he is on the scene but also the love that persists when he is gone—in the endless struggles of *viraha*.

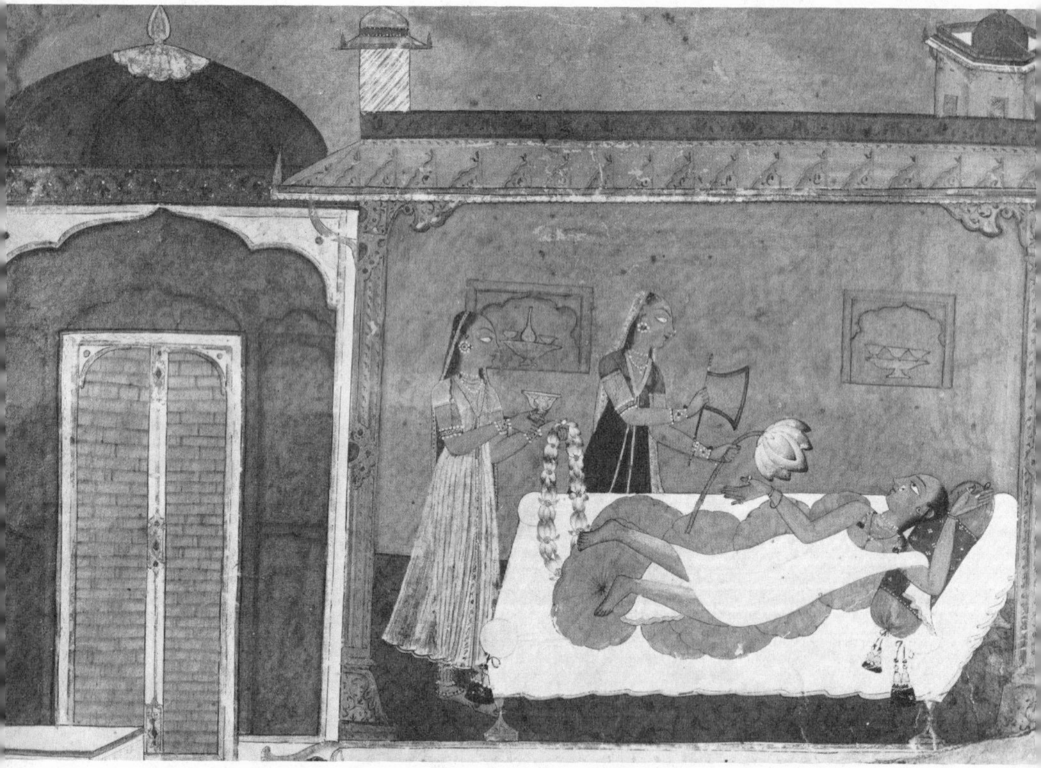

Virahiṇī nāyikā, a woman afflicted with the pain of being separated from her beloved. Basohli, late seventeenth century. Courtesy of the Museum of Fine Arts, Boston (Ross-Coomaraswamy Collection, 17.3113).

CHAPTER 4

Viraha: Separation and Simple Religion

NO THEME in the early *Sūr Sāgar* can rival *viraha* in prevalence or intensity. The longings and sufferings caused to the women of Braj by their love for Krishna provide what is clearly the dominant voice in which Sūr chose to express himself. The earliest reaches of the *Sūr Sāgar* are almost entirely unembellished with the softer, more irenic poems that one meets so frequently in the Sabhā edition. The message of these earlier poems is saltier and more stark, for in Sūr's world Krishna is gone almost before he arrives. His birth, it is true, is attended by great celebrations; his mother sings him loving songs at the cradle and wakes him for the joy of serving him his breakfast; he plays with animation. But it is not long before animation turns to mischief and, once he has begun to capture the hearts of *gopīs* old and young, to pain. Sūr was less fascinated by the gradual increments of growth that brought Krishna from infancy to youth than were later poets who composed in his name, though of course some of the most distinctive poems in this genre were his own. He was enthralled at least as much by the elusiveness of the child as by his loveliness—his pranks and stratagems, his fondness for stealing butter, his escapes. And by the time Sūr's Krishna becomes old enough to engage in real love play (some of the early poems imply that it did not take long), he is known less in his presence than in his absence. Like the *gopīs* who earlier saw him eating butter at a distance and chased futilely after him, the women of Braj now see the object of their newborn affections with the eye of memory and desire; for Krishna has run off somewhere else (S 2490):

Gopāl has slipped in and stolen my heart, friend.

He stole through my eyes and invaded my breast
  simply by looking—who knows how he did it?—
Even though parents and husband and all
  crowded the courtyard and filled my world.
The door was protected by all that is proper;
  not a corner, nothing, was left without a guard.
Decency, prudence, respect for the family—
  these three were locks and I hid the keys.
The sturdiest doors were my eyelid gates—
  to enter through them was a passage impossible—
And secure in my heart, a treasure immeasurable:
  insight, intelligence, fortitude, wit.
Then, says Sūr, he'd stolen it—
  with a thought and a laugh and a look—
    and my body was scorched with remorse.

As time passes, the ruts in the road deepen: the devious rake is unreformed. We hear the young women of Braj asking time and again where he is. Has he spent the night with someone else? Here is the bitter, sarcastic lament (S 3255):

I know, I know what fine qualities you have,

So what have you to hide? I beg you to tell,
  tell me her name, who has so utterly felled you.
Look at yourself: those all-night crimson eyes,
  your face and body wasted with the lethargy of love;
A bright red *tilak* mark has strayed to your cheek
  and passion has scratched its jagged nailmarks
    on your chest.
What a fine strapping lad! Nanda's purest son!
  Tell me, whose heart have you taken captive now?
And how can you stand there, knowing what I do,
  and swear, Sūr's Lord, that it just isn't true?

Before long he is gone altogether. A messenger comes from evil King Kaṃsa in Mathura bidding Krishna and his brother Balarām to join in a tournament. Everyone knows it is a ruse, but the boys are unafraid and go off to lift the weight of wickedness from the kingdom by killing its potentate. All that is to the general good, but it spells only despair for those who have grown to love the cowherd boy more than they love themselves. Krishna soon becomes Mathura's crowning glory, but Braj is emptied of its reason for being (S 3815):

Every rhythm pulses to a different beat

Now that our lovely Gopāl has gone;
  nothing in Braj survives unchanged:
Our homes are now caverns, lions' divans,
  and the beast is panting for its prey.
You know how they say that moonbeams are cool
  and soothing, friend, but they've scalded us all,
And no matter how much we shower ourselves
  with *kumkum* and sandalwood paste on the breast
And musk from the deer, it comes to naught
  in face of the fever of being apart.
We've heard that love is a life-giving vine,
  but now, says Sūr, it bears poisonous fruit,
And deprived of the light from Hari's lunar face
  the lotus of our hearts declines to bloom.

The voice of lament raised by Yaśodā, Krishna's foster mother, is among the most poignant, but no one complains more loudly or more frequently than the *gopīs*. These are the poems that later editors and critics have attributed in such great numbers to Rādhā. Here are two typical laments, both of them intensified by a note of hope, but in each case the hope proves barren. In one we hear the words of Yaśodā as she catches sight of Nanda returning from a mission to bring Krishna back from Mathura (S 3746):

Seeing that Nanda has returned
  and anxious to know whether he has come
With little Kānh, her darling son,
  Yaśodā falters, in joy and fear.
"Where is he? Where has my butter thief gone?"
  she asks, as her head bows low,
Stunned that instant like a lotus on the pond
  whose bloom has been bent by snow.
"So it's true: that day has come,
  as Garga the astrologer said it would.
His fussing and fighting and grabbing the churning rod,"
  says Sūr, "—has it all gone?"

In the other poem (S 3935) we hear not Yaśodā's voice but that of one of the milkmaids. The girl decides she must send a message to her lover, who has become king of the Yādavs in Mathura, and revives at the thought. After all, as another of Sūr's poems reminds us, a king is made king by virtue of his concern for his subjects' welfare. Is not Braj within the domain of Mathura? But she does not know, as we do, that her effort is in vain. When the first line—the refrain—is repeated at the end of the poem, as it always is when these poems are recited, the audience will clearly recall that "Hari has gone away."

The season of rains has come

but Hari has gone away.
Thunder rumbles deep
as lightning lights the dark sky;
Peacocks screech for joy in the wood;
the frogs are alert, alive;
Cuckoos swoon with a high piercing sound,
and I, friend, I could die.
Rainbows brandish arrows;
they shoot, and full of ire
They loose their pointed raindrops:
how can I endure?
Quick, dispatch a letter
by some traveler, then, says Sūr,
So that my Yādav prince may know
what torture I've been through.

LOVE AND YOGA

For Sūr, the pangs of separation have a religious valency. The people of Braj, above all the *gopīs*, are forced by Krishna's absence to an intensity of concentration that would otherwise have been hard to conceive. *Viraha* deepens their love, or at least forces it to expression, in the same way that the invisibility of God is responsible for so much of the intensity and generality of the religious emotions. The *gopīs* watch for Krishna to return from Mathura as if the very act of watching could somehow cause him to materialize; after all, what other tool do they have? It is as if they were yogis, making use of the only leverage they possess—their own bodies—to force the divine hand through practices of meditation and renunciation. Indeed Sūr makes this comparison quite explicitly, but at the same time he contrasts the simple religion of the heart that the *gopīs*' actions epitomize with the elaborate contortions of formal religion of which yoga is the exemplar and culmination.

For Sūr the extreme complexity and rarefaction of which Hindu religion is capable lies at the periphery of Krishna's world; sometimes it is even made fun of. At the center are the simple demands of the heart that the *gopīs* represent. The utterances of Sūr's *gopīs* make it clear that the tension between simple faith and the more complex manifestations of religion is as much alive in Hinduism as in any tradition. Indeed, some of the most vivid statements that these women make in defense of their position are stimulated by the visit of a representative of the opposite camp: Ūdho, the scholar and yogi whom Krishna has sent to dissuade them from their straightforward lamentations. As the *gopīs* argue with Ūdho we hear the echoes of a broad debate that divides many religious traditions—between those who hold that true worship is a single, simple thing and those who feel that in a world as complicated as this, religion too must be something complex and manifold. Other sets of oppositions group themselves naturally around this central polarity. On the one hand there is the notion that true religion involves direct contact with the divine realm, on the other the conviction that a more indirect approach is necessary. On the one hand there are those who argue that salvation must have an immediate quality to it, on the other those who believe it to be a matter of process. If one rotates the axis of opposition slightly one finds similar debates about faith as against works and interiority as against external practice, and another slight turn reveals the debate that sets the path of devotion over against the path of knowledge. Yet another rotation and one sees the opposition between those who feel that religion is something by nature totally devoid of technique and those who hold that it is centrally concerned with developing the proper techniques and disciplines. Not far away is the debate about whether faith is something childlike or mature, something easy or difficult. And, as the confrontation between Ūdho and the *gopīs* particularly suggests, there has also been a tendency to identify one side of all these oppositions with the nature of women and the other with the nature of men. Collectively we might call this series of polarities a debate between simple religion and its opponents.

Within the Hindu tradition no pericope represents this confrontation more expressly than the one that Sūr exposits. The *gopīs*' situation is clear. As the story goes, all their trials in love had finally had their reward. They had known with Krishna, if only briefly, a degree of fulfillment so overwhelming that for many Hindus it has come to symbolize the union with the divine that is the ultimate goal of the religious life. Attracted to him through no merit or action of their own but rather by the irresistible call of his miraculous flute, surprised by his mischievous presence at the very moment they undertook a vow of chill early morning bathing to earn him as their husband, finally they were granted the intimacy each of them had sought. Indeed, it exceeded every expectation. At the sound of his flute they abandoned their homes and mundane occupations and hurried into the depths of the forest to join in a circle dance (*rās*); and by some divine magic Krishna managed to multiply himself around the circle so that each one had the sense of being the only focus of his attention. It was ultimate community and ultimate intimacy all in one breath.

Now, however, he is gone. All that is left is grief and memory. At this point Ūdho, the well-educated, well-placed expert in yoga, comes to them from Mathura with words of consolation. Ūdho is Krishna's confidant at court, and Krishna himself has dispatched him on his mission. He is to console the *gopīs* by raising their consciousness, by persuading them that in truth they have nothing to lament, for they must understand that in this world of illusion it is only the outer manifestation of Krishna who has left them. The real Krishna—the pervasive, divine, spiritual Krishna—is with them still, embedded in their inmost souls. What they need to do is to adopt a yoga, a discipline of concentration that will make them aware of the fact, and their troubles will be over.

In the earliest version of this meeting, that recorded in about the tenth century in the *Bhāgavata Purāṇa,*[1] the exchange between Ūdho and the *gopīs* is amicable enough. The *gopīs* do utter words of complaint about Krishna's having abandoned them, but these are addressed to a passing bee, not to Ūdho. The *gopīs*, in their distress and disorientation, confuse the two. Both Ūdho and the bee are travelers; both are messengers; but since the bee shares Krishna's black color, the women take it rather than Ūdho as their lover's stand-in. Because they direct their laments to the bee, their utterances have come to be called the *bhramargīt,* the songs of—or more properly to—the bee. Ūdho says his piece; but ultimately

1. *Bhāgavata Purāṇa* 10.47.

he is so impressed with the women's concentration on Krishna, and the degree to which their love has been tested and refined by their separation from him, that he declares they have already attained yogic status and are not in need of his teaching. It is a victory for simple religion.

In subsequent poetic treatments of this theme[2] the confrontation between Ūdho and the *gopīs* becomes much more sharp and the victory for simple religion correspondingly more vivid. For one thing, the two sides are directly pitted against one another in debate. The *gopīs* no longer address their complaints to the bee but to Ūdho himself, whom they speak of as a messenger bee, and they fault not only Krishna for his absence but Ūdho for his yoga. In the Sabhā edition of the *Sūr Sāgar* theirs is a massive victory indeed: some seven hundred poems contribute to it (S 4029–4712), and of these only a handful represent Ūdho's point of view. In the earlier levels of the *Sūr Sāgar* the relative proportion of poetry devoted to this encounter is even higher, and the outcome so clear that Ūdho is not even given a chance to speak.[3]

The debate between Ūdho and the *gopīs* is a standoff between love and yoga, or to be more specific, between *viraha* and yoga. There is little in Sūr's poems to define exactly what is meant by the latter term, though in the course of time there was a growing tendency to identify yoga specifically with the practices of the Nāth Yogīs.[4] In the early *Sūr Sāgar,* however, the word yoga functions

2. A listing is provided by Ronald Stuart McGregor, *Nanddas: The Round Dance of Krishna and Uddhav's Message*, pp. 47–48. McGregor translates a prominent example of the genre, the *bhramargīt* composed by Nand Dās, in the next generation after Sūr (pp. 85–105). A modern dramatic recounting of the episode is recorded and translated by Norvin Hein in *The Miracle Plays of Mathurā*, pp. 179–221. Kenneth Bryant, in *Poems to the Child-God*, translates several poems from the *Sūr Sāgar* that are related to the incident (pp. 201–4), and there is an abundant literature on the genre in Hindi, both commentarial and analytic. Examples are Rājnāth Śarmā, *Bhramar Gīt-Sār*, and Devendrakumār, *Bhramargīt aur Sūr*.

3. See chap. 2, n. 58.

4. See S 4156.2–4; 4219.8–13; 4221.2; 4308.3; 4311.4, 12; 4312.3–5; 4430.3; and 4501.4. The point has been noted by Hazārīprasād Dvivedī in *Sūr Sāhitya*, pp. 61–63, and *Nāth Sampradāy*, p. 18, and has recently been investigated by Kenneth E. Bryant in "The *Bhramargīt* of Sūrdās," paper presented to "The *Sant* Tradition" conference, Berkeley, May 1978. Only five of the poems cited above, however, occur in the manuscripts of the period we are considering (S 4221:B3, J4, A1; S 4308:B3, U1, J2, J4, A1; S 4311:J4, J5, K1; S 4430:J4; S 4501:J1, B1, B2, B3, U1, J2, J4, J5), and I think it safe to say that in the great majority of poems in the old *Sūr Sāgar*, where no specific qualifications are introduced, Ūdho represents yoga in general. On this point, see also Dvivedī, *Sūr Sāhitya*, pp. 64–65. Even to

as a general term to indicate practices of ever-increasing discipline that, combined with ever subtler knowledge of the nature of reality, lead to ultimate spiritual concentration. For Sūr the object of that concentration must be Krishna, who is God himself, hence it is fitting that its spokesman be an associate of Krishna. Traditionally, and in the poems of Sūr, yoga exemplifies one side of all the oppositions we have listed above. Yoga devotes specific attention to integrating (or, to use the cognate term, yoking) what is complex; it defines a graded process; it emphasizes knowledge and practice; it is thought of as mature and difficult; and it is almost entirely the province of men. Moreover the most basic meaning of the Sanskrit term associates it with technique.

Those who take the other side of the battle, in this pericope, are the *virahiṇī*s, the victims of *viraha,* and Sūr often uses these terms to describe their condition. The word *viraha* is convenient in this respect, for it connotes not only separation but the affect that goes with it: yearning, longing. But another term occurs almost equally often: *viyoga.* Semantically it is somewhat more restricted than *viraha*; it suggests the situation of separation more than its experience. But grammatically it could not be more apt, for it is the opposite of yoga. *Viyoga* literally means an unyoking, a disjunction; in Sūr's language, of course, it refers to the disjunction between the *gopī*s and Krishna, the undoing of a prior bond. Their physical separation from him, however, does nothing to diminish the totality of their attachment, and it throws into bold relief the starkness of their position. Their love for him is so fundamental that no outward change of circumstance, not even his own departure, can alter it. It is the total orientation of their life, and as such it is offered by Sūr as a model of true religion. Specifically it is a religion characterized by utter simplicity; and as

identify Ūdho specifically as a Nāth Yogī, however, is to cast him as a yogi of what for that period was the most common type. The Nāth sect, at the time possessor of great numbers of monasteries in east and north India, traced its lineage back to the early medieval saint Gorakhnāth and ultimately to Śiva himself. Its teachings incorporated certain tantric strands and emphasized a regimen of *haṭha yoga* culminating in an immediate, "spontaneous" (*sahaj*) experience of truth in which the True Guru (*satguru*) made himself known to and in the adept. The sect continues today, but its numbers and influence are greatly reduced. For further information, see Dvivedī, *Nāth Sampradāy*; George Weston Briggs, *Gorakhnāth and the Kānpaṭha Yogīs*; and Charlotte Vaudeville, *Kabīr*, 1:85–89. A catalogue of references to Nāth Yogīs in the Sabhā *Sūr Sāgar* may be found in Nirmalā Saksenā, *Sūrsāgar Śabdāvalī*, pp. 243–45.

devotion to the Lord in separation from him, as *viyoga*, it admirably summarizes the various elements we earlier associated with simple religion—as fully as yoga epitomizes their opposite.

One can readily identify the features of simple religion as they appear in Sūr's portrait of these *viyoginīs*, victims of separation. The *gopīs* are unable to entertain any complexity or qualification. Direct contact with Krishna is all that matters to them—the real Krishna, not some shadowy, tasteless, subtle substitute. Salvation was theirs with immediacy when Krishna was with them; in his absence they refuse to settle for any process that would mediate his presence. Theirs was a salvation by grace alone, and it continues to be so insofar as Krishna is still vividly with them in the intense emotion that accompanies his absence. In no way were they able to earn his presence in the first place, and no regimen is able to recover it now. The signs of their state of grace—their gestures of faith—are entirely involuntary: they can do nothing else but talk of their longing for Krishna, and they hallucinate his presence. Their actions manifest an interior reality rather than appropriating an external model. They know only what they feel, and they are entirely resistant to any talk of technique or discipline. Their attachment is so total as to appear childlike. And, finally, they are women, representatives of a group whose religion, indeed whose very nature, is often depicted as essentially simple. In fact the only feature in their portrait that does not conform to a general description of simple religion is that their separation from Krishna is by no means easy for them. But even in that respect it can be observed that their entry into Krishna's thrall, responding as they did to his naughtiness and then to the call of his flute, once had a quality of perfect spontaneity. About that we shall have more to say.

When yoga and *viyoga* meet one another in the debate between Ūdho and the *gopīs*, then, it is a full-fledged confrontation between developed, differentiated, sophisticated religion and the religion of simplicity, and the latter easily wins the day. At the end it is not Ūdho who has converted the *gopīs* to his version of the proper discipline of the spirit, but they who have persuaded him of the depth and cogency of their path. He returns to Krishna in Mathura with a sense of the uselessness of yoga and all subtle and specialized knowledge. He praises the devotion of the women of Braj and in some poems openly berates Krishna for having left them in such a dire condition. Here is an example of the genre (S 4762):

Mādhav, give ear to what love is in Braj.

I've studied it now for fully half a year,
 the milkmaids' way of life,
And all the time, Syām, you and Balarām
 refuse to vacate their hearts.
Their tears are a torrent of holy oblations,
 their windblown saris the cooling whisk;
For offering vessels they tender their breasts,
 their hands bear votive lotuses,
And their lips are alive with hymns that recall
 the playful deeds you displayed.
Their homes and emotions, their physical frames
 they offer to your lotuslike eyes.
Says Sūr, one look at love like theirs
 and how tasteless it seems to be wise.

The word used here to describe the *gopīs*' devotion is *prem* ("love," v. 1), and the competing habit of mind is called *gyā̃n* (Sanskrit, *jñāna*, "wisdom," v. 8). This is to restate the age-old opposition between two of the great paths that religion can take, and the extended comparison between the *gopīs*' way of life and the various features of temple worship makes it clear that the poet has in mind precisely this opposition. In terms of the most influential way in which Hindus have expressed this tension, the *gopīs* score a victory over *jñāna* (the word itself is used) on behalf of *bhakti* (loving devotion, mentioned as *bhajan* in v. 8 of U1 and J4). Theistic Hinduism abounds with arguments intended to establish this ranking of *bhakti* over the other forms of religion, to assert that *jñāna* and *karma* (action) find their pinnacle and consummation there.[5] But

5. They cluster particularly in commentaries on the *Bhagavad Gītā*, where *jñāna*, *karma*, and *bhakti* are set alongside one another. See, e.g., Yāmuna, *Gītārtha-saṃgraha*, *śloka* la. On Rāmānuja's elaboration of the same point in his *Gītābhāṣya*, see J. A. B. van Buitenen, *Rāmānuja on the Bhagavadgītā*, pp. 20–24, and Robert C. Lester, *Rāmānuja on the Yoga*, pp. 52–54, 64–141. Vallabha's commentary on the *Gītā* is not extant, if ever it existed, but clear evidence of his position comes from elsewhere in his writings. He classifies *jñāna* and *karma* as instrumental in nature (*sādhana*), as against *bhakti*, which is sometimes not (*niḥsādhana*, *siddha*), and relegates the former two to the status of *maryādāmārga*, which in Vallabha's parlance means the path of limitation, whereas the latter is substance of the *puṣṭimārga*, the path of fulfillment. Cf. Peter Johanns, S. J., *Vers le Christ par le Vedanta*, 2:41–42.

Sūr's position is even more extreme. Poems such as this one imply not only that *jñāna* and *karma* are next best, but that ultimately *bhakti* is everything. Here yoga, which goes hand in hand with *jñāna,* is not only a propaedeutic to faith, as Rāmānuja and others argued, it is pictured as the positive enemy of faith, the arch-temptation.[6] For Sūr Dās, therefore, there is no real dialogue between Ūdho and the *gopīs*.

THE YOGA IN *VIYOGA*

Sūr makes this point in a telling way. On a number of occasions he makes it clear that the *gopīs* have no reason to listen to Ūdho the yogi because, appearances notwithstanding, they are yogis themselves. Indeed they have gone farther down the yogic path than he has, and they have done so precisely as exponents of *viyoga.* As *viyoginīs* or *virahiṇīs*, women separated from Krishna, they are the true yogis of this world, paradigms of the spiritual life. The states of consciousness to which the best-trained yogis aspire through whole lifetimes of renunciation come with maddening ease to these untutored and, to add insult to injury, female rustics. Time and again (but always retrospectively or from sufficient distance to allow perspective) Sūr describes the happiness that is theirs when they are in the presence of Krishna by saying that it equals that blissful, self-transcendent state that yogis and sages have always sought but failed to achieve. He is fond of quipping that this exalts them even above Śiva, the ascetic god who is captain and exemplar of all yogis. Now when they are left without Krishna it is even plainer how completely they have stolen the yogic crown from Śiva and his legion.

Ūdho is not the first envoy from Mathura whom they have had to endure. Earlier there was Akrūr, the messenger Kaṃsa sent to Braj to bring Krishna to his city so that he could be killed in a tournament Kaṃsa was arranging especially for the purpose. Krishna accepts the challenge willingly, since he has projected himself as an avatar into this world precisely to redress the insults

6. Vallabha also takes this position. In his "Saṃnyāsanirṇaya" he rejects any form of renunciation other than the self-renunciation that is experienced naturally in the hearts of those who love Krishna when he is absent. Love in separation is held up as the true form of ascetic renunciation (*saṃnyāsa*), and the *gopīs* as model renunciants. See Vallabhācārya, *Kṛṣṇaṣodaśagranthāḥ*, treatise 14. An English summary is given in Mrudula I. Marfatia, *The Philosophy of Vallabhācārya*, pp. 237–39.

of tyranny and return the world to *dharma*: he goes off to fight a man's battles. This leaves the women behind, bereft, and as the royal chariot disappears from view with Krishna in it, they begin to manifest a heroism of their own by displaying the traits of yogis. They complain that their hearts are suddenly like *vajra,* the impervious, adamantine substance in which yoga culminates; they say they would far rather their hearts would burst and break (S 3623.2). They also experience the emptiness that is the object of certain forms of yoga. They go about their daily tasks with nothing but the husk of a self to guide them. They find themselves completely dissociated from the mundane world, like fish out of water (S 3880.2, 4236.8), lotuses beyond the pond (S 3859.3); but as these images attest, theirs is a painful state, not the stuff of salvation and release.

Sometimes the dissociation they experience is so extreme that their senses cease to make any claim on them; thus they haplessly attain another of yoga's goals. Krishna has so thoroughly displaced every other awareness that they hallucinate his presence even when he is not there, as in the following poem addressed to Ūdho who, as Krishna's messenger, is likened to a black bee. Ūdho comes to reason with them, but what need have they of learning and yoga? The object of these disciplines, the peace and composure that comes with awareness of the ultimate, is already attained (S 4174):

It's a wondrous thing to live in Braj,

O honeybee, where our Kānh's in charge
  of herding the cows and the calves,
And however dense the din of Brindavan,
  his thunderous flute comes through.
And when he stands beneath the tree
  demanding his buttermilk tax,
We sing and praise, we worship his fame,
  as deep inside our love takes form.
The Lord of Sūr means so much to us:
  he gives our life its breath.

In the same vein, they sometimes respond to Ūdho's arguments (usually only implied in the text) with a prior caveat. They say that there is really no point in debating with them since they have no mind (*man*) left by means of which they could engage in discursive discussion (S 4343, 4348). They have gone beyond the world of subject and predicate, mine and yours: they are selfless.

So far the comparison between these *viyoginīs* and yogis has remained implicit. In other poems it comes directly to the surface. Nothing is more characteristic of yogis than a concentration of *tapas,* the heat they try to generate, maintain, and channel for their own ends through ascetic rigors. For the victims of separation, however, there is no necessity to generate *tapas*: they are engulfed in the fire of separation, whether they like it or not. Hence it is ludicrous for Ūdho to press yoga on them, as the last verse of the following poem demonstrates. The burning in them is so intense that it cannot be extinguished even when they have at hand the constant services of their own fire department, a plentiful flow of tears (S 4408):

If Hari dwells in each of us, within,

How can you make demands on our hearts?
  That would be insulting him!
When he was here our hearts did not burn,
  but now the yearning crackles hot,
For he has left our hearts abandoned
  and ablaze: will they never cool?
We're doused and drenched each second, every day,
  in torrents of tears, like Indra's rain;
With mountainous chill our bodies shiver
  and crumble, but he lifts not a finger.
(Then fingering their bangle-mirrors they saw
  they were racked and deadened by pain.)
No yogic cure can bring us life, says Sūr:
  we're scorched with separation.

Heat is one favorite term of comparison between yogis and *viyoginīs*; wakefulness is another, for it is the ideal of the yogi never to sleep. This is a capacity that Krishna's women have no need to cultivate: it thrusts itself upon them. Here are the words of one victim of insomnia (S 3599):

He's gone—to Mathura, I hear.

Shame will not let me share my thoughts by day,
 it muffles these hidden heartbeats,
But now, full-formed, they charge my lips.
 I look: the midnight's gone.
Sleep won't come this endless night.
 When will I rise and see the dawn?
The son of Suphalak has slipped away
 as water slips down a lotus petal,
Taking him far away, the Lord of Sūr.
 Who will make my blessedness return?

The *gopīs* frequently fix the blame for their sleeplessness on their eyes. They accuse them of having turned traitor and aided the enemy's (Krishna's) cause. They are robbers and looters, these turncoats, allowing every inner emotion to be stolen, and pirating sleep itself. In one of the more moderate poems of this ilk Krishna, the object of sight, appears as more the villain than the eyes and eyelids; but the two of them in league have left the poor *gopī*'s body defenseless against love (Kāma, "Śiva's foe") and moonlight, and they in turn rob her of any chance to sleep (S 4004):

Nandakumār's no longer in Braj.

That clever, handsome, knowing one,
 this body's bodyguard,
Had daily guarded the door—these eyes—
 repelling all else with the staff of his beauty.
Now, my friend, this house—my heart—
 has been invaded by Śiva's foe,
Who pains me, knowing that no one can stop him:
 he knows the house is vacant.
If sighs and tears should slip away,
 what does it matter to the vanished guard?
At night the latch of the eyelids lies open
 and the moon steals in, steals my inmost self.
My life is crippled, says Sūr, but time
 strides on with the crutch of remembrance.

This sleeplessness that is the *gopīs*' lot, more than a reflex that bears comparison to yoga, is sometimes deliberately induced by yoga. Once again the eyes are the offenders: they have taken on the role of yogis. As the Braj women say in the course of debating with Ūdho (S 4184),

Having seen Hari's face, our eyes are opened wide.

Forgetting to blink, our pupils are naked
 like those who are clad with the sky.
They've left behind the teachings of home,
 burned up the sacred thread of decorum;
Family and veil are all cast aside:
 our eyes scan always ahead, toward the wood,
And there for the love of beauty they pledge
 they'll never, forever, close their lids.
It comes to this: an ascetic's death.
 Our families are spent in reproach.
So Ūdho, though your speeches touch
 our minds, and we understand,
Nothing can argue with our eyes, says Sūr,
 so obstinate and fixed, so blind.

Disciplined by their eyes, these *viyoginīs* have abandoned the world and taken up the ascetic's life. The familiar forest[7] where they had danced and enjoyed Krishna's sensual presence has now become the wilderness where their yogi-eyes wander. Or, in a shift to another feature of the yogic repertoire, they say their eyes move not at all, but stare out unblinking, as if they had undertaken a vow of one-pointed concentration. Their only focus is Krishna and they wait for the moment when he will reappear from Mathura (cf. S 3870). So has it been ever since they have been initiated by the sight of him. Wandering or static, they are complete *digambar*s: Jain ascetics who are, as the term literally says, "clad with the sky." They eschew even the film of clothing that a blink would provide.

And so it will be to the end. In a clever play on words their *sahaj samādhi,* their "spontaneous concentration," is at the same time their "simple yogi's funeral," their "ascetic's death." Yogis are not cremated at death, since their death rites have already occurred at the moment when they separate themselves from every societal bond and norm. Similarly these *gopī*s have left all social convention behind—"Our families are spent in reproach"—and the end they

7. *Ban* (wood, S 4184.4) in this context is *brindā-ban,* the luxuriant basil forest that the present town of Brindavan memorializes.

earn is an ascetic's, a yogi's. If one understands the analogy as referring to most ascetics, the meaning is that the stream of their tears is so incessant that their eyes are constantly being submerged, as a yogi's body typically is at death. If, however, as is more likely, the reference is to the Nāth Yogīs who were so important in the religious life of medieval North India, then the implication is that these motionless *gopīs* have attained that state of naturalness and spontaneity (*sahaj*) that is the final goal of all the rigorous practices of the Nāth Yogīs and is so called (*sahaj samādhi*). At death such adepts are interred in the lotus pose to signify that their attainment of this state of simplicity has made them immortal; their tombs are called *samādhi*s. Krishna's *gopīs* attain both the simplicity and the tomblike pose by a far more direct path—the path of love they survey even now.[8]

But their eyes are not the only yogis on the scene, not the only *digambar*s. Ever since the moment when Krishna stole their clothes as they bathed in the River Jumna they have gone naked body and soul. *Digambar*s wear only the sky; they, so to speak, wear only Hari. Hence, with every decoration of worldly morality already discarded, it is hardly appropriate that they be asked to take on the superficial paraphernalia of the yogic life. The reality these are meant to signify is theirs already. They snap back at Ūdho (S 4501):

Follow your own advice, why don't you?

Deck yourself out in your splended yoga
  for a ten-day trial: let's see if Hari comes.
Don your coiled coiffure, your yogic rags;
  slather your face and body with ash;
Take your staff and whistle, your antelope skin,
  keep those unanointed eyelids closed,
And tell us, Ūdho, of the truth we know is true:
  love's dominant tone that thunders through the monsoon
When one's lover is lost. From yoga to no love
  is a distance so deadly we've perished in its span—
From arrows of passion fired straight in our faces
  that have left us wise but wounded, no more free to flee,
Naked as the day Sūr's Lord found us as we bathed
  and stole away our clothes, made us renounce all shame.

8. S 4184.5. On *sahaj samādhi* in the Nāth Yogī context, see Mircea Eliade, *Yoga: Immortality and Freedom*, p. 307, and Briggs, *Gorakhnāth*, pp. 39–43.

The rigors of love have steeled them beyond anything yoga might do. Love is harsh, they often tell Ūdho. If he doesn't believe them, let him try staying in Gokul where they live, away from the presence of Krishna, and see how long he survives. If he practices what he preaches, an Advaitin brand of yoga aimed at cultivating the awareness that no phenomenal reality is truly different from any other, then the physical distance should be of no consequence. The *gopīs* make this clear in the sequence that follows (S 4231). Note the slighting references to Vedantin theology, which are explicit in line 5, where the term *māyā* (illusion) is used, and implicit in line 6, where the *gopīs* cleverly appropriate the idea of *advaita* in referring to the absence of difference but do not employ the word itself.

"First teach yourself, you black honeybee,

before you start teaching others.
If you had lived through it, then you'd know
how exacting love can be.
You say your mind is still at Hari's feet,
though you've brought your body here,
But without the living presence of his lotus eyes
who ever has found the true way?
So stay here in Gokul! What do you care,
since to you this world's an illusion?"
This was their challenge to Ūdho, says Sūr:
"See if there's any difference between us."

In the last analysis, for all the yogic traits that Sūr discovers in the *gopīs' viyoga,* there is a difference between them, "a distance so deadly we've perished in its span." And out of respect for that fact the *gopīs* beg Ūdho to be silent if he cannot bring them the one thing of sufficient enormity to address their condition, Krishna himself (S 4346):

Ūdho, hearts like ours can't change:

They're dyed with Syām's pure blackness
and there's no way to wash it away.
Spare us then your artful speeches
and let's get down to the root of the matter:
That yoga you preach means no more to us
than *campā* flowers do to you bees—

How could an insipid thing like that
  erase the fate that is furrowed in our hands?
Show us Syām instead, our delight;
  one look, says Sūr, and we'll come to life.

In most of the poems in the early *Sūr Sāgar* the comparison between yoga and *viyoga* is implicit, not spelled out in so many words; that is part of the art. But there are exceptions, times when Sūr allows himself the luxury of a direct juxtaposition. Apropos of the *gopīs*' total experience of separation, for example, he says (S 3399.4):

Viraha-viyoga, like the greatest of yogis,
  passes hours and ages always awake.

Or the poet may bring rhyme into play, as in the following couplet (S 3910.1-2). A *gopī* begins her speech to Ūdho by explaining that the separation (*biyog*) she has experienced is indeed a form of yoga (*birah jur jog*: "the yoga of yearning"):

Day after day I've endured this separation

Until this body is no more my own, friend,
  bound and burned in the yoga of yearning.

Such explicit use of the parallel between yoga and *viyoga* was not lost in later levels of the *Sūr Sāgar,* where familiar formulae had great appeal.[9] Yoga and *viyoga* (the pangs of being alone) are the rhyming words in the following salvo (S 4316.1-2):

Ūdho, why should we take up your yoga?

We who have drunk the nectar of Syām,
  why must we suffer the pangs of being alone?

9. At the same time, however, the comparison between *viraha* and yoga also remains in force at the implicit level. One senses it especially in the liberality with which the verb *tyāgnā* (to leave, renounce) is used to describe the sacrifices that the *gopīs* have had to make in the service of their love for Krishna. They have renounced home, family, propriety, even their very bodies, and their senses have renounced them in a similar way. Examples of this usage from the later *Sūr Sāgar* are S 2249.1, 2272.4, 2309.2, 2527.5, 2874.4. Earlier poems sometimes use the same expression.

In the early *Sūr Sāgar,* however, one usually finds a less obvious use of the rhyme between yoga and *viyoga* and a less direct appeal to the conceptual analogy it conveys. In the poem that follows, for instance, Sūr refers to the way in which Ūdho urges yoga on the *gopīs* with the aim of releasing them from the harshness of their *viyoga,* but manages to skew the directness of the rhyme by placing it in the mouth of a *gopī* who doubts that yoga and *viyoga* are true analogues at all. The parallel announced in the poem's rhyme—between *jog* (yoga, S 4208.3) and *biyog* (distance from Syām, 4208.4)—is negated by its sense: the *gopī* finds it weak and annoying. She proceeds to obfuscate its clarity by bringing to bear other rhyming words intended to suggest that the one is so anxious to cure the *gopīs*' *viyoga* with Ūdho's yoga is really motivated by a desire to cover up his own sexual license (*sambhog* or *samyog,* depending upon the manuscript, 4208.5), his social disease (*rog,* 4208.6). Or at the very least he has lost all perspective about the depth of his own perverse promiscuity:

Those Mathura people, they're rife with vice,

My friend: they've taken our beautiful Syām,
  and the fast, jaded ways they've taught him!
Ūdho, they say, has arrived in our midst
  to peddle his yoga to poor young maidens;
His postures, dispassion, his eyes turned within—
  how can they shorten our distance from Syām?
We may be just herders, but this much we know:
  Syām's coupled in passion to a hunchback girl!
What kind of doctor, says Sūr, is this,
  who has no idea what true illness is?

In poems such as this the comparison between yoga and *viyoga* is developed, discussed, even denied—but never lost. And as one moves toward the final layers of the early *Sūr Sāgar* it continues to form the basis for poems in which the *gopīs*, as covert yogis, emerge as the champions of faith. In the following poem, which was introduced into manuscripts of the *Sūr Sāgar* toward the end of the seventeenth century, the *gopīs* declare in even more vivid detail than before that Krishna has visited upon them a fate tantamount to yoga, and a number of the accoutrements they list—the old rag worn around the neck (*mekhalā*), the dingy glass earrings (*mudrāvali* in Kl; *mudrā* in J4, J5), the crook that supports them at the elbow (*adhārī*), and the animal horn through which they blow (*siṅgī*)—reveal that they have in mind particularly the version of yoga practiced by members of the Nāth sect.[10] They do not begin by brandishing the rhyme between yoga and *viyoga,* but the thought is certainly evident, and they extend this implicit play on words by complementing it with another: two references to the term *nāth* (Lord) itself. They depict Krishna not as the Lord of yoga he pretends to be but as the Lord of worldly Mathura, and when they style themselves yogic initiates they specify that their guru is the Lord of Passion, that is, Kāma. Their brand of yoga, then, is love's *viyoga,* and their two masters (*nāth*s)—Kāma and Krishna, two beings in one—are experts in the field. The catalogue they provide of the features of the unique ascetic discipline that they represent is so complete and forthright that their words serve as a fitting final statement of the parallel between yoga and *viyoga* (S 4311):

Ūdho, yoga is something we've had to endure

Ever since that day when Mohan went to Mathura
 and left us here, oh honeybee.
Love and dreams have oiled our hair
 just as yogis smear themselves with ash.
We're ascetics draped from ear to ear
 in tattered, mended rags
And with earrings made from thick dingy glass.
 We rest our weight on a mendicant's cane.
We've wandered in search of a vision,
 begged with our wide-open eyes,
Worn bamboo flutes as our yogis' horns,
 sounded the songs of remembrance,
And wielded love's wound as the fearless wicker staff
 that sends scared dogs to scrambling.
The Lord of Passion, our matchless master,
 has rested his blessed hand on our heads
Like a guru, and given us our initiations
 of sermons and powerful, secret words.
So carry this message away to your Lord,
 wily, uncanny, Mathura magician:

10. In the version recorded by J4 and J5, but not in that given by K1, this identification becomes specific. The name of Gorakh, the principal guru of the Nāth Yogīs, is mentioned in the line reckoned by the Sabhā as verse 12. For a translation, see Notes on the Translations.

That when we walk and walk in the midnight groves,
  it's not in pleasure, but in sorrow.
Love from our loved ones, a family visit,
  even a moment, is more than we can bear.
Where, oh where are those happy women
  whose husbands are present and hallow their lives,
Whose easy world is in need of the burden
  of your yogic message? None of them here.
For we've mastered already the mystical arts,
  the signs of the discipline of your Lord.
So go, says Sūr, and testify to him
  the worth of our constant meditation,
And bee, please take to someone else
  your useless, used-up, ruthless truths.

SIMPLE RELIGION, WOMEN'S RELIGION

One can scarcely read a line of Sūr's *bhramargīt* poetry without being aware that to make the *gopīs* models of faith is not just to exalt simple religion but specifically to praise the simple religion of women. It may seem that such praise masks an act of condescension: males have often portrayed women as untutored and childlike because they did not understand them and did not care to do so. And there can be no denying that Sūr's picture of the *gopīs* confronting Ūdho, though it gains some of its vividness from pitting the urban against the rural, depends mostly upon a stereotype that represents men as complicated and subtle and women as plain and transparent. One does not have to look far, moreover, to find that familiar religious pattern according to which feminine models are held up for emulation at the same time that real women are devalued. Vallabha, for instance, clearly recognized Krishna's *gopīs* as the model of devotion. At the same time, however, he insisted that women must become reborn as men before they are fit to worship Krishna the way the *gopīs* do.[11] Even the increasing veneration of Rādhā in subsequent years displayed this pattern to a degree: the higher she became, the less she partook of the nature of earthly women.

11. *Subodhinī* 10.14. The point, however, is not a simple one: see Marfatia, *Philosophy of Vallabhācārya*, p. 222. David Kinsley has drawn attention to a similar pattern in the *Devī Bhāgavata Purāṇa.* Kinsley, "The Image of the Divine and the Status of Women in the *Devī-bhāgavata-purāṇa*" (paper presented to the American Academy of Religion, New York, 1979). See also A. K. Ramanujan, "On Women Saints," in *The Divine Consort: Rādhā and the Goddesses of India,* ed. Hawley and Wulff, p. 324.

For Indians who hear the *bhramargīt* poems of Sūr, however, the link between the emotions of *viraha* voiced there and the experience of real women is immediate and self-evident. In the *bhramargīt* genre Sūr brings to focus a tradition of women's songs that reaches back further than memory, though it has only rarely been committed to writing. Folk culture all across North India is rich in songs of women's lamentations; one of the most prominent genres, the *bārahmāsā* (songs of the twelve months), records the sufferings and longings of women whose husbands are away.[12] In the poems of the *Sūr Sāgar,* as in some of the women's songs themselves, these longings are transposed into a Vaiṣṇava key: the absent husband is Krishna.

Such a transposition implies that these outpourings are the proper stuff of religion, and the leap is not so extreme as it might seem. In India the canons of religious and social behavior have long specified that men should define the arena in which women act.[13] A woman is expected to regard her husband as a god.[14] When Sūr proposes that the *gopīs* are to be understood as models of the religious life, then, he is not merely reinforcing a caricature of the female role. Rather, by modeling many of the motifs in his songs upon those that appear in women's own songs, he is highlighting an authentically female element in a women's tradition.

In comparing the austerities of yoga to those of love's separation, furthermore, he sometimes suggests another element that is

12. On *bārahmāsā* songs, see Charlotte Vaudeville, *Bārahmāsā*; Dusan Zvabitel, "The Development of the Baromasi in the Bengali Literature," *Archiv Orientalni* 29 (1961):582–619; and Susan Snow Wadley, "The Rains of Estrangement: Understanding the Hindu Yearly Cycle" (paper presented to the American Anthropological Association, Los Angeles, 1978). Vaudeville records and translates a selection of *bārahmāsās* of various types. A helpful collection of Bhojpuri *bārahmāsās* is to be found in Kṛṣṇadev Upādhyāy, ed., *Bhojpurī Lok-Gīt,* 1:407–28; 2:165–93. Very little has been written on the *caumāsā*, a similar genre, and few examples have been presented in print. See, e.g., Vidyā Cauhān, *Lokgītõ kī Sāṃskṛtik Pṛṣṭibhūmi,* p. 239. The *virahā* genre, despite its name and the time of year at which it is sung, does not contain an especially high proportion of songs of separation. See, e.g., Upādhyāy, *Lok-Git,* 1:439–50 and 2:270–98. Upādhyāy groups songs of women's sufferings that do not easily fit in one of the standard genres under the heading "Pīḍiyā ke Gīt" in 2:62–83. On women's songs generally, see also Winifred Bryce, ed., *Women's Folk-songs of Rajputana*; Rāmnareś Tripāṭhī, ed., *Grām-Sāhitya,* 1:257–372; and various folklore collections.

13. The classical formulation is *Mānavadharmaśāstra* 5.147–149, Georg Bühler, trans., *The Laws of Manu,* p. 195.

14. *Mānavadharmaśāstra* 5.154, Buhler, trans., ibid., p. 196.

genuinely at the heart of women's religion: the *vrat* or vow. The undertaking of such vows at regular intervals is a ubiquitous feature of women's piety in North India and much more characteristically a part of women's concerns than of men's.[15] Usually the purpose of the vow is to benefit some or all members of a woman's family, especially her husband and son, but it can have more general aims as well. Its most pervasive feature is fasting, but other voluntarily imposed hardships are also frequent.

In the Krishna story one such *vrat* has an especially honored place: the *gopīs*' vow to bathe in the chill waters of the Jumna each morning for a month so as to be granted Krishna as their husband. This *vrat,* classically, prepares them both as a group and as individuals to come into his intimate presence, to become his mates at the highest level by participating with him in the great circle dance, the *rās.*[16] Sūr, however, seems to extend the mood of the *vrat* far beyond this one incident (e.g., S 2286.4). The fasting and waiting that the *gopīs* endure for the sake of the man in their lives, and the songs they sing in the process, are like a *vrat* that has been extended to encompass all of life, one that has deepened from the voluntary to the involuntary level. It is no wonder that their lives should be compared to those of yogis, for in India the *vrat* is a woman's analogue to yoga. Unlike yoga, however, it is practiced by many, not just a few. That anyone can undertake a *vrat,* particularly any woman, clearly identifies it as an aspect of simple religion, although its rigors may seem as extreme as those of yoga.

In drawing upon two facets of women's experience—women's songs and the *vrat*—Sūr's *bhramargīt* poems make a legitimate claim to interpret simple religion as the religion of women. The effect is profound. One comes to see that simple religion is not so

15. A helpful index to scholarship on *vrats* can be found in Barron Holland, ed., *Popular Hinduism and Hindu Mythology*, pp. 120–21. A recent addition to the literature is James M. Freeman, "The Ladies of Lord Krishna: Rituals of Middle-Aged Women in Eastern India," in *Unspoken Worlds: Women's Religious Lives in Non-Western Cultures*, ed. Nancy A. Falk and Rita M. Gross, pp. 110–26.

16. In the *rās līlā,* the great circle dance. See *Bhāgavata Purāṇa* 10.22.25–27. On the relation between the *gopīs*' *vrat* to the goddess Kātyāyanī and the *rās līlā* as explained by Vallabhācārya, see James D. Redington, "The Meaning of Kṛṣṇa's Dance of Love According to Vallabhācārya" (Ph.D. diss., University of Wisconsin-Madison, 1975), pp. 18–19, 350. This framework of interpretation is sometimes assumed to be present in the *Sūr Sāgar* as well. See Vrajeśvar Varmā, *Sūr-Mīmāṃsā*, pp. 110–23.

simple—that is to say, not so easy—at all. In fact, to love God simply is as hard as, even harder than, yoga.[17]

In arguing that point, Sūr is drawing on a considerable tradition. The eleventh-century philosopher Abhinavagupta, for instance, compared the value of yoga with that of aesthetic experience.[18] At about the same time vernacular poets like Vidyāpati began to compare the intensity of the emotions borne by Rādhā with the austerities of yogis.[19] In Sūr's own time these theoretical and literary strands came together in figures like Rūpa Gosvāmī, the theologian of the Caitanya Sampradāy, who was chiefly responsible for transposing Abhinavagupta's aesthetic analysis of experience into theological terms. On the one hand Rūpa was able to show theoretically why devotion, while as stringent as yoga, is superior to it; on the other hand he carried on the tradition of Vidyāpati's poetic expressions of the same theme, transposing it into Sanskrit. Here are some lines translated from the *Vidagdhamādhava* by Donna Wulff, in which Rūpa reflects on Rādhā's yogic qualities:

> Seeking to meditate for a moment upon Krishna,
> The sage wrests his mind from the objects of sense;
> This child draws her mind away from Him
> To fix it on mere worldly things.
> The *yogī* yearns for a tiny flash of Krishna in his heart;
> Look—this foolish girl strives to banish Him from hers![20]

17. Wilfred Cantwell Smith has made a similar point in regard to Shinran Shonen's interpretation of faith. "Introduction to World Religion," lectures, Harvard University, 1969 and 1971. A parallel statement in the Indian context, focusing as does Shinran on the repetition of the divine name, can be found in poem 65 of the *Vinaya Patrikā* of Tulsī Dās. It is translated by F. R. Allchin in *The Petition to Rām*, p. 134.

18. Abhinavagupta, *Dhvanyālokalocana*, ed. Paṭṭbhirāma Śastrī, in Ānandavardhana, *Dhvanyāloka*, p. 155, as quoted in J. L. Masson and M. V. Patwardhan, *Aesthetic Rapture*, 2:37–38, n. 234, and translated by Donna M. Wulff, "*Rasa* as a Religious Category: Aesthetics and Supreme Realization in Medieval India" (paper presented to the conference honoring Wilfred Cantwell Smith, Center for the Study of World Religions, Harvard University, 1979), p. 8.

19. See, e.g., Kṛṣṇadev Śarmā, ed., *Vidyāpati aur unkī Padāvalī*, *pad* 210, p. 351. A translation is available in Richard Alan Hartz, "A Metrical Translation of Selected Maithili Lyrics of Vidyapati" (M.A. thesis, University of Washington, 1979), p. 128. The poem goes on to show how Rādhā's love leads her spontaneously to fulfill a number of acts of ritual punctiliousness. Thus her love supplants not only the yogi but the Brahmin.

20. Rūpa Gosvāmī, *Vidagdhamādhava* 2.17, translated in Donna M. Wulff, "Drama as a Mode of Religious Realization: The *Vidagdhamādhava* of Rūpa Gosvāmin" (Ph.D. diss., Harvard University, 1977), p. 321.

In comparing the *gopīs* to yogis, then, Sūr was heir to two traditions: one in which women expressed their own experience, including their religious experience, and one in which that experience was compared to yoga. But did he merely level a broadside at yoga as it had come to be popularly conceived, further derogating what in many quarters had already become a degenerate form of the religious life, or did he genuinely attempt to reconsider and recast a significant part of his religious heritage?

A measure of both, I would say. Certainly there is humor in the *bhramargīt* poems, but we should not underestimate the role humor can play in reformulating religious traditions, or its role in the religious life generally. This is particularly the case in a tradition where *līlā* itself, play, is one of the most important categories. Indeed humor is sometimes required to illuminate the seriousness of the issue at hand. Sūr uses the intrinsically comical situation of Ūdho's encounter with the *gopīs* to make it clear, as he could scarcely have done otherwise, that simple religion is no simple matter, certainly no shallow matter. Nand Dās, half a generation later, already loses some of the magic of this formula by turning his *gopīs* into genuine debating artists: both their simplicity and the depth it implies become less believable.[21]

As for yoga, we should not conclude that because Sūr pillories it he dismisses it. To the contrary, the more one thinks about poems such as these, the more one is forced to reflect on the improbable congruences between yoga and *viyoga*. On one level, to be sure, yoga is debunked and dismissed as trivial and peripheral. But on another level the comparison with yoga reveals the depth of the sufferings and strictures of the life of love. The difficulties and high aspirations of yoga, though ultimately misguided from Sūr Dās's viewpoint, still serve to measure the profundity of the life recast by simple and total contact with Krishna. Karl Barth, the twentieth-century Reformed theologian, has sometimes spoken in a similar vein, suggesting that the lengths to which the human search for God can lead—however misguided, irrelevant, or even harmful from his point of view—serve nonetheless to illuminate the far greater reach of divine revelation. In Sūr's poems too there is a sense of the depth of the human response to the divine presence. The difference is that there is a grandeur in the deprivation of that presence that rivals even the effulgence of the presence itself. Hence yoga, the disciplined aspiration for a condition not

21. A number of critics have noticed this transition from Sūr Dās to Nand Dās. E.g., Dvivedī, *Sūr Sāhitya*, pp. 134–37; McGregor, *Nanddas*, p. 53.

yet achieved, emerges as a more apt yardstick for faith in Sūr's comparison than human religious strivings can be as a measure for revelation in Barth's.[22]

Udho the yogi, then, is the occasion for much more than comic relief. His presence does lighten the tone of a corpus of poetry that explores the depth of human pain when God, once present, is absent. But it also sharpens the focus. Never do the *gopīs* articulate their position so crisply as when they have Ūdho to tell it to, which explains why Sūr devoted such particular attention to the *bhramargīt* genre and why these poems are so highly regarded and well remembered right up to the present day.

Ūdho and the great yogic tradition that he stands for, however trivial they seem by comparison with *viyoga,* provide some standard for indicating how great the stakes are when humanity and divinity fall in love. And in some measure all types of formalized religion do the same—mirroring, however imperfectly, and sometimes even inversely, the extraordinary power of simple faith.

22. See Karl Barth, *Church Dogmatics*, 1, pt. 2: 280–361, especially pp. 301–2, 310, 340–44.

Sants conversing. Kangra hills, early nineteenth century. Courtesy of the Museum of Fine Arts, Boston (17.2615).

CHAPTER 5

Sant and Sinner

WHEN SŪR ESTABLISHES the claims of simple religion by focusing on the *gopīs*' separation from Krishna and reporting the words of despair and derision that they direct against Ūdho, he seems to place himself firmly on one side of a great theological divide. The simple devotion that he praises is *saguṇa bhakti,* the worship of God through his appearance and attributes, through his manifest form. There are times when the *gopīs*, Sūr's spokeswomen, are savage and sardonic in their derogation of the opposite camp. As they insist on experiencing Krishna in his full earthly form, they ridicule the *nirguṇa* position, which holds that God can truly be worshipped only in the absence of attribute and form, since these are qualities projected onto him by sense-bound humans but not intrinsic to the divine nature. In the "songs to the bee" the *saguṇa* approach emerges as direct and real, capable of incorporating the powerful force of love in the realm of religion. The *nirguṇa* approach, by contrast, is caricatured as senselessly difficult, aimlessly rarefied, and in the end simply dull. By making Ūdho the representative not only of yoga but of the *nirguṇa* persuasion in general, Sūr seems clearly to cast his own lot with *saguṇa bhakti.*

Before leaping to this conclusion, however, we need to look more closely at another group of poems that emerge with great force in the early *Sūr Sāgar.* These are Sūr's *vinaya* poems—compositions he addresses to the Lord apart from any narrative context; songs in which he offers some combination of praise, petition, and self-remonstration. The emphasis falls in large measure on the latter two, for these poems are in spirit much less expressions of satisfaction at the divine presence than they are laments at its absence. In a word, these too are songs of *viraha,* but played in a different key. Because they are not voiced from within the context of Krishna's Braj, they fall much less clearly within the *saguṇa* camp than do Sūr's other *viraha* poems, and indeed it is not impossible for the poet to address God with epithets that echo the *nirguṇa* point of view. Titles such as *avigat* and *avināsī* (changeless, indestructible) suggest that one cannot really speak about or comprehend the divine essence. Furthermore Sūr seems to place himself in the company of those whose habit it is to worship God in the *nirguṇa* manner. These are the *sant*s (saints) whose contributions to medieval Indian religion are best remembered in the poetry of such figures as Nāmdev, Nānak, and Kabīr. And many of these *sant*s composed poems that are very much in the spirit and form of Sūr's *vinaya* outpourings.

Having examined Sūr's defense of *saguṇa* religion by exploring one genre of *viraha* poetry, then, we are now faced with the question of how he can place himself in the company of *nirguṇa* poets in another. Why should Sūr should associate himself with the *sant*s? In this chapter I hope to show that there is nothing really anomalous about such a seemingly unlikely creature as *sant* Sūr Dās; but at the same time it will become evident that important differences do set Sūr apart from poets of the time who are more customarily called *sant*s than he. For instance, although Sūr assumes communities of *sant*s (*satsaṅg*) as part of his world and labels them as such, indicating that he participates in the general *sant* milieu, he accords little significance to such groups. What matters to him more is a direct confrontation with the divine. This relative indifference to the virtues of *satsaṅg* would seem to separate Sūr from *sant*s such as Kabīr, but at the same time the radical edge in Sūr's point of view suggests a strange alliance. Here, as in the *bhramargīt* poems themselves, Sūr's is a message of unqualified faith, no less stringent than that preached by caustic Kabīr. It would be confusing, no doubt, to call this an expression of *nirguṇa bhakti* per se, for that label could hardly mean what it does when applied to a *sant* like Kabīr. But Sūr's stance is closely analogous, and in its own way no less extreme.

SUR AND THE *SANT*S

The familiar taxonomy for popular devotion in medieval North India rests on a theological distinction between *nirguṇa* and *saguṇa*. *Saguṇa bhakta*s worship through the attributes of the objects of faith, hence they can easily be distinguished not only from *nirguṇa bhakta*s but also from other members of the *saguṇa* camp according to their emphasis on either Rām or Krishna. By the same token this theological rubric suggests that there is no further need to differentiate among the partisans of *nirguṇa* religion (*nirguṇīs*): as worshippers of a God whose formlessness is his most significant property—the term and the ranking are, of course, misleading—they too resist formal differentiation. Still, they are allied with one another not only on the basis of what they lack—a consistent Krishnaite or Rāmaite orientation—but on the basis of certain shared emphases: an inward faith, the conviction of the importance of the guru (whether external or internal), sometimes an explicit social protest, and ever so occasionally the mention of one by another.

The contrast between *sants* and Vaiṣṇavas, *nirguṇīs* and *saguṇīs*, however, is not always so neat as this taxonomy would imply. This is clearly evident in the social arena. One might logically predict that Vaiṣṇava religious movements claiming one or more of these *bhakti* saints as their founders or inspirers would have engendered more well-defined organizations than their *sant* counterparts, since the community could be so directly shaped around a specifiable, "qualified" (*saguṇa*) object of devotion, Rām or Krishna. Scholarship in Hindi typically speaks of a rather ill-defined *sant* persuasion (*sant mat*) for just this reason.[1] But as more detailed investigations show,[2] religious movements representing this *sant* persuasion bear organizational patterns no less definite than their Vaiṣṇava counterparts. The Dādū, Kabīr, and Nānak (i.e., Sikh) Panths are as well articulated as the Caitanya, Vallabha, and Rādhāvallabha Sampradāys. Indeed, it is the Rāmaite com-

1. It is not clear when this term came into common usage, but it seems definitely not to have been an expression known in the medieval period itself. There is some suggestion, in fact, that it may be as recent as the eighteenth century. It appears frequently in the phraseology of the *Ghaṭ Rāmāyaṇ* of Tulsī Sāhib (1: 1, 22, 126, 158; 2: 21, passim), a work composed early in the nineteenth century, and emerges as a standard feature in the historical self-understanding of the Radhasoami Satsang later in the nineteenth century. The Radhasoami Satsang looks to Tulsī Sāhib as the guru of its first guru and may have been chiefly responsible for the wide currency that the term *sant mat* enjoys today. See Mark Juergensmeyer, "The Radhasoami Revival of the Sant Tradition," in *The Sants: Studies in a Devotional Tradition of India*, ed. Karine Schomer and W. H. McLeod, forthcoming. The latter work is a valuable general resource on the *sants*, bringing together some of the most recent scholarship in the field. It serves as good background for this chapter and an excellent place to turn for further study and bibliographical assistance.

2. E.g., the comprehensive work of Paraśurām Caturvedī, *Uttarī Bhārat kī Sant-Paramparā*. See also W. G. Orr, *A Sixteenth-Century Indian Mystic: Dadu and His Followers*; G. H. Westcott, *Kabir and the Kabir Panth*; Kedārnāth Dvivedī, *Kabīr aur Kabīr-Panth*; David N. Lorenzen, ed., *Religious Change and Cultural Domination*; and W. H. McLeod, *The Evolution of the Sikh Community*.

ponent of medieval *bhakti,* not the *sant,* that has failed more than any other to spawn clearly recognizable sectarian communities, with the case of the Rāmānandīs as the single notable exception, and even that a bit mystifying.[3]

Such difficulties of classification are fortunate, for they alert us to the likelihood that the religious world in which the medieval *bhakta*s participated and which they so shaped was much more fluid in its organization than that of subsequent generations.[4] To divide the principal figures of this period (ca. 1400–1650) into Rāmaite and Krishnaite *bhakta*s on the one hand and *sant*s on the other is to run the risk of obscuring the important connection that related them to one another and made them in significant ways parts of the same movement.[5] There were differences, of course: the *bhramargīt* poems of Sūr and Nand Dās plainly make fun of the *nirguṇa* position, at least insofar as yogic, ascetic types are understood as its spokesmen. The remarkable thing, however, is that someone like Kabīr, who is normally classed as *nirguṇī* and on occasion uses a Nāth Yogī term of address, *avadhūt* (renunciant), in a roughly collegial sense, is scarcely less sparing in his criticism of yogis. Or to take the contrary case, while Kabīr was uncompromising in his opposition to worship through images, some of the most forceful poems attributed to the supposedly likeminded Nāmdev associate him with a particular manifestation of divinity, Lord Pāṇḍurāṅg of Pandharpur—and do so in seemingly *nirguṇī* terms.

We are forced to conclude, at the least, that we ought to think of the most influential poets of this formative period in North Indian religion as arrayed in a spectrum rather than clumped together in well-defined camps. Kenneth Bryant's distinction be-

3. On problems relating to the connection between this sect in its more recent forms and the shadowy Rāmānand, see Charlotte Vaudeville, *Kabīr,* 1: 113–14; Richard Burghart, "The Founding of the Ramanandi Sect," *Ethnohistory* 25, no. 2 (1978): 121–39, and "Wandering Ascetics of the Rāmanandī Sect," *History of Religions* 22, no. 4 (1983): 361–80.

4. See Wilfred Cantwell Smith, "The Crystallization of Religious Communities in Mughul India," in *Yād-nāme-ye Irāni-ye Minorsky,* ed. Mojtaba Minovi and Ijar Afshar, pp. 1–24.

5. In what follows I will occasionally have to refer to the movement as a whole, and will call it the *bhakti* movement, reserving the term *sant* for a stream within the whole. This usage, though conventional and in accord with the precedent set long ago by Nābhājī, can be misleading. I must ask the reader to remember that if one gave greater weight to what its participants called one another, the term *sant* would be equally appropriate as a designation of the whole.

tween *sants* and Vaiṣṇavas in rhetorical terms provides one way of describing the extremities of the spectrum: Kabīr's appeal is to personal experience, particularly on the basis of his own, whereas Sūr's appeal is to a shared dramatic legendry.[6] One will find more explicit reference to the everyday world, therefore, in the poetry of Kabīr, Dādū, and Nāmdev than in Sūr or Tulsī, and there is a strong suggestion that such *nirguṇīs* inherit much from the emphases of the Nāth Yogīs.[7] Yet they share a surprisingly similar range of perspectives. In almost all cases, not just at the Vaiṣṇava extreme, *viraha* is interpreted as the true and rigorous form of yoga; the Kabīr who speaks in the *Bījak* and in the *Gurū Granth Sāhib* is the only exception that comes to mind.[8] And the yogic goal of *mukti,* release from this world as such, is at some level called into question by all. To be sure, Nāmdev, Kabīr, Nānak, and Dādū—the *nirguṇīs*—are the ones who speak most familiarly of the *satguru,* the "True Guru" who is at once an internal presence and at the same time available in a teaching succession. But Mīrā refers to the *satguru* as well, and there is even a hint or two in the poetry attributed to Sūr. Sūr, Tulsī, and later Tukārām—the *saguṇīs*—make a great deal of the Lord representing himself as a savior of sinners, but so does Nāmdev near the other end of the spectrum. Finally, the hallmark of the whole group, from Sūr at one end to Kabīr at the other, is a trust in the absolute power of the name of God; and all agree that whatever other designations are also possible, that name can be called Rām.[9]

Later generations, with more narrowly defined loyalties, were often forced to awkward extremes in accounting for the catholicity of their revered predecessors. The case of Kabīr is well known.

6. Kenneth E. Bryant, "*Sant* and *Vaiṣṇava* Poetry: Some Observations on Method," in *Sikh Studies: Comparative Perspectives on a Changing Tradition,* ed. Mark Juergensmeyer and N. Gerald Barrier, pp. 65–74.

7. In regard to Kabīr see Vaudeville, *Kabīr,* 1: 120–48. Also P. D. Barthwal, *The Nirguṇa School of Hindi Poetry,* pp. 140–52. In regard to Nānak, see W. H. McLeod, *Gurū Nānak and the Sikh Religion,* pp. 157–58, and Hazārīprasād Dvivedī, *Nāth Sampradāy.*

8. See Linda Hess, "Studies in Kabir: Texts, Traditions, Styles and Skills" (Ph.D. diss., University of California, Berkeley, 1980), p. 50.

9. Two examinations of the exaltation of the sheer name of God from a seemingly *saguṇa* perspective are: Norvin Hein, "Caitanya's Ecstasies and the Theology of the Name," in *Hinduism: New Essays in the History of Religions,* ed. Bardwell L. Smith, pp. 15–32, and F. R. Allchin, "The Place of Tulsī Dās in North Indian Devotional Tradition," *Journal of the Royal Asiatic Society,* 1966, pts. 3 and 4, pp. 128–29.

The puzzle was how Kabīr, as a member of a caste that had embraced Islam, could have sung the name of Rām, for by 1700 or so that name had come to be thought of as a particularly Vaiṣṇava province. Hence one has, in Priyā Dās's commentary on the *Bhaktamāl,* the story of how Kabīr, the Muslim weaver (*julāhā*), elicited an inadvertent initiation from Rāmānand by placing himself in the great teacher's path so that Rāmānand would stumble over him and shout out "Rām, Rām!" Kabīr, so the story goes, took this involuntary ejaculation as his initiatory mantra.[10] Later, as so often happens, a tale developed to establish that Kabīr was really a Brahmin all along, and *julāhā* only by adoption, which makes the whole affair impeccably legitimate—or would if it were not for Kabīr's own disdain for Brahmin pretensions.[11] Similar chroniclers evidently wondered how Nāmdev could have been at once a passionate devotee of Pāṇḍurāṅg (Krishna) and at the same time capable of condemning sectarian allegiances of all sorts. Nāmdev was primarily remembered as a *nirguṇī sant,* so the solution was to periodize his life in such a way that he grew away from his attachment to the Lord of Pandharpur and adhered to a more strictly interior religion, as taught by *sant* Visobā Khecar.[12]

In the case of Sūr the interested parties were *saguṇī* rather than *nirguṇī,* so the opposite transformation was effected. As we have seen, partisans of the Vallabha Sampradāy demarcated Sūr's life into two phases separated by an encounter with Vallabha which entirely reoriented his perspective. The poems of Sūr that did not describe the sports of Krishna then become the documents of his life before enlightenment, and the Krishna poems followed. It was

10. Nābhājī, *Śrī Bhaktamāl,* p. 481.

11. The motif of brahminhood in a former life is a familiar one in the *bhakti* literature of non-Brahmin saints. Normally there is nothing to indicate that the poet himself might have made such a claim. Kabīr's case, however, is otherwise. In one of the verses attributed to him he challenges the behavior of a Brahmin by saying that he too once lived the life his interlocutor leads, preoccupied with meaningless ritual affairs, only to find himself reborn on that account as a low *julāhā* in his current life. The spirit of the remark, of course, is just the reverse of what the *Bhaktamāl*'s story of Kabīr's earlier, nobler birth seeks to establish. By mentioning his former birth and its consequences, Kabīr denigrates rather than exalts himself. See P. N. Tivārī, *Kabīr-Granthāvalī,* vol. 2, *pad* 188.2.

12. I am not sure what is the earliest attestation of the story of Nāmdev's devotion to Pāṇḍurāṅg and subsequent *dīkṣā* at the hands of Visobā Khecar. It does not appear in the *Bhaktamāl.* Standard works report it without citation, e.g., Rāmcandra Miśra, *Sant Nāmdev aur Hindī Sāhitya,* p. 61, and Paraśurām Caturvedī, *Uttarī Bhārat kī Sant-Paramparā,* p. 110.

inconceivable to the Vallabhite theologian(s) who shaped the *Caurāsī Vaiṣṇavan kī Vārtā* that the two could mix.[13]

But in fact they did. In Sūr's *vinaya* poems it becomes clear that even the poet who held up the *nirguṇī* position to such ridicule in his *bhramargīt* poems has a dimension that brings him into the company of the *sants*.

EARLY *VINAYA* COLLECTIONS

In the Sabhā edition of the *Sūr Sāgar* one locates Sūr's *vinaya* poetry—his poems of petition, his prayers—with considerable difficulty. The reason is that the manuscripts that were the principal models for the Sabhā editors, dating to about 1800 A.D.,[14] went even further in their attempt to cast Sūr in the Vallabhite mold than had the *Caurāsī Vaiṣṇavan kī Vārtā* itself. They categorized the whole of Sūr's poetry in such a way that each poem would fit (sometimes awkwardly) into one of the episodes described in the twelve books of the *Bhāgavata Purāṇa,* thus implicitly displaying Sūr's indebtedness to Vallabha's commentary on that work. The *vinaya* poems are distributed among several headings appropriate to the first two books.

In the early manuscripts no such system pertained. These *vinaya* poems, like most poetry from the *bhakti* movement, were occasional poems, and they were collected in a variety of ways—most commonly by theme, but also by raga, and even by loose alphabetical groupings. Although these *vinaya* poems were placed in close proximity to one another in the early manuscripts (except, of course, in the case of those organized by raga), there was no consensus as to what they should be called. The *vinaya* label that has become current recently (in the Gītā Press edition, for instance) seems to have been borrowed by analogy from the famous work of the first

13. An influential modern-day scholar and critic of Hindi literature, Hazārīprasād Dvivedī, has adopted a comparable perspective in regard to Kabīr. The problem was how the same poet could have composed the trenchant, seemingly nonsectarian *sākhīs* associated with the name of Kabīr and at the same time the softer, more yielding Vaiṣṇava lyrics bearing the same signature. Dvivedī's solution was that indeed the two were not composed at the same time. He proposed that Kabīr's initiation by Rāmānand be understood not as an event of his youth but as something that happened a bit later in his career. The *sākhīs*, then, come naturally before the poet's Vaiṣṇava initiation and the others after. H. P. Dvivedī, *Kabīr,* pp. 159–60; translated and discussed in Hess, "Studies in Kabir," pp. 56–61.

14. See chap. 2, n. 1.

great poet to collect compositions of this type: Tulsī Dās. Tulsī's *Vinaya Patrikā* was largely a reworking of earlier poems which he, like Sūr, had composed independently.[15] The term *binti* (or *vinti,* "prayer, petition"), a close relative of *vinaya,* does indeed occur in early Sūr poems of this genre,[16] but as it happens none of the early scribe-editors seized upon it to characterize the group as a whole.

Of the seven manuscripts that provide substantial collections, four omit any designation at all. In two cases the poems are distributed through the manuscript according to their ragas (B2, J2); in the others (J5, A1) they are numbered in separate series and then listed one after another, but without headings. U1 is the first manuscript to provide headings, and it does so by distinguishing ten poems of petition voiced by figures in the *Mahābhārata* and the twenty-five couplets called *sūrpacīsī* from the general mass, 137 poems labeled *bhagat* because they have to do with *bhakti.* At almost the same time the scribe of B4 (or the manuscript he copied) made a different distinction, between 112 poems of petition addressed to the Lord, which he designated *karunā,* and 23 poems of inner dialogue and remonstration, which he called *pramodh*—the poet's attempt to instruct and correct himself.[17]

There are other early manuscripts that conform, seemingly, to the Vallabhite perspective on Sūr and contain either only a very few *vinaya* poems (B3 has four; K1, six) or none at all (B1 and the two related manuscripts, J3 and J4). Given that this is sometimes the case, however, it is striking that when the *vinaya* poems do appear they are present in considerable numbers; they account for anywhere from 10 to 22 percent of the total. In the case of J5, furthermore, we have a text that is entirely devoted to the *vinaya* genre, and the middle portion of the oldest dated Sūr manuscript, J1, is an independently numbered *vinaya* anthology that intersperses some of Sūr's *vinaya* poems with those of other poets. Only one manuscript of the *Sūr Sāgar* adopts the scheme that was later to become orthodox and places the *vinaya* poems at the beginning of the collection, as if they were to be understood as superseded by a conversion at the hands of Vallabha. Not sur-

15. The *Rām Gītāvalī,* on which see F. R. Allchin's introduction to his translation of Tulsī Dās, *The Petition to Rām,* pp. 37–38.

16. S 4.14, 42.1, 162.5, 170.2, and 201.2. The Sabhā edition has *vinaya* in S 124.12, but the manuscripts read *bintī* or *vintī* (B2: *vantī*).

17. These bear general comparison to poems of Kabīr. See, e.g., *pads* 48, 50, 53, 55, 86, and 93 in Charlotte Vaudeville, *Kabīr,* vol. 2.

prisingly, this manuscript (K1) is one of the most recent in the group and was compiled at Pachor, near the important Vallabhite seat at Kota, in which city it is now housed. In all other cases the *vinaya* poems are either distributed throughout the collection, as in manuscripts organized by raga, or, more commonly, placed precisely where they should not be from a sectarian Vallabhite point of view: at or near the end.

In the early manuscripts, then, we seem to have a clear difference of opinion as to whether Sūr's *vinaya* poems were to be regarded as an integral part of the poet's message, with the majority feeling that they were. This would tend to give credence to the argument that in the early years most people did not regard Sūr as being of an entirely different stripe from those of his contemporaries who are now known as *sant*s. Other evidence bears on the same point. A number of anthologies, many of them small but some more extensive, survive from this early period, and in not a few of them the compositions of poets who were later to be called *saguṇa bhakta*s are included along with the compositions of those whom we have come to think of as *sant*s. Sūr and Tulsī appear alongside Nāmdev and Kabīr, and in varying orders. Those who made collections of the poetry of various *bhakta sant*s in this early period had a natural tendency to include a significant number of *vinaya* poems, usually a higher proportion than one typically finds in independent collections. Both the fact of such groupings and their content, then, call into question too strong a dichotomy between *sant* and Vaiṣṇava.[18]

It was some years before this dichotomy was systematically observed. By the middle of the seventeenth century the Vallabha Sampradāy was insisting that when Sūr met Vallabha he left behind all of his poetry that was not specifically bounded in the world of Krishna-*līlā*—that is, he gave up the poetry that had tied him most directly to the *sant*s. Nonetheless poems continued to be contributed to the less sectarian, *vinaya* portions of the *Sūr Sāgar*. These

18. The manuscripts in question are usually untitled and referred to in the catalogues under headings such as *phuṭkar pad*, *padāvalī*, or *khaṇḍit prati*. Examples of Hindi anthologies predating *vikram* 1800 in which the *sant*/Vaiṣṇava or *nirguṇa*/*saguṇa* line is crossed are: nos. 39687, 6992, 34235, 39680, and 30587 in the Rajasthan Oriental Research Institute, Jodhpur; no. 3322, Royal Palace, Jaipur; an unnumbered manuscript entitled *bhajan ādi*, Jiwaji University, Gwalior; no. 2062, Rajasthan Oriental Research Institute, Udaipur (though its early date is not assured); and nos. 148 and 4863 in the Rājasthānī Śodh Saṃsthān, Chopasini (Jodhpur).

later poems, in fact, make clearer and more frequent reference to such features of *sant* piety as *satguru, satsaṅg,* and the ineffable divine word (*sabad, śabd*) than one finds in earlier poems of the same group. In such poems one observes a tendency for the poet to be "routinized" along *sant* lines.[19]

But the bulk of the development and routinizing of the *Sūr Sāgar* after 1700 came, of course, from the sectarian Vaiṣṇava side. This leaves us with the odd and notable fact that of all the sections of the Sabhā *Sūr Sāgar,* the one containing the highest proportion of poems from the early manuscripts is the *vinaya* section, the part that fits so uneasily into the structure of the work as the Sabhā editors conceived it. And this is particularly the case in the poems that lie at its core, the boasts and complaints of Sūr the sinner. One can rarely open the Sabhā *Sūr Sāgar* and be confident that all of what one reads is attested in the early manuscripts, but that does happen in the *vinaya* section. If one opens to pages 44–45 of the 1972 edition, all nine poems (S 131–139) date to about 1700 or before.

SANT THEMES IN *VINAYA* POETRY

The most numerous, and in many ways the most impressive, of Sūr's *vinaya* poems are those that can be strictly described as *vinaya*: compositions in which the poet calls upon the Lord of salvation. To assume that they are in the same vein as the petitions of the *Vinaya Patrikā,* however, is to miss the distinctive characteristic of many of them, for they bespeak anything but the humility (however measured and confident) of a Tulsī Dās. These are poems of bitter complaint and strenuous contest in which the poet demands that the Lord follow through on promise and precedent and save him, a sinner, or relinquish any claim to being known as savior of the fallen. Other moods, represented in less numerous poems, array themselves around this theme. There are

19. In S 407.2, for instance, the term *satguru* is explicitly associated with the concept of *sabad.* In 360.7–8 *satsaṅg* is praised in the most familiar sort of way. The earlier *sādhi samādhi* (B4) becomes the fomulaic *sahaj samādhi* in later readings of the same poem (S 312.2), and a similar shift toward familiar usage may be observed in S 356.8. In its only manuscript reading (J4, a relatively late attestation) it has the *sants* as the objects or beneficiaries of songs to be sung in praise of Hari (*santan ko*); in the Sabhā version they are rather, as one would expect, the context in which such songs might be sung (*santan mili*).

poems in which some of the protagonists of the *Mahābhārata* also call upon the Lord—particularly Draupadī, whose situation is the most extreme and the most scandalous. Her Pāṇḍava husbands bargained her away in a game of dice, leaving her defenseless before the appetites of their Kaurava cousins, one of whom attempted to disrobe her in public. At that she raised a helpless plea to Krishna, who supplied her with endless lengths of cloth. Such petitions as these are complemented by a number of others in which reassurance is given that the Lord is attentive to cries of distress. The Sabhā labels these *bhaktavatsaltā*: Krishna's solicitude for his devotees, like a parent's for a child. In the opposite vein there are poems of deep remorse, in which the poet laments a life wasted in absorption with the things of this world, contemplates death, and finds that it is too late to change. These are poems of unusual sobriety, and unlike most later additions to the genre, they are not often relieved by a message of hope. The act of giving voice to one's condition before the Lord provides the only glimmer.[20] In a companion series the poet's reflections turn to self-accusation and he remonstrates with his own heart.

Among these outpourings are several motifs that place Sūr firmly in the company of the *sant*s. There is the frequent mention of death, particularly as the god Yama[21] or as the devouring "snake of time" (*kāl-vyāl*),[22] accompanied in both cases by the plea to be released. And because death is so pressing a concern, those whom the Lord has saved from its noose and jaws, Ajāmil and Gajendra respectively, figure with special prominence when Sūr is listing the recipients of the Lord's grace. Ajāmil it was who, though born a Brahmin and properly married, deserted his family and caste obligations to elope with a low-caste prostitute and live a life of sin. Only once did he ever call upon the name of the Lord, and that was by accident. As the terrors of mortality assailed him on his

20. In commenting on a parallel genre in Bengali, poems of self-deprecation called *kākuvāda* or *kākukti*, Joseph T. O'Connell proposes that the act of throwing oneself at the Lord's feet has a hidden and intrinsic salvific power because it reveals the proper ontological relation of humans to the divine, namely servanthood. O'Connell, "Gaudiya Vaisnava Symbolism of Deliverance (*uddhara, nistara* . . .) from Evil," *Journal of Asian and African Studies* 15, no. 1–2 (1980): 126–27, 131–32.

21. E.g., S 67.6, 111.2, and 334.6. Attention to the last moment of life as such, however, is more a feature of later additions to the *Sūr Sāgar* than of these early poems. E.g., S 80.4 and 85.4.

22. E.g., S 117.12 in B4, and 312.12 (B4, J5: *kāl var vyāl*; U2: *kāl bal vyāl*; cf. J2: *byāl*, B3: *jam jāl*); also 326.8, which is translated in chap. 6.

deathbed, he shouted out for his son Nārāyaṇ—but it was Krishna (also called Nārāyaṇ) who answered by bringing Ajāmil the assurance of a totally unearned heavenly salvation. Gajendra the elephant was in similarly dire straits. A crocodile had grabbed hold of his toe and was pulling him steadily beneath the water. He too bellowed out for Krishna, who arrived in split-second haste and saved him at a stroke from death and his deadliest foe. Ajāmil and Gajendra figure frequently in *sant* poetry, providing object lessons not only about God's grace but specifically about his power over death, a pressing *sant* concern.

Other expressions of the struggle against death also tie Sūr closely to the *sants*. A number of figures of speech common in *sant* poetry appear when Sūr looks back—sometimes explicitly in the face of death—on a life that has gone to waste. In poems full of bitter remorse we find the dogs, jackals, and vultures that often symbolize the voracious world of the senses in *sant* compositions (e.g., S 150.6). There is also mention of the bird of the soul, who has been so callously entrapped in the snares of this world (e.g., S 337). In the example that follows, it is the dog who comes to the poet's mind: he finds himself suspended between his canine soul and the master it has foolishly forsaken (S 103).

Master, my mind is absent and lost.

It's left your lotus feet, that treasury of all,
  and taken to the scavenging habits of a dog.
It wanders without aim, scratches after food
  in barren houses and near burning pyres
With a desperate thirst it can never quench—
  the thirst that stirs from inner depths.
And wherever it goes, it's in ever-present fear
  of hurled stones, sticks, and well-placed kicks.
How many animal insults has it suffered, poor dumb dog?
  How many vicious slurs for a mouthful here and there?
Lord, all merciful, you guard the very world,
  and every heart you master as your own;
Surely, says Sūr, only a foolish dog like me
  would leave your home to join the company of the lost.

Another familiar theriomorphic image for the misguided soul is that of the parrot who watches carefully over the ripening of the silk-cotton (*semar*) fruit. The parrot waits with anxious greed until the fruit appears juicy and full, and pecks it at last—only to have the inedible cottony substance inside fly away in the breeze. So do we nurture our affections in this world, and they, like the silk-cotton, are ultimately indigestible. Here are two poems among many that draw on this image, one by Sūr (S 59) and one, for comparison, by Kabīr.

My soul, abandon the blandishments of flesh.

Why yearn like a parrot for some silk-cotton fruit?
  In the end, you know, it evades your grasp.
Waves of elusive passion—women and wealth:
  they slip through the sieve of your hands.
Fool, dispense with pride and pretension
  and take refuge in the name of Rām
    before you leave and you're lost to the flames.
As you've heard the words of the True Guru,
  now you're witness to these words of mine:
If ever you would reckon the treasurehouse of gems
  that is Rām, dear soul, the time's at hand.
Unless you reflect on Hari, the Lord of Sūr,
  you'll be like those yogis—like monkeys they are—
    you'll wriggle on a leash, and dance.

Fool soul, jettison the flesh,
Save a second's thought for God.

Fearless fool, refusing Hari,
You've cast off the life raft of Rām.

This world, fool soul,
This elephant effigy
Is made by the Lord to lure you
And lead on your elephant lusts:
  the goad
  to prod your dense head.

Fool soul, jettison the flesh,
Save a second's thought for God.

The monkey, fool soul,
Stuck in his hand,
Searching for grain in a narrow-necked pot,
And it stuck, and he couldn't get it out,
  he was caught,
  and ever after danced from house to house.

Fool soul, jettison the flesh,
Save a second's thought for God.

The parrot, fool soul,
Is lured to silk-cotton;
  likewise the lure of illusion:
It flies in the face,
A fistful of color,
Of safflower powder
  that spreads in the winds.

Fool soul, jettison the flesh,
Save a second's thought for God.

Fool soul,
There are rivers and rivers
In which to bathe
And gods and gods to praise,
But none will set you free,
  says Kabīr:
  freedom is in the service of Rām.

Fool soul, jettison the flesh,
Save a second's thought for God.[23]

23. For an alternate translation, see Vaudeville, *Kabīr*, vol. 2, *pad* 50. The line concerning the parrot and its prey presents textual difficulties, since none of the major versions actually uses the term "silk-cotton." In present-day editions of the *Gurū Granth Sāhib* and the *Bījak* one finds instead *nalanī* ("lotus"), and P. N. Tivārī's critically edited *Kabīr-Granthāvalī*, reflecting the Rajasthani recension, reads *lalanī* ("alluring woman"). The latter is a general enough term and the former a close enough analogue, however, to indicate that the poet had the silk-cotton image basically in mind, as the parallel with safflower almost requires. So Vaudeville, evidently (ibid., n. 4). Cf. Tivārī, *Kabīr-Granthāvalī*, vol. 2, *pad* 97. *Sākhī*s 163–65 of the *Bījak*, each of which concerns the image of the parrot and the *semar* tree, are translated by Linda Hess in collaboration with Shukdev Singh, in *The Bījak of Kabir*, p. 108. For the original, see Kabīr, *Bījak*, with commentary by Khemrāj Śrīkṛṣṇadās, pp. 466–67.

Sūr and the *sant*s share not only images of dogs, jackals, and birds drawn from the great storehouse of common speech, but whole proverbs as well. Take, for instance, two widely known sayings having to do with human obduracy and heedlessness: "You can't pierce a stone with an arrow," and "If you dye a blanket black, the color will never change." Both formulae make their way into the rhetoric of Kabīr and Sūr, but the effect is not quite the same. Here are two *sākhī*s of Kabīr, as translated by Vaudeville:

The Bowman kept aiming and aiming,
but his shots never pierced:
All his arrows fell to the ground,
so tossing away his quiver, he left.[24]

If you keep company, then do so with discernment,
associate with your own kind:
Even if the blanket be torn to pieces,
still it will keep its own color![25]

And here is a *pad* of Sūr, which concludes by incorporating both images (S 332):

Soul, turn your back on those who shun the Lord.

Tell me, what good is there in giving cobras milk?
Serpents can never surrender their venom.
Why waste camphor by feeding it to crows
or squander the water of the Ganges on dogs?
Why array an ass in an aromatic scent?
Why bejewel a monkey or dress it in clothes?
Do you really think an arrow can pierce a fallen stone,
even if you empty your quiver of them all?
Once you've dyed a blanket black, says Sūr,
there's no point hoping for a different hue.

24. Vaudeville, *Kabīr, sākhī* 22.4, 1: 272. Kabīr, *Bījak, sākhī* 313, p. 539.

25. Vaudeville, *Kabīr, sākhī* 24.17, 1: 279. Tivārī, *Kabīr-Granthāvalī, sākhī* 24.17, 2: 221.

The motifs of arrow and blanket are the same from poet to poet, but they are employed in characteristically different ways. When Kabīr speaks of the bowman and the arrow, he has something quite specific in mind. The archer is the *satguru,* the divine interior teacher in whom the *sant* tradition placed such confidence, and his arrow is the *sabad* or *śabda,* the inner word through which he speaks to those who seek him out:

> The Satguru is the true Hero,
>   who loosed off a single Śabda;
> The moment it struck, I fell to the ground
>   and a wound opened in my breast.[26]

Sūr's use of this image is more general. He never explicitly identifies the arrow in question with the *sabad* and, as the passage above shows, the meaning would not necessarily be clear if one made that interpretation.

Where the blanket is concerned, it is Sūr's world rather than Kabīr's that gives an added specificity to the meaning: for black is Krishna's color, and the *gopīs* are hopelessly dyed. As they themselves say (S 2276.5–6),

> Our lives, it seems, have immersed themselves
>   in the sea of Syām, the dark one;
> And once they touch that color, says Sūr,
>   you'll not squeeze a drop of white from them again.[27]

Sūr and the *sants*, then, share much, but he retains—as many of them also do, individually—a particular perspective.

A comparable difference emerges in regard to the issue of equality before God, with the closely associated criticism of social hierarchies that one finds in the utterances of many of the *sants*. Sūr apparently has as little use for institutionalized inequality as Kabīr, but his style of expressing himself on the point is different. In-

26. Vaudeville, *Kabīr, sākhī* 1.9, 1: 153–54, Tivārī, *Kabīr-Granthāvalī, sākhī* 1.9, 2: 137. Cf. Vaudeville, *Kabīr, sākhī* 1.21–23, 1: 156–57.

27. The Sabhā's mention of red (*arun*) in the last line is absent in all manuscripts, but *dhām* ("town") is a respectable alternative for *sindhu* ("sea") in verse 5, since it is not only the Sabhā's reading but that of B1 and U1 as well. Cf. S 4380.5–6 and many other poems in the *bhramargīt* section on blackness.

stead of lashing out at the meaninglessness of social distinctions and the hypocrisy of the great, Sūr cites example after example in which the Lord, primarily as Krishna, has preferred the company of the lowly and outcaste to that of the pure and well-placed. In the following poem (S 19), one of a great many similar poems, he alludes to four such vignettes: the time Krishna was out in the forest and accepted food at the hands of the wife of Vidur, who though wise was a half-breed; the time he came to the aid of the Pāṇḍava brothers when they had been exiled from their rightful throne and reduced to the status of wandering mendicants; the time he granted wealth to Sudāmā, the penurious Brahmin who had been his boyhood friend; and the time he had mercy on Kubjā, the hunchback of Mathura, and healed her deformity.

Syām is solely the patron of the poor.

Our Lord is the one who fends for the wretched,
who answers the needs of those whose love is true.
For what storehouse of wealth did Sudāmā possess?
Why was Hari drawn to a hunchback's charms?
And what sort of splendor graced the Pāṇḍava house?
Still he volunteered as Arjun's charioteer.
Or Vidur: what high-caste status was his?
Yet Hari ate his food—it was offered in love.
Sūr Dās's Lord is a Lord whose inner fire
burns away the trials of the true.

The *sants*, especially Kabīr, are remembered for their trenchant perceptions about human depravity. Their perspective is tough and realistic, and the path to salvation that they describe is often regarded as more difficult than that presented by Vaiṣṇava poets.[28] But there is a sense in which Sūr's assessment of human need is even more radical than Kabīr's—particularly in what he says about himself. In Kabīr, especially as we meet him in the *Bījak,* there is a definite self-confidence. This is the man who takes it upon himself to address others in phrases such as the following, assembled from various poems in the *Bījak* and translated by Linda Hess:[29]

28. Cf., e.g., McLeod, *Gurū Nānak,* p. 152: "the easy path of traditional bhakti."
29. Hess and Singh, *The Bījak of Kabir,* pp. 10–11.

Pandit, you've got it wrong.
Monk, stop scattering your mind.
Pandit, do some research . . .
Morons and mindless fools—
Enchanted madman . . .
You simple-minded people . . .
Saints, once you wake up don't doze off.

And last but not least, the following salvo:

Son of a slut!
There: I've insulted you.
Think about getting on the good road.

This is hardly the language or attitude of Sūr. In the old poems of the *Sūr Sāgar* he never places himself in the position of criticizing others. It is only himself he ventures to call a fool, leaving his listeners to draw their own conclusions about themselves.[30] He is similarly diffident about according himself any sort of status in relation to the Lord, even the lowest sort, that of a servant or slave. Tulsī Dās, by contrast, does not hesitate to claim such status for himself (VP 271.1):

Whatever I am, I am yours, O Rām,
  your servant; do not desert me.
Ocean of mercy, Kośala's overlord,
  guardian of those who come begging shelter,
Shield me, I pray, with your shield.[31]

Only rarely is Sūr confident enough to declare himself a servant of the Lord, and even then he does not speak as if such slavery were his hereditary right, making him a member of the Lord's household. This is often Tulsī's starting point, as in the example just quoted, but if Sūr claims servitude it is on the basis of his bad character, which has caused him to be auctioned and bought. He reinforces his sense of lowly status by dwelling on what for Indians is its most obvious and distasteful manifestation: the requirement that his food should consist of another's leftovers (S 171).

30. E.g., S 77.8 (*saṭh*), 103.8 (*mahā saṭh*, in U1, B4, J4), and *man pramodh* poems such as S 337, where this is the general theme.
31. Cf. also VP 154.3, 155.5, 249.3, and 263.1.

Nandanandan has bought me, redeemed me,

Cut me clean from the fetters of death
  and shown me what fearless freedom can mean,
Decked my forehead with a *tilak* mark,
  settled a sprig of *tulsī* in my ear,
    and wrapped my body in close embrace;
Shaved my hair, my initiate's head,
  draped fresh flowers around my neck,
    and branded me with his holy signs.
Everyone now calls me the Dark One's slave;
  hearing it my heart breathes cool and free,
For what, says Sūr, could measure the pleasure
  of living on leftovers,
    scraps from such a plate?

In a similar vein, the question of having attained an experience of plenitude (*pūrā*), a state Kabīr is willing to claim for himself, simply does not arise for Sūr in the *vinaya* context. One poem in which Kabīr makes this affirmation, in fact, is quite revealing in the contrast it makes to its counterpart in the *Sūr Sāgar*. In both poems the speaker takes on the role of a dancer who has performed so long that not another step is left in him. For Kabīr this emptying of every human desire and versatility yields, paradoxically, the plenitude that is the presence of Rām. For Sūr, however, there is no such release, and the poem ends in a devastated petition to the Lord to do away with this ignorant, misguided life (*avidyā*). Here is Kabīr:

Too many, many roles,
  these parts I've played,
    and now
  I'll part from them.
Too tired of all pretense,
  tuning, tuning the strings,
  and now it's over, done—
    thanks to the name of Rām.
I haven't another dance to dance
  and my mind
  can no longer maneuver the drum.

Life's postures, love, hate—
lost to the flames;
the craving-filled kettle drum
finally burst.
Lust's veil, this body,
is tattered with age;
every errant shuffle is stilled.
All that lives and dies—
why, they're one,
and the this and that,
and haggling,
are gone.
What I have found,
says Kabīr,
is fullness itself,
a finality granted
by the mercy of Rām.[32]

And here is Sūr (S 153):

Now I have danced too much, Gopāl.

Dressed in anger and lust, and garlanded
with a necklace of passions at the throat;
Girded with the ankle-bells of sham and delusion
(how sweet their slanderous sound),
I am bound at the waist with a sash of illusion,
and a beauty mark of greed crowns my brow.
Cravings roar inside my body
in a clash of competing rhythms
And my mind, a drum dusted with confusion,
beats to a dissonant pulse.
I've marshaled and flaunted every artful step
and filled my sinful net:
Sūr's learned his ignorance well, Nandalāl—
take it, take it all.

Sants such as Kabīr are extremely pessimistic about human nature, if left to its own devices. They train on it a barrage of ex-

32. *Gurū Granth Sāhib, rāg āsā,* Kabīr *pad* 28. For an alternate, annotated translation, based upon the *Kabīr Granthāvalī* edited by P. N. Tivārī, *pad* 50 (2: 29), see Vaudeville, *Kabīr,* vol. 2, *pad* 133.

hortations about the need for concentration and repentance. Sūr's tone, if one reads the *Sūr Sāgar* as a whole, seems less barbed, more relaxed. But in the *vinaya* poems it becomes obvious that on this point too Sūr is among the most radical of the *sant*s. Kabīr, after all, was at least willing to give open praise to the human capacity for love (*prem, prīti*)[33]; whereas Sūr is more guarded. Among the early poems in the *Sūr Sāgar* there are only occasional instances in which love is singled out as the element in the human psyche to which God responds (for instance S 19.2-3, translated above[34]), and even then the initiative rests on the divine side of the interaction. For Sūr it is the fact of Krishna that equalizes all beings before him more than any quality inherent in people. In a similar way Sūr places much less emphasis on the unique privilege of the human condition, namely the potential for ultimate salvation that it offers, than one would think from reading the Sabhā edition. Poems that make a point of the countless births it takes to be born human are rare in the earlier years of the Sūr tradition.[35] On the contrary, Sūr is likely to be found lamenting how many lives—human, presumably—he has wasted cursing others or otherwise misbehaving (e.g., S 52.2). Sūr is suspicious, evidently, of all status, even Darwinian hierarchies: what matters in life has nothing to do with one's position. When Sūr talks of status there is irony in his voice, as when, paradigmatically, he styles himself the best of sinners. If one must have hierarchy, better to be low than high.

SŪR ON THE *SANTS*

In accord with all this there is little praise for the *sant*s as such. Hari is Sūr's refuge, not they; what importance they have derives purely from the fact that they sing the Lord's name(s). In this respect Sūr is measurably different from his *sant* compeers. Kabīr, for example, frequently plays on the meaning of the familiar term *sādh* (*sādhu*) so as to point his listener toward its original designation. It means not the ascetics of this world, as in common parlance, but the good; their company, says Kabīr, is heaven.[36] This

33. E.g., Vaudeville, *Kabīr*, *sākhī*s 1.21, 14.15, and 14.31–35, 1: 157, 222, and 225–26.

34. Cf. also S 13.1 (*prīti* in B3, J2; *prīt* in A1).

35. As against later entries such as S 68.8 or 317.5; cf. Tulsī's VP 83.1 and 84.2 in the same vein.

36. Vaudeville, *Kabīr*, vol. 2, *pad* 103.5.

interiorizing conception of true religion is by no means foreign to Sūr, but one meets it by and large in the *bhramargīt,* where Krishna's *gopīs* are the models, rather than in the *vinaya* poems where the community of ordinary human "saints" (*satsaṅg*) might have been expected to play such an exemplary role.

The Sabhā *Sūr Sāgar* does contain poems that praise the *sants*, but they are overwhelmingly more recent additions to the corpus. Kabīr's redefinition of *sādhu,* for instance, is echoed in a poem that proposes that *satsaṅg* is the true form of ascetic practice (*sanyās*), giving life rather than leading to death, and offering to its practicants the trackless forest into which they should truly abandon themselves—the endless singing of the name of Rām (S 340). One can also read that to offer hospitality to a *sant* (the term means here a religious specialist, a wanderer) is to perform an action as worthy as countless pilgrimages (S 360). Such statements, however, are entirely foreign to the early strata of the *Sūr Sāgar.* Nor is there much emphasis on the notion, so frequent in later poems, that the Lord is the benefactor particularly of the *sants* (S 282), that he comes into the world to tear away the net of death for their sake (S 74.6); such praise of a person or community is quite beside the point.[37] In the later reaches of the *Sūr Sāgar* one finds that the *sants* have become powerful enough in the Lord's sight to exercise an intercessory function, much as in the history of the Christian church the term "saint" was gradually transformed from a designation that applied to all believers into something more rarefied and special, designating an independent status and favor. One hears, for instance, that the influence of the saints (*saṅgati pratāp*) had a great deal to do with persuading the Lord to come to the aid of Gajendra, the elephant in distress (S 190.6):

Just a moment's prayerful song
at the instance of the saints,
and he released the deadly grasp
and set the elephant free.[38]

37. In S 282, Draupadī directs a plea to Krishna that culminates in the affirmation that Krishna is *santani ke hitakārī,* "the benefactor of the *sants.*" A version of this poem does occur in B2, but this phrase is tellingly absent.

38. The phrases *sant kī saṅgati* (S 208.6 in J4) and *sādh kī saṅgati* (S 208.6 in J5; S 297.5 in J4) begin to appear in the more recent manuscripts included in the early *Sūr Sāgar* and make clear the meaning of the expression *saṅgati pratāp.* In later strata of the *Sūr Sāgar* such phrases become frequent: *sādh saṅgati* in S 309.3; *sādhu saṅgati* in 45.3; and *sādhuni kī saṅgati* in 340.6.

But when one turns to older versions of the poem in question, one finds mention only of the thought of the poor elephant in the face of his extremity, which has the effect of locating the agency of salvation directly with Krishna himself:

At just a moment's thought
  from one cursed with mortal danger,
he released the deadly grasp
  and set the elephant free.[39]

Sūr does recommend good company—*satsaṅg,* or rather *sant samāgam* or *sādh samāgam,* as he often calls it[40]—but what he means by that has little to do with virtue of any sort. That company is made good, it seems, simply because it provides the place where Hari's name is sung and heard. In perhaps the earliest instances in which Sūr recommends the company of the *sant*s, the mention of the Lord's name directly precedes that of his devotees. In one case the poet refers to "songs of the Lord, gatherings of the good" (S 292.4), and disparages himself for ignoring both:

Life has filtered away in a thousand tiny bothers—

Matters of state, of salary, of sons.
  Without my even noticing, my life has ambled off
And tangled in illusion, in a snare so foolproof
  that I can never break it or wriggle it loose.
Songs of the Lord, gatherings of the good—
  I left myself hanging in air without either,
Like an overeager acrobat who craves just one more trick
  as if his ample cleverness could hide his skimpy clothes;
Like a sad abandoned strumpet, says Sūr,
  who sways and swings her hips when her lover is gone.[41]

39. The first half of the line reads *chin citavat śrāp saṅkaṭ te* in U1. Cf. *cin citavan saran saṅkaṭ te* in B4, and *vin cit cakra caran saṅkaṭ te* in J4.

40. E.g., S 233.6.

41. The phrases translated here are *hari bhajan* and *sādh samāgam* (J1, B2, U1, J4, U2), to which compare the Sabhā's *hari bhakti* and *sādhu-samāgam.* J5 has *sant samāgam* as its second component, and B3 and A1 have an altogether different *tripti biṣaya.* All retain *hari bhajan.* Note that the opening lines of the poem cannot be strictly autobiographical if we understand Sūr's life as legend has presented it. Either there is a measure of the rhetorical "I," as Linda Hess has suggested in commenting on this poem (private communication, May 1982), or the author's life departed from the mold assigned to it by legend.

In the other case (S 233.6) Sūr adopts a locution that would be a bit awkward but for the need to mention the Lord at this point. He interjects the term *prabhu* (Lord) into a line that would make easier grammatical sense without it. Without the interjection the poem would have read as follows:

Life goes well for those who sing of Hari.

The lowest dog-devourer is ennobled in his service,
  that Cowherd's. Without him
                    what Brahmin birth has worth?
Fine points of doctrine and the fruits of yogic vows—
  they're useless, they only serve to fritter life away.
Sing songs of the Lord of the World—just that,
  and the four fruits of life are effortlessly yours.
Why flutter about to every corner of the earth
  when every inch bears the prints
                    of his lotus-flowered feet?
Instead, says Sūr, in the gathering of the good
  you can beat the drum of joy and shout of no more fear.

This is not, however, quite what we hear. Instead Sūr has prefaced his mention of "the gathering of the good" (*sādh samāgam* in B4, J5; *sant samāgam* in U1, J4), and therefore qualified it, by making mention of his Lord (*sūrdās prabhu* in U1, J4; *sūrdās svāmī* in B4). So the final line emerges somewhat changed:

The Lord of Sūr Dās and the gathering of the good
  are cause to beat the drum of joy and shout of no more fear.

Or, in an alternate translation:

Sūr says, among the good who gather for the Lord
  you can beat the drum of joy and shout of no more fear.

Another early citation calls the *sant*s "wise" or "knowing" (*sujān*, S 235.7), but once again the divine priority is retained. It is not the inherent intelligence of the *sant*s that renders them wise, but that they have heard the glory of the Lord:

Songs to Hari work great wonders:

They elevate the lowly of the world,
  who celebrate their lofty climb with drums.
To come to the feet of the Lord in song
  is enough to make stones float on the sea.
No wonder that even the meanest of the mean—
  hunters and harlots—can mount the skies,
Where wander the infinite company of stars,
  where the moon and the sun circle around,
And only Dhruv, the polestar, is fixed,
  for he as a lad had sung his way to Rām.
The Vedas are verses, testaments to God—
  hearing them makes the saints saintly and wise—
And what about Sūr? I sing too.
  O Hari, my shelter, I've come for your care.

Only in the most recent manuscripts of the early *Sūr Sāgar* does this pattern begin to relax. In A1 the poet states that without the devotion (or singing) that is possible in the company of the *sant*s this body is useless (*sādhu saṅgati bhakti binā tanu akārathu jāy,* S 330.3). And even here it is not righteous company per se but the act of praising God that makes the difference.

In the early *Sūr Sāgar,* then, the virtues of the *sant*s are extolled derivatively or negatively. Sūr does on occasion advise himself to keep away from those who turn their backs on Hari (*hari bimukhan,* S 332.1), but this never becomes the frequent refrain it is for Tulsī Dās. Certainly Sūr has no such category as Tulsī's *kusaṅgati* (VP 84.2)—"bad company"—against whose example the righteous *satsaṅg* are held up for praise. When Sūr speaks of such people, calling them for instance "non-saints" (*asat-saṅgati,* S 144.6 in J4), he does so with the intention of confessing that he is one of them, and a ringleader at that! Hence it is no surprise that the cliché one hears so often in *sant* poetry—"join the *satsaṅg,*" or as the Braj literally says, "do *satsaṅg*"—is quite absent from the early *Sūr Sāgar.* It begins to appear only in more recent levels of the collection, where it is frequent.[42] In the early *Sūr Sāgar,* by contrast, the *sant*s appear less as moral examples than as an accepted part of the religious landscape. Twice we find them as part of a series with

42. S 86.10, 360.8, etc. Cf. *bhakti karihau* in S 329.1.

Vedas, Puranas, and the like, and in both cases pointing to Hari as the central figure. On one occasion the poet praises the name of Hari as "Śiva's wealth, the subject matter of the Vedas and Puranas, and everything the *sant*s have to their name" (*santan kau sarabas,* S 114.5). On the other he asks to be given the grace of Krishna's presence, a foundation as basic for the Vedas, Puranas, Smṛti, and the *sant*s as water is for a fish (S 204.3).

Similarly, references to the guru in these early poems are rare and tend to be nontechnical. On one occasion, for instance, Sūr remarks, rather formulaically, that he is "insubordinate to the guru" (*guru drohī,* S 124.5). Another line, in a more substantial reference, characterizes the guru as the source of that illumination by means of which the heart is able to churn its raw material, curd, to *ghī* and eliminate the inessential, watery buttermilk substance left behind (S 351.3 in B4, U1, J4, J5). Such imagery is also familiar to others of the *sant*s.[43] As we approach the end of the period we have designated as "early," we do encounter a passage in which the guru is credited with urging the devotee to sing the name of Govind, that is, Krishna—perhaps implying that he had transmitted it as a mantra.[44] In another passage of comparable age gurus are described as charged by God with the mission of facilitating the tortuous passage that their pupils must make over the terrifying sea of existence (S 208.2 in J4, J5). But not until much later additions are made to the *Sūr Sāgar* is the guru singled out as the entire subject of a poem of adulation (S 417). Only at this point is the service of one's preceptor placed on what is seemingly the same plane as that of remembering Hari (*hari sumiran,* S 155.2). And certainly it is not until this stage in the development of the *Sūr Sāgar* that one finds the guru mentioned in the same breath and on the same plane as Govind (S 65.3), much as he is in the famous couplet attributed to Kabīr:

> Suppose I encountered Govind and my guru:
>   of them both, whose feet should I touch?
> I think I would prostrate first to my own,
>   for it's he who has shown the way to Govind.[45]

43. It occurs, for instance, in a *pad* of Kabīr, but without mention of the guru, as it happens. See Vaudeville, *Kabīr,* vol. 2, *pad* 84.

44. S 311.6, which occurs only in A1; S 375.4, which occurs only in J4.

45. Cf. Vaudeville, *Kabīr, sākhī* 1.28, 1: 158.

The term *satguru* (True Guru) does occur at least once in the early *Sūr Sāgar*—surely there is no anathema attached to the concept, as if it represented the theology of a distinctly rival camp—but again it is a casual reference. The *satguru* is not the object of explicit reverence. Rather, Sūr sets his own counsel on a par with that of the *satguru* as he desperately addresses his heart (S 59.5):

> As you've heard the words of the True Guru,
> now you're witness to these words of mine:
> If ever you would reckon the treasurehouse of gems
> that is Rām, dear soul, the time's at hand.

All these references to the *sant*s and their milieu are slightly offhanded, indicating a generally understood environment rather than an object of direct concentration. It is not the *sant*s or their *satsañg* as such that are essential for Sūr, but the presence of the Lord that they may make possible. That is the ultimate *satsañg,* and the poet rails against himself for not having recognized that this more radically intimate companion (*suhṛd*) has been at his side through his entire life (S 77):

> *What did you do to deserve that day?*
>
> For what purpose but God's were you born?
> Give it some thought, you miser-minded one;
> remember, if you can, and reflect.
> Think of the pain, the harsh karmic past
> that thrust you into the world that day
> And smeared you with your mother's blood
> as you came into the womb again.
> It's a tortuous place, where no one can go,
> dreadful, daunting, dark,
> Full of fear, in every way vile.
> What dirt you had for food!
> Does the sense of this begin to descend?
> Everything living had first to be born—
> Your mind, your strength, the family line
> that bore you, whose honor you prize.
> It all goes back to that same disastrous
> space that kept you, fed you, bred you,

And gifted you with your precious face,
  your eyes and nose, your hands and feet.
Ingrate, listen, who then do you think
  has stayed by you both day and night,
Befriending you, though you long ago forgot—
  that is, if ever, you knew?
Even today he stands at your side,
  ready to bear your birth-born shame,
Always wanting for life to go well,
  and loving you as his own.
In sum, says Sūr, he's lord and jewel,
  guardian brother and intimate friend;
So listen, fool, there's no need to stay
  with your cheating, lying, willful ways.

The Quintessential Sinner

Sūr is loath to describe himself as anything but a stranger to virtuous company (S 124.9–12, 130.7 in B4, J4). The Lord to whom he appeals is not the Lord of the good and faithful—of *sādhs, sant*s, and *bhagat*s, as later poems in the *Sūr Sāgar* often picture him—but rather the Lord of sinners. Obviously Sūr is, at least in part, reaching for dramatic effect when he characterizes himself as the worst (or as he rather says, the best!) of sinners. But the underlying point, as with Luther's famous dictum, "Sin boldly!," is a serious one, and one that seems to have fit ill with the more routinized, less scandalous predispositions of later generations. Later versions of earlier poems are often sharply reoriented through the alteration of a few words: evidently singers and scribes could not quite believe what they heard or read.

S 19 is such a poem. Its older versions praise the Lord who comes to the aid of those who seem least to deserve it, the meek and outcast of this world. In the version we have already translated, that of B2 and U1, these people are ultimately called "the true," the *sant*s, because of their unyielding devotion to Krishna. Evidently their goodness—their *sant*-hood— is inextricably bound up with their humility. The B4 version of the poem, in which the position of several lines is altered, makes the point even clearer. Its final, summary line focuses not on the worthiness of the recipients of the Lord's mercy but upon the extremity of their condition (*ārat ke dukh,* not *santan ke dukh*):

Syām is solely the patron of the poor.

Our Lord is the one who fends for the wretched,
who answers the needs of those whose love is true.
Take Vidur: what high-caste status was his?
Or the hunchback; yet Hari was drawn to her charms.
What sort of splendor graced the Pāṇḍava house
that he should volunteer as Arjun's charioteer?
And what storehouse of wealth did Sudāmā possess?
No, Hari seeks genuine affection instead.
Sing, then, says Sūr, a song to him, the Lord
who burns away the trials of the low.

The Sabhā version is closer to that of B4 than to that of B2 and U1, but several minor alterations reveal an appreciable change of attitude. In the last line the vocative *saṭh* appears: "fool." Whereas in earlier poems Sūr seems to affirm his likeness to the fools of this world, here we find him castigating them and setting himself apart:

Sing, fools, says Sūr, a song to the Lord
who burns away the trials of the low.

In the same vein, the Sabhā version fails to mention the hunchback of Mathura, probably the most repellent among those who receive Krishna's ministrations. Instead we find a reiteration of the comfortable sentiment that Hari is drawn to true love (or, alternatively, truth and love: *satya prīti*). Inadvertently or not, the scandal has been removed.

The tone of the early *Sūr Sāgar* is different. There Sūr addresses himself far less to the Lord of the good than to the Lord of the unfortunate, the poor, the deformed, even the evil. And the style of the appeal, while consistent in some respects with Kabīr's and Tulsī's prayers, has a pointedness uniquely Sūr's own. He does not typically confess that he has fallen away from constant devotion, as Tulsī does, and hope confidently that the Lord of the fallen (*patit-pāvan*) will accept him back in the fold of the faithful (e.g., VP 92.7). He does not send a letter of petition from a respectful distance to the resplendency of the divine throne. The petitionary letter (*vinaya-patrikā*), which became so famous at the hands of Tulsī

Dās, does not appear in the old poems of the *Sūr Sāgar.*[46] Instead of a letter sent from afar, from the outer fringes of the community of saints that surrounds the heavenly throne, we have a petition addressed to God at closest range, as if the poet has burst in upon the holy audience. An example is the following poem (S 134), in which we hear the wails and contortions of a desperate and unruly beggar, a personal challenge that bypasses the community of the saints altogether. This reprobate deals in blackmail, holding Krishna ransom by his sinner-saving name (*patit-pāvan*), which is the implied backdrop of this poem. In verse 4 there is even the suggestion, made explicit in its Sabhā version, that he will go so far as to do a striptease until he is paid to depart. If he is allowed to do so and remains unredeemed, he will strip Krishna of his own most precious garment—his savior's reputation:

Today's the showdown, and I'm not going to flinch

From the fight to the end between you and me.
  You urbane, clever one, I've faith in myself,
For I am heir to a sevenfold lineage of failure
  and to conquer this fallen one you'll have to go as low.
Now I bare my all: I want you to know
  that unless you rescue me you wreck your reputation.
You lack the nerve to try! I have you now—
  oh Hari, hard diamond, I have you.
Sūr Dās says, I will only rise and go
  when you offer me the betel prize and laugh at the show.

Sūr's access to God is an outsider's access, like a bawdy dancer's. It is his sin, not his sainthood, that wins its way into the divine throneroom. How different this is from Tulsī Dās, who, even when he is calling upon the Lord on the basis of his fallenness, cannot refrain from summarizing his plea in terms of the "numerous ties" (*nāte anek*) that bind the Lord to him (VP 79):

46. Nor, so far as I have been able to ascertain, does it occur in the *vinaya* poetry of Nāmdev, Kabīr, Raidās, Dādū, or Dhannā. Contrast S 142 and 143, later poems in which the petitionary letter does figure.

You are the pitying, I the pitiful one,

you the beneficent, I the one who begs;
I am notoriously fallen,
and you can dash away mountains of sin.
You are the father of those without fathers,
and who could be more orphaned than I?
No one is so downtrodden—none more than I—
and you are the one who lifts the heavy weight.
You are all life, I am one life;
you the master and I the servant;
You are mother and father, teacher and friend:
in every connection my lot is relieved.
We are bound by numerous ties, you and I,
so choose whichever you please.
Somehow, says Tulsī, oh you who send mercy,
let me find at your feet a refuge of peace.

Sūr's approach, in contrast to such complementarities, is all contest and combat. In poem after poem he singles himself out as a hero among sinners, the king, the great one among them, the crest-jewel, the best, the lord of them all, the one whose renown in the community of the fallen is unequaled, the head performer of the group, the one who has danced to the tune of Māyā as no one else has.[47] The following expression of self-congratulation—a desperate lament as well—is typical (S 138):

I, only I, am best at being worst, Lord.

It's me! The others are powerless to match me.
I set the pace, forging onward, alone.
All those other sinners are a flock of amateurs,
but I have practiced every day since birth,
And look: you've abandoned me, rescuing the rest!
How can I cause life's stabbing pain to cease?
You've favored the vulture, the hunter, tyrant, whore,
and cast me aside, the most worthless of them all.
Quick save me, says Sūr, I'm dying of shame:
who ever was finer at failure than I?

47. S 108.2, 131.2, 134.3 (cf. 138.2), 138.1, 139.1, 144.1, 146.1, 147.1, 149.1, 153.1, 192.1, 197.1, 198.1, 200.6.

Tulsī Dās sometimes writes in this vein too, but the outcome is altogether different. In the following poem (VP 91)—and in the refrain, as in many similar poems of Sūr—Tulsī also singles himself out as the worst. But worst of what? He depicts himself not as the worst of sinners but as the worst of the *mand,* the dull (VP 92.1), and he explains his condition as the result of a lapse of knowledge (*ajānyo,* VP 92.2) rather than an act of will:

Mādhav, you'll find none duller than I.

The moth and the fish, though lacking in wit,
  can scarcely approach my slow standard:
Transfixed by the shimmering shapes they meet,
  they fail to discern the dangers of fire and hook,
But I, who can see the perils of fiery flesh
  and still refuse to leave it, have wisdom even less.
I've drifted along in the grand and entrancing
  river of ignorance, a stream that knows no shores,
And abandoned the rescue raft of Hari's lotus feet
  to grapple and grasp after bubbles and foam,
Like a dog so hungry that he lunges for a bone
  grown ancient and marrowless; and bitten so tight,
The bone scrapes his mouth and draws blood—
  his own blood—yet he tastes it with delight.
I too am trapped in jaws. The grip that clamps
  and claws is that of a merciless snake, this life,
And I yearn for relief, poor frog, but have spurned
  the one chance I had: the bird that Hari rides.
Here and there other water creatures float;
  we are snared together in a tightening net:
Watch them, how greedily on one another they feed,
  and they never sense that next may be their turn.
Goddess of Learning, count up the sins
  of my countless lives if you think it can be done,
But Tulsī Dās places his trust in the One
  who rescues the destitute, and in trusting hopes to live.

In utterances such as these Tulsī apologizes for himself. Sūr, by contrast, vaunts himself. He demonstrates that he is the best of sinners, and that status provides him with whatever leverage he has on his Lord. For Sūr as the unredeemed offender stands to falsify the very core of Hari's claim to lordship: *prabhu kī prabhutā,* as one poem calls it (S 124.10), "what makes the Lord the Lord," namely, his capacity to save sinners. This is why he is so often called *patit-pāvan,* "the rescuer of the fallen." It is not one name, really, but many that collectively constitute the divine name, or to put it another way, many versions of the same name. The Lord as *patit-pāvan* is also the merciful one (*karunāmay*), the lord of those who have no lord (*anāth-nāth*), the refuge of those who have no refuge (*asaran-saran*), pitier of the poor (*garīb-nivāj*), and so on. In addition, as we have seen, there are many stories of salvation that seem almost to have become part of the divine signature.

Sūr shares with other *bhakta*s of the period, *sant*s especially, the perception that, as Tulsī was to put it, the name of God is more crucial than God himself;[48] but he attaches a different meaning to that affirmation. Sūr is uninterested in a mystique of the name as such. By comparison with Tulsī or Kabīr he is relatively unimpressed with the benefits that accrue from hewing to the name of Rām, *rām nām.*[49] Only in later additions to the *Sūr Sāgar* does one find poems that repeat and encourage the repetition of the names Hari or Rām. In older poems the form of Sūr's repetitions is more likely to be a detailing of acts of divine mercy or of names that refer to that quality (e.g., S 7, 120, 132, 133) than a chanted repetition of the name as name. This is because for Sūr what is transcendent about the name of God is not its sound but its meaning: radical salvation.

Sūr's disinterest in identifying the ultimate with a particular series of vocables, even "Hari" or "Rām," is hardly apparent from a reading of the Sabhā *Sūr Sāgar,* for many poems included there begin with variations on the formula "remember Hari, Hari, Hari, Hari" (*hari hari hari hari sumiran karau*; S 224, 236, 245, 306, 344, 348, 382, 394, 395, 397, 399, 416, 420). None of these poems is old. Others that seem to take for granted the practice of repeating the name of Rām sometimes turn out on inspection to have had a different form in the old manuscripts. One version, after mentioning devotion to the name of Rām at the beginning, ends with a line in which the poet counsels himself to take the name of Rām to his lips (*rām nām mukh let*) since, after all, it costs nothing

48. Tulsī Dās, *Rāmcaritmānas,* 1.23–25. On this point see Allchin, "The Place of Tulsī Dās," pp. 128–29.

49. For a somewhat different assessment on this point, see Ronald Stuart McGregor, "Some Materials from the *Sūrsāgar* Bearing on the Evolution of the Sūr Tradition," in *Early Hindī Devotional Literature in Current Research,* ed. W. M. Callewaert, pp. 109–11.

(S 297.8). If one scrutinizes the earliest manuscript occurrence of this poem (B4), however, one finds that both references to the great name are absent. The first is simply omitted and the second reads as an exhortation to take Rām and Krishna to one's lips (*rām kṛṣṇa mukh let*), rather than the name of Rām as such. Sūr seems unwilling to acknowledge any special point of access to the divine such as the name would provide. Similarly on the human side of the salvation formula, as we have seen, Sūr does not believe that there is any quality as such that makes a person potentially the recipient of salvation. All that matters is the state of fallenness itself; the sheer fact of absence from the divine creates the conditions for the manifestation of the divine presence.

Sūr's way of making this point is to style himself the worst of sinners and to force his audience to recognize that this and only this is at issue. As he does so, however, he employs a second sense of the divine name—name not only in the sense of designation or description, such as *patit-pāvan,* "the savior of the fallen," but name in the sense of reputation as well. The Lord has a name to live up to so as to be the Lord. If he cannot save Sūr, he loses his name, and there is no sense in the panegyrics (*birad*) that his worshippers (whom Sūr often calls *sant*s or *sādh*s) address to him.[50] This is the repute that Sūr's naked dance in the divine throneroom stood to falsify (S 134.4). On the one hand, Sūr sets himself over against the *sants*, styling himself a lapsed soul who is sharply separated from the just and convinced; on the other hand, he asserts that the entire logic of *satsaṅg* depends on just such a one as he. The act that makes *satsaṅg* what it is—the recalling of the divine name, broadly conceived—requires the existence of sinners such as Sūr, for the Lord has named himself by the fallen, and that good name, his reputation, depends on their salvation.

Just as Sūr's recognition of his own distance from "saints" such as these in one sense makes him their essential companion in another (indeed to the point that Sūr's songs were and are sung in *satsaṅg,* redefining and deepening what it means to be a part of such an association), so his distance from the Lord is what brings him before the divine presence. In his "best of sinner" poems, which stand at the core of many early Sūr *vinaya* collections, the poet confronts the Lord with a direct challenge. He stages a con-

50. S 124.2, 130.12, 131.6, 132.2, 133.1, 137.3, 137.5, 157.1, 188.8.

test, full of bitterness, complaint, and irony, trying to shame Hari not only with his helplessness but also with his shamelessness in boasting of his sins.[51] Every evil quality he can recount puts a question mark after that long list of mercies his divine rival is supposed to possess.

Sometimes individual lines of poetry square off the sides. In the following line, for instance, the familiar title *patit-pāvan* is pulled apart so that the repetition of *patit* in the section before the caesura creates the expectation that *pāvan* will follow in rebuttal (S 131.2):

> Notorious me, a sinner [*patit*] among sinners [*patitani*];
> and you, you're supposed to be the savior [*pāvan*]!

Sometimes series of words are arranged so as to have the same answering, challenging effect, as when the Lord's ineffable "non" qualities (*ajit, anādi*: "unconquerable, beginningless") are measured against the lapses that make Sūr just as much a "non" (*ajān, matihīn*: "unknowing, mindless")![52] Or entire poems take their structure from this test of strength. Such a contest can be the explicit subject, as in the struggle between Sūr the naked dancer and his well-reputed patron (S 134). Or the poet can go on at length about the Lord's mercies to heinous sinners and end by wondering how he could have been left off the list (S 132, 133, 135, etc.). Finally, Sūr may detail his own excesses and leave God and his audience with the question, implicit or explicit, as to why he did not also receive salvation. Was the Lord too weak to grant it after all? The mention of "the fallen" in the first line of the following poem alerts our ears to the fact that the whole composition is such a challenge to "the savior of the fallen"; the last line particularly signals a readiness to deal with any advance on the part of his rival (S 144):

51. E.g., S 111.2, 120.2 (U1's *lāl* for *lāj* seems an error), and 150.1. These bear contrasting with another mood, which becomes prominent in a different strand of poetry, somewhat more recent and less widely shared, in which the poet is ashamed to come before the divine presence, e.g., S 128.3 (B3, A1) and 137.4 (B4, U2).

52. S 181.5 in J1, U1, J2 (twice), and B3. This can be expanded to two full lines, as in S 128.3–4 and 111.10–11, where one line details Sūr's depravity, and the other the Lord's transcendence.

In the realm of the fallen, Hari, I am king,

Regent of a world filled with folk
  who live to beat the drums of slander.
An animal thirst is the liquid of this land;
  desires are the servants, the senses torturers,
And lust, ever ready to proffer good advice,
  is the chief adviser in this dismal state.
Snarling anger serves as bodyguard;
  and what could be a more suitable steed
Than that unvanquished victor, the elephant of pride?
  And the parasol of greed provides a regal shade.
As king I've fled from any native truth I ruled
  and enthroned myself lord of a legion of liars
Who sing of my glories, how I've conquered
                through delusion,
  how my evil is unequaled, how criminal my name.
Sūr says, I'm garrisoned in self-congratulation—
  an unyielding fortress: only death suggests a door.

Other *bhakti* poets, *sant*s among them, also employ this motif of contest between the exemplar of sin and the savior of sinners,[53] but there is something uniquely radical in Sūr's usage. Perhaps the closest comparison is to be found in a poem in the *Vinaya Patrikā,* in which Tulsī, like Sūr, demands the betel at the end of his performance (VP 75). But with what a difference. Tulsī makes this demand not in consequence of his status as the most victorious sinner but because he has been unswervingly faithful in his allegiance to Rām: he has come to no other for refuge (VP 75.2). Tulsī is confident that his Lord, unlike the other gods, will honor his part of the bargain and provide shelter. Sūr's approach is diametrically opposed. Instead of trusting to his Lord's trustworthiness, he suggests that the Lord himself is guilty of unfair dealings. After all, hasn't he saved everyone else but Sūr?

THE *NIRGUṆA* SIDE OF SŪR'S SENSIBILITY

The effect of this view of access to God is to recast the terms in which *satsaṅg* makes sense. Tulsī and Kabīr emphasize how pointed

53. Linda Hess notes that the motif of self-abasement in the presence of a merciful Lord is to be found only in the western collections of poems attributed to Kabīr, with one possible exception. See "Studies in Kabir," pp. 52–54, 243–44.

and harsh the path of faith is by saying it in so many words, and Kabīr tries to startle his listeners into believing it and joining the *satsaṅg*. Sūr takes a different tack, not so much drawing his hearers away from their sin as acting out his own to show that before the Lord there is no retreat. That, for Sūr, is the meaning of the blistering road of faith. Sūr treats the matter in characteristically dramatic fashion—with implied dialogue, with outrageous confrontation, and with style as he dances in the presence of the magic-making Lord with a magic all his own. But it is crucial to note that this dramatic approach does not blunt or diffuse the directness of the message; rather, it concentrates it.

Too often it has been assumed that the *nirguṇī*s of this world, and of medieval India in particular, are the ones who approach God most directly, much more so than their *saguṇī* counterparts. The evidence is that they refuse to attend to the intermediating connections and qualifications that classical philosophies of Brahman in the *saguṇa* mode have described. They prefer not to turn to the points at which the Ultimate has made itself manifest in this world to facilitate their faith. But in the *vinaya* poetry of Sūr we have a message as barren of qualification as anything Kabīr or any other voice of the *via negativa* ever broadcast. Sūr's sense of unmediated confrontation with the divine can well be seen as the *saguṇa bhakti* analogue to the *nirguṇa* position. In that it flouts any real attention to the community of the faithful, in fact, it emerges as an even stronger denial of qualifying circumstance than Kabīr was prepared to offer. True, Sūr's position takes very seriously the Lord's qualities (or at least his reputation for such qualities!). In this objective sense it is *saguṇa bhakti.* But in the subjective sense, in the way in which those qualities are addressed, there is no sense of qualification or mediation whatever. As far as the transaction between humanity and divinity is concerned, Sūr's faith might fittingly be called *nirguṇa.*

This peculiar "*nirguṇa*" side of Sūr's sensibility is not confined to the *vinaya* poems; we meet it elsewhere as well. At the most obvious level Sūr uses clusters of negative *nirguṇa* adjectives to point up the irony and wonder of the Lord's particularity against the background of his ineffability.[54] The following poem, for in-

54. Later contributions to the *Sūr Sāgar*, e.g., S 1719, 2138, 2221, or 3445, tend to play out this incarnational irony even more explicitly. On this mood in the *Sūr Sāgar* see Bryant, *Child-God*, pp. 12–13, 35–39, passim. In regard to the coalescence of *nirguṇa* and *saguṇa* elements in the theology of Tulsī Dās, see Allchin, "The Place of Tulsī Dās," p. 127.

stance (S 746), is built on a series of contrasts between the Lord's great majesty and his utter accessibility. Colossal as he is, he allows himself on the night of his birth in this world to be carried across the Jumna in a winnowing basket as a tiny baby, to escape the wrath of the king of Mathura. More startling still, the umbilical cord from which he generates the universe is transformed into one that ties him as a baby to a human mother. All this might be considered as shedding light on two poles of the *saguṇa* side of divinity, majesty and accessibility, but in the poem's opening salvo it is clear that God's majesty phases imperceptibility into what is utterly indescribable. And as the composition develops, it becomes clear that even the Lord's human characteristics are riddled with paradoxes that are hard to grasp:

Ponder the Imponderable, the paths of the Unfathomable.

Consider the way he has taken human guise.
He holds in his womb the universe, the whole,
yet he curls up in the corner of a winnowing pan.
From his navel spring Brahmā and all the gods,
toward whom every vow and work of art are aimed,
Yet a woman of Braj has cut that navel cord
and bandaged it up with a strand of silken twine. . . .[55]

At other points too this sense of contradiction is felt. Take the very use of the term *guṇa,* "quality." One expects, in a *saguṇa* point of view, that the Lord's qualities will be appreciated, and indeed by Sūr's time the word *guṇa* had come to mean explicitly that: not just "quality" but specifically "good qualities." In the *Sūr Sāgar,* therefore, there is quite a measure of talk about the Lord's *guṇa*s in this sense, in particular the lengths to which he will go to rescue the wayward. But there is at least an equal fascination with *guṇa*s that can hardly be said to fall in such a group. When the *gopī*s cite the "fine qualities" (*guṇa*s) for which Krishna is so renowned, they have in mind anything but his beneficial actions, and speak with the broadest irony. Recall the poem that begins with the following challenge (S 3255):

55. The translation follows B4, the only manuscript to contain the poem. Its important differences from the Sabhā version are: *dekhau adbhut* for *adbhut avigat* (v. 1); *jaisau veṣu* for *kaisau rūp* (v. 1); *kalā* for *jog* (v. 3); *kāṭi* for *chīni* (v. 4); *pāṭ* for *bā̃ṭi* (v. 4).

I know, I know what fine qualities you have,

You charmer of hearts, so what have you to hide?
And where did you get so tattered and worn?
Look at yourself: your all-night crimson eyes,
and your body spent from having labored at love. . . .

In recitation one would hear the refrain again and again, heightening the irony: "I know, I know what fine qualities you have."

Another expression of this same sense of contradiction in regard to Krishna's *guṇa*s becomes evident when one compares certain words and phrases in the *vinaya* poems with those that appear in poems that give voice to the *gopī*s' *viraha.* We expect that Sūr will use harsh terms to characterize human (and his own) misbehavior and selfishness, but it comes as a matter of some astonishment that the same terms are used by his *gopī*s to characterize the object of their love, who is God himself. In Sūr's vocabulary Krishna and the sinners of this world are tarred with the same brush. Both are burdened with characterizations such as "crooked, deceiving" (*kapaṭ*), "false, lying" (*jhūṭh*), "obstinate, unbending" (*haṭh*), and "sly, naughty" (*ḍhīṭh*). Even the term *naṭ*, referring to the lowly acrobats who travel about clad in the scantiest garb to display their feats on street corners, can be used both of Krishna and of the misguided and brazen of this world. Among the very few exceptions to this rule of universal derogation are the following: Krishna can never be called a simpleton (*saṭh*), as sinners sometimes are (e.g., S 1420.6 in K1); and common sinners, Sūr included, are rarely clever enough to qualify for the title *ṭhag,* which designates a wily and deceptive thief and is such a favorite label for Krishna.[56]

There emerges in all this the sense, very strange from the *saguṇa* point of view, that if Krishna is the Lord, then he must be so precisely in spite of quite a number of his qualities. Or to see the matter in a slightly different light, it is the very range of his qualities, both good and bad, and even their seeming contradiction of each other, that signal his lordship. An awareness of contradiction in the nature of things has often been understood as a significant stage along the path to an awareness of the qualityless reality that lies beneath the whole phenomenal edifice. In Sūr's poems this sense of divine self-contradiction becomes dramatically real. It should come as no surprise, then, that the tone and format

56. See John Stratton Hawley, *Krishna, the Butter Thief*, pp. 151, 159, 163.

of many of the *vinaya* poems echo the complaint and contest, the longing and irony, that stand at the center of the *Sūr Sāgar* as a whole.

For Sūr, evidently, there was no question of choosing between being *sant* or Vaiṣṇava, *nirguṇī* or *saguṇī*. This indeed is one of the meanings of the conviction that we have explored at length, that the person who struggles with *viyoga* is the true yogi. Life in the *saguṇa* world, as it turns out, does not have the effect of distancing its subjects from a qualityless God who stands mysterious and afar, like the Wizard of Oz behind some indescribable cosmic curtain. Instead, paradoxically, it brings its victims—who are at the same time its beneficiaries—into direct confrontation with the One whom they have lost. And this unmediated confrontation, whether it be on the part of Sūr the sinner facing the Lord of sinners, or of the *gopīs* facing their vagrant lover, is as stringent and stark as any that *nirguṇa bhakti* has to offer.

Sūr Dās "observing" the *līlās* of Rādhā and Krishna. Detail from an illustration for a poem from the *Sūr Sāgar,* Mewar, 1720–1730 A.D. Courtesy of the Los Angeles County Museum of Art (Nasli and Alice Heeramanick Collection, M.71.1.11).

CHAPTER 6

Song as Salvation

WHAT EXIT IS THERE in a world so riddled with contradiction, where the Lord who should be present is absent, where *saguṇa* and *nirguṇa* come ultimately to the same thing? In two different modes now—*bhramargīt* and *vinaya*—we have heard the persistent voice of complaint that Sūr raises in face of the assessment he makes of the human condition. But where, if anywhere, is the way out?

In this final chapter I would like to argue—or perhaps it is more a suggestion than an argument—that we have been seeing, or rather hearing, the way out all along. If anything in the *Sūr Sāgar* spells release and salvation, it is the act of singing itself. It is penultimate perhaps—the *gopīs*' condition is never remedied—but it is a constant, hidden comfort. Even when the song is a lament, the act of voicing it and directing it to its Source brings a measure of fulfillment, a degree of closure, a taste of deliverance. Song, for Sūr—singing to the Lord—is as close as one can come to salvation.

THE DANCE OF DELUSION

Not every form of aesthetic creativity enjoys such a handsome reputation in the *Sūr Sāgar*: Sūr was neither an indifferent observer of the arts nor an uncritical partisan of art for art's sake. In fact, the art forms with which singing is most intimately associated come in for considerable criticism in the poems of the early *Sūr Sāgar*. These are dance and drama, and they have at best an ambivalent potential. There are a certain number of songs describing the happy abandon with which Krishna and his *gopīs*, or specifically Rādhā, dance; sometimes these moments are identified as phases of the *rās līlā,* sometimes not. But there are an equal number of songs in which dance and drama symbolize not the integrative core of life but its unraveled edges—life at its height of deception, confusion, and distraction. Since dance and drama lend themselves so easily to staging and decoration, since they are so colorful and include so many elements, these arts are natural symbols for the froth and indulgence that draw a person away from the Lord into a vortex of self-absorption. As we have seen, Sūr does not hesitate to depict the frenetic indirection of his own life in precisely such terms.[1]

When he does so, he usually places the responsibility for a life of profligate art squarely on his own shoulders. We recall the instance in which his weapon against an unheeding Lord was a brazen, naked dance (S 134). We also remember the famous and well-loved poem in which Sūr takes a more plaintive tone, lamenting that "Now I have danced too much, Gopāl" (S 153). He lays at his own feet, evidently, the responsibility for having summoned up "every artful step." Who else would have robed him "in anger and lust" and placed "a necklace of passions at the throat"? Still, the complaining tone of the first line ("Now I have danced too much") and the fact that it is addressed to Gopāl suggest that he may not have been alone in precipitating the masquerade. Sūr's summary description of the whole show confirms this hint: he uses the term *avidyā* ("ignorance"). Kenneth Bryant appropriately reflects the sense of Sūr's own responsibility that is so evident in the poem as a whole by translating this term "sinful ignorance," and I have done the same by supplying the verb "learned" to govern the noun. But the root meaning of *avidyā* is more ambiguous and may suggest that the fault is not entirely Sūr's.[2] However willful and obstinate the poet depicts himself, there is still a sense in which he is caught in something not altogether of his own making.

In other poems Sūr implies even more clearly that he has danced his tireless dance not for his own pleasure, but at another's behest—the Lord's (S 174):

Danced, I have danced before you,

Gracious, generous jewel of the gods.
  I've mastered the court's artful manners,
Expanded my repertoire, traveled the world,
  like a clown with a tawdry show.

1. For a radically different evaluation of dance within the *bhakti* tradition, see A. K. Ramanujan, *Hymns for the Drowning: Poems for Viṣṇu by Nammāḻvār*, pp. 115–17.

2. Cf. Daniel H. H. Ingalls, "Śaṁkara on the Question: Whose Is *Avidyā*," *Philosophy East and West* 3, no. 1 (1953): 69–72; Allen W. Thrasher, "Mandana Miśra on the Indescribability of *Avidyā*," *Wiener Zeitschrift für die Kunde Südasiens* 21 (1977): 219–37.

Into every nuance I've delved, reached beneath,
  to lay bare the truth that's inside;
And did it please you, this posturing and probing?
  No. It pleased you not at all.
Say it then, say "Sūr, that's enough!"
  Why kill me by driving me on?

Finally there are times when Sūr, after castigating himself for having been led every which way by the pull of his senses, clearly states that Māyā is responsible for pulling the strings behind the scenes. She is the dance mistress, the playwright, and last but not least the madame who has lured him into an endless and ultimately empty series of cheap performances (S 42):

I'm pleading with you to turn, hear this wretch

  who cries to sing your praises.
That minstrel Māyā has got out her stick
  and put me through a monkey's paces:
Door to door she's goaded me to dance
  in every sort of skit and show.
She curtains her face black to hide from you
  and pirates my mind and power away,
Floods me with waves and waves of longing,
  stirs and wakens me all night long,
And if ever I sleep she tortures me wild
  with dreams of fabulous wealth.
The world's greatest temptress, she saddles my heart
  and leads me away down the wayward path;
She lures like a madame beguiling some bride
  to peddle her innocence to another man.
But you, you're my husband, the goal of my life:
  where could I find another like you?
Sūr Dās says, if *you* have no mercy,
  who else can make me forget my pain?

These songs debate among themselves as to who the agent of all this is. Sometimes we hear that Sūr has bound himself with the sash of Māyā (S 153.6). Sometimes it is she who has tethered him with the leash that *naṭ*s, *naṭī*s and *bājīgar*s (that class of traveling acrobats and impromptu performers to whom we have been introduced in other *vinaya* poems) attach to the monkeys they parade around with them.[3] Sometimes it is not clear who is running the show. On occasion the poet is content simply to analogize his whole life, with all its aimlessness and dependency, to that of a *naṭ-bājīgar,* who sleeps where he can, eats what he can, is rich one minute and poor the next (S 293.4); the agency for this condition is indeterminate. Elsewhere he seems to cast the blame in the direction of the senses, attributing to them the commanding role of the *naṭī,* the female *naṭ* (S 201.7–8 in J4, cf. B2, B3, B4; missing in A1). Or again, he will sum up a poem on the lures of the senses by pleading with himself to remember Hari unless he wants to dance like a monkey on a (*naṭ*'s) leash—or, in a second sense that takes us back to a familiar theme, like some marionettelike monkey-of-a-yogi (*jogī-kapi jyau nacibo,* S 59.6). Finally, and not unexpectedly, there are times when he accuses Krishna himself of having inspired this dumb show (S 174.5, except for B3). But the phenomenon is always the same: the dance of delusion.

In a few poems this dance is interpreted as having specifically to do with reincarnation. It is the meaningless dance of an endless series of lives (e.g., S 205.8, 354.6). But the base metaphor remains the same—dance, and often dance performed in a dramatic context. As we have already heard on two occasions (S 42.3, 174.3), this dance takes its place as a leading feature of the informal acts and sketches (*svā̃g*) that are the bread and butter of the *naṭ*s.[4] Such performances depend for their effectiveness not on their depth or refinement but rather on the number of punch lines, special effects, and showy steps that they can amass. These are what Sūr refers to generically as "the arts" (*kalā*) and their effect is anything but edifying (S 153.8, 292.5). They merely titillate, for their salient feature, apart from ornament, is their number. In each of the poems we have quoted, there is a strong sense of repetitiveness and multiplicity (S 42.2, 134.3, 153.1, 174.1). Like sensory cravings, the arts are powerful because they are legion—they survive by always presenting something new—and in this realm as in that, there inevitably comes a time of surfeit and disgust.

3. Cf. S 292.3–5. Some manuscripts prefer to think of the knot or snare in which the poet is entangled (S 292.3) as that of *māyā* (J1, J2, J4, J5); others prefer associating it with *moh,* "delusion" (B2, B3, U1, A1, U2).

4. Cf. also S 136.5, 356.6, and among more recent poems, 45.6. On the modern usage of the term *svā̃g* see Darius L. Swann, "Three Forms of Traditional Theatre of Uttar Pradesh, North India" (Ph.D. diss., University of Hawaii, 1974), pp. 225–311, and Ved Prakash Vatuk and Sylvia Vatuk, "The Ethnography of *Sāng*, A North Indian Folk Opera," *Asian Folklore Studies* 26, no. 1 (1967): 29–51.

This is the level to which the dance and drama of life can fall, and there is no more appropriate person to complain to about the state of these arts than Krishna, for Krishna is renowned as a dancer himself. He is, of course, the centerpiece of the *rās līlā*; but he is no less often described as a very different sort of dancer. Krishna himself is a *naṭ,* the *gopīs* say (e.g., S 2913.6, 4023.6), and even when he is not on stage in some way the characteristic yellow cloth he wears, his "*naṭ*'s costume" (*naṭvar bes,* S 2837.9, 3705.2, etc.), serves as a reminder of his quickness and skill in sleights of hand. He is capable of all the trickery, display, and cunning that Sūr alternately berates himself for and boasts of, and the words that describe these imperfections of character are substantially the same in both cases. Plainly this Lord is akin to Māyā herself, as theistic strands in classical Hindu theology have typically affirmed.

Sūr poses this as a challenge to the great trickster. Let him turn aside from the many misleading beckonings with which he fills the world and come forth with the clear voice of salvation. Sūr has danced enough; he has shown that he can spring forth with a gesture to elaborate every murmur and whim of creation. Now, having tried to match the Lord's virtuosity with an exhausting obbligato of his own, he would rest; and in artistic terms the rest he seeks is song. In words we have already heard, "I'm pleading with you to turn, hear this wretch/ who cries to sing your praises." Or as the original more literally pleads, ". . . how may I sing your praises?" (S 42.1).

AN ANSWER IN SONG

For Sūr, then, song is not so much the accompaniment to drama and dance as it is their antidote. Even in the generic sense it seems that Sūr regards song as a thing of inherent purity. Unlike dance, it evidently has no potential perversity. The verb *bhajnā,* which carries some of the religious overtones that one senses more patently in the related nouns *bhajan* (devotional song) and *bhakti* (devoted love), is the term Sūr most commonly uses to speak of singing, but one finds the more neutral verb *gānā* as well. And except on the rarest occasions, a positive, even specifically religious meaning is always associated with these verbs. It appears that in Sūr's mind there is an intrinsic link between singing and the life of faith. Considering the all but unbreakable association between Krishna and his flute, that constant companion of whom the *gopīs* are so jealous, perhaps this is no wonder. A number of songs in the early

Sūr Sāgar are emphatic in underscoring not only Muralī's proximity to Krishna, but also her undefiable influence over the entire Braj landscape. When Muralī sounds the women of Braj come running, whether they like it or not.

Song, it seems, is a way to harness this aural energy in the service of humanity. And when Sūr speaks not just of singing in general but specifically of singing to the Lord (*bhagavant bhajan,* as he sometimes called it, and as it came formulaically to be termed in poems added to the later *Sūr Sāgar*), he clearly associates this form of artistic expression with the positive aims of life. Unlike the other arts, *bhagavant bhajan,* singing to the Lord, has the power to cut through the cycle of death and rebirth itself. Without it life is in disarray. This is a matter of considerable emphasis. In the Sabhā edition of the *Sūr Sāgar* no fewer than sixteen *vinaya* poems[5] begin their final line *sūr dās bhagavant bhajan binu* (Sūr Dās says that without singing of the Lord), and many others use similar locutions. Most of these verses then describe the various forms of perdition that ensue in the absence of song. Though formulaic phrases are considerably rarer in the older layers of the *Sūr Sāgar,* there too this expression is used on multiple occasions.[6] Similar phrases expressing the same thought are also frequent.

One might legitimately suspect that we have fallen prey to a quirk of language in pointing to the unique importance, for Sūr, of *bhajan.* Though strictly speaking this much-used word means song, perhaps all Sūr intends by it is what its etymological cousin *bhakti* denotes, namely, loving devotion. It is true that the two are related, and important that their common root is *bhaj,* "to share," for both retain that element in significant measure. But I am convinced that this is not just a case of synecdoche, in which the act of singing merely indicates the whole stance of devotion. I think Sūr means what he says when he praises *bhajan* at such length. After all, the form *bhakti* (or *bhagati*) is known and used in the early *Sūr Sāgar* and is metrically equivalent. If Sūr speaks much more often of *bhajan* instead, it is presumably intentional.

To a degree Sūr's preference for *bhajan* as against *bhakti* may

5. S 34.10, 35.12 (though the manuscript in which it occurs, K1, reads otherwise), 37.10, 58.6, 65.8, 79.8, 80.4, 86.12, 303.8, 317.6, 323.6, 324.8, 326.8, 329.8, 331.8, and 357.6. Variants include *sūr dās prabhu tumhare bhajan binu* (S 41.6), *sūr śrī gobind bhajan binu* (309.8), *kahat sūr bhagavant bhajan binu* (335.6), etc.

6. S 41.6 in U1, 326.8, 335.6, and 357.6. Cf. S 309.8, 323.6, and 324.8, all of which come into manuscripts of the *Sūr Sāgar* in the eighteenth century.

be a function of their etymological relation. *Bhajan* is an action noun in form, whereas *bhakti* is abstract. Hence it may be natural that *bhajan* will be used more easily with the frequent verb "to do" (*karnā*) than will *bhakti.* Indeed it is only in the later *Sūr Sāgar* that one finds instances of the latter expression, *bhakti karnā* "to do devotion," that is, to be devoted.[7] To speak in that way is to reify *bhakti,* to suppose it is something you can intend and do; earlier poems resist such a reification of faith.[8] What one can do, legitimately, is to sing (*bhajan karnā*), and that they wholeheartedly recommend.

Also worthy of attention are the many instances in which Sūr uses *bhajan* in the absence of a verb of action, as in the formula we have cited, "Sūr Dās says, without songs of God. . . ." There it would seem to have been entirely conceivable for him to choose the term *bhakti* if that is what he had meant. In one old manuscript (U1) he does just that, urging on his audience the importance of doing *bhakti,* loving God, devoting oneself to him (S 357.1). But note that even there Sūr retains the term *bhajan* in the last line, specifying a definite form that the act of loving God should take:

Unless we love the Lord we're like dogs and pigs,

Like meat-eating owls and vultures and cranes:
  such are the animal bodies we bear.
Like lynxes we are, like a mongoose or fox—
  they all live in homes just like ours;
All have their houses, their wives and sons—
  what makes us better than they?
To fill their bellies they kill living beings
  and feed on pleasures for which no one should yearn.
Sūr says, unless we sing to the Lord,
  we're camels and asses—that's what we are.

7. E.g., *bhakti kab karihau* in S 329.1: "when will you do devotion?" The past tense occurs in S 333.2 and 316.8. The latter is of particular interest in that the older poem of the same pattern, 315.8, has, instead of *hari kī bhakti kīnhāi* ("did Hari's devotion," S 316.8), either *hari ko bhajan kījai* ("do Hari's song," J2, A1, cf. B4) or, as if specifically to avoid matching the term *bhakti* with the verb "to do," *hari sāu prīti kījai* ("do Hari's love," i.e., "love Hari," U1).

8. It is worth noting, however, that although *bhakti* is sometimes paired with *kar-* in the later *Sūr Sāgar*, verbal expressions with *bhajan* or *bhaj-* remain much more frequent. E.g., S 80.2, 304.6, 305.6, 317.2, 342.7, 344.4, 346.1, 366.6, and 374.1.

SONG AS MEMORY—AND MORE

Sūr's preference for *bhajan* over *bhakti* can be attributed only partially to the term's implications for action. To a much greater extent his use of the word reflects its specific meaning as song, and the unique power of singing in his poetry. Sūr has no use for the classical concepts of sacrifice and yoga, the two disciplines with sufficient force to cut through the world's misleading variety, its birth and decay, and pierce to the seed of immortality that lies at the core of existence. For Sūr, both of these are replaced by song. In the countless songs of challenge and confrontation that Sūr directs to Krishna, whether in his own voice or through that of the *gopīs*, sacrifice is supplanted; for these songs, like sacrifice, are at root rituals of transaction in which human and divine beings interact. Sūr's songs of contest are clearly intended to provoke divine response. In the case of yoga, there is no question that its replacement with another form of piety is one of the main messages of the *Sūr Sāgar*. As we have seen, yoga is frequently the subject of derision and amusement in the *Sūr Sāgar,* and what makes a saint a saint is certainly not ascetic practice. The saints of this world are sanctified by one thing alone: they sing to the Lord. As for the *gopīs*, the ultimate (and very unsaintly) saints, their yoga is *viyoga,* and we receive eye-witness accounts of the many austerities of love to which they have wittingly and unwittingly subjected themselves. But the acts of steadfast repetition to which we ourselves bear witness are those that we can hear, not see. These are the *gopīs*' songs of separation, directed either to Krishna or to Ūdho in his stead.

It would be natural enough to suppose that this wholesale substitution of song (particularly *viraha* and *vinaya* songs) for yoga was made possible by one genre of devotional singing closely resembling yoga in a significant respect. *Kīrtan,* especially *nām saṃkīrtan* of the style that Caitanya taught, involves the repetition of the divine name as if it were the *mūl mantra,* the core of yogic concentration. God's name provides an unchanging focus for meditation. An occasional poem at the margin of the early *Sūr Sāgar* implies that song is the legitimate yoga for just this reason (S 375.3–4, found only in J4), but this is scarcely the spirit of the whole. Not one of the many poems in the Sabhā *Sūr Sāgar* that draw on a *kīrtan* style appears in the old manuscripts. Poems involving such incantational formulae as *hari hari hari hari sumiran karau,* which are so prominent in the Sabhā edition and familiar in analogous forms in the writings of other *bhakta*s and *sant*s, for example Tulsī Dās, were either unknown to Sūr, or rejected by him as unfit examples of the sort of *bhajan* he intended to project.

Yet there are a number of instances in the old poetry of the *Sūr Sāgar* in which the poet lauds the divine name or bewails the fact that he has not. Most familiarly he gives the name as Rām and Hari,[9] but also as Govind and Gopāl, and on one occasion the divine name, its vocables unspecified, is said to be the boat that can ferry one across the waters of existence (S 99.8 in B3, U1, J2, J4; cf. J5, A1), a common motif in medieval poetry.[10]

As we saw in the previous chapter, however, the name of the Lord as such held little mystique for Sūr, certainly by comparison with other poets of his period. Sūr's way of "remembering the name of the Lord," a phrase he uses, was not to repeat it alone but to invoke its salvific power by recalling incidents in which that name had meant something in action. Furthermore, as we have seen, Sūr refrained for the most part from according a particular exaltation to the name of Rām (*rām nām*), and apparently for much the same reason. It was not the transcendent theological fulcrum for him that it was for Tulsī Dās, hence did not provide in its own scope the access to immortality that yoga had always claimed. For Sūr the mystique of the name is reduced almost to practicalities. It is the means by which creatures may call upon God and, as the Śrī Vaiṣṇavas of South India are fond of saying, it provides the

9. Leaving aside the *rāmcarit* poems, one finds the following occasions on which the name of Rām is praised in the old manuscripts: S 59.4–5 (J1 [twice], B2, U1, B4, J4, J5); 57.1 (B2, U1); and 313.3 (B2, U1, J5). A1, somewhat later, adds 311.1–2 (the mention of Hari does not occur in v. 2, as in the Sabhā text), 330.10, and 151.18 (in the margin). S 233 and 296 are poems with venerable pedigrees and include references to the name of Rām in their Sabhā versions (233.1, 297.7). These, however, present complications in their manuscript forms. In S 233, only J5 reads *rām*; the remaining manuscripts have either *gopāl* (B4) or *hari gun* (U1, J4). In S 296, it is again only J5 that corresponds to the Sabhā reading (*rām nām*). J4 has a similar *rām sumiri* but B4 has the hybrid *rām krisan* and J2 has *hari ko nāu*. The term Hari occurs in S 57.6 (B2, U1); 114.3 (B2, U1, B4, A1, U2); and 347.1 (J1, B2, B3, U1, J2, J4, J5, A1). S 152.2 simply has *nām tumhāro* (B3) or *nām tumhārau* (A1): "your name."

10. The same phrase (*nām naukā*) recurs in a single version of S 155.10, that given in folio 169 of A1. Other manuscripts, however, give some form of *pad naukā* (B3, J2, J4, and fol. 163 of A1). Cf. the later S 202.8; also S 175.9 and 212.4, in which Hari's feet and memory have been identified with his name and they in turn become the *naukā*. S 175 occurs in B4, J4, and A1, but the line in question has been added later.

Lord with an excuse for coming to the rescue. For Sūr it is that divine readiness that gives power to the name—and that makes it appropriate for Sūr to defame and challenge it when that quality seems absent. Song, with its discursive as against incantational capabilities, provides a vessel in which both these aspects can be explored, and to that degree it derives some of its power from the mystique of the name.

Another way in which song conquers the storms of this world, as yoga would, has to do with the person to whom it is directed, Krishna. Song becomes the antidote to death and time because it is Krishna's nature to defeat them; song is the means for fastening onto him. It is the call for help that can be raised by one who is drowning in the sea of existence, pummeled by waves that bring birth after birth. It goes out to the one who has shown himself capable of intervening in every age and in every stage of life, irrespective of considerations of time and death (S 17.13). For countless lapses of his own, Sūr is able to match examples of Krishna's saving power, and song permits him the medium in which he can do so in a greatly condensed form. In his songs of petition and praise, a number of which we quoted in the last chapter, he typically mentions such incidents in only a word or phrase, at most a couplet, as is appropriate in a cry for rescue. Song affords him a medium in which he can steady himself by calling to mind the reality that is unaffected by change and circumstance. In that respect it is again the analogue of yoga.

There is a final avenue through which song gains its power, a third way in which it functions as saving memory. It is true enough that the power of song derives in part from its being a way to "remember the name," as Sūr says (*nām sumiran,* S 17.8), and in part from its being an effective way to remember Krishna (*hari sumiran,* S 52.1, 59.6).[11] But many of Sūr's songs of petition carry the strength they do, not because they recall something memorable but because they remember what has been forgotten. There is a mysterious sense in which to record in song the very process of forgetting the Lord, if one does it with sufficient intensity, constitutes a saving memory.

Any one of a number of poems in which Sūr remonstrates with himself (the *man pramodh* or *man prabodh* genre) will serve to il-

11. Or Rām (*rām rām sumiran* in S 330.1, recorded in A1). Note, however, how late and isolated this citation is in comparison with those just listed for *hari sumiran,* both of which occur in half a dozen manuscripts extending back to B2 in the case of S 52 and J1 in the case of S 59.

lustrate the point. Take, for example, the following poem (S 326), which is more effective in the original than in translation because the poet always uses the reflexive pronoun. It is personal, first-person speech, yet Braj Bhāṣā poetry is supple enough that nothing in the diction prevents listeners from generalizing to include themselves.

Time after time I've deceived myself,

Instinctively clawed after sensual carrion
  and squandered the jewel of Hari within,
Like a deer in a desert chasing a mirage,
  who aggravates his thirst with every assault.
Birth after birth I have acted and acted
  and acting, entangled, imprisoned myself
Like the parrot who nurtures the silk-cotton bud,
  stalking it constantly, obstinate, vigilant,
Till one fine day he pecks the ripe fruit
  and it's empty: like cotton it flies in his face;
Like the monkey the minstrel-magician has leashed
  so he'll dance for crumbs at each neighborhood market—
Sūr Dās says, sing to the Lord, sing or else
  you're feeding your tail to the viper of time.

As one follows along with catalogues of omissions and commissions such as this, there is typically—especially in poems added later to the genre—little signal that the sequence is about to end. The *pad* is an elastic enough poetic form and Sūr, to hear him tell it, a grievous enough sinner, that the recital could go on at indeterminate length. The pattern is slightly more complex in the poem we have just quoted, since the poet constructs it by alternating errors in his own life with illustrations from the world at large. Even so there is no clear signal that closure is ahead until one hears the poet's signature. After a generalizing refrain the sequence builds, verse by verse: error, illustration, error, illustration, illustration. It could well continue with another statement of error and a series of three illustrations, and so on.

Only one sure relief is in prospect, as the poet and the experienced listener know. At some point the sheer weight of all these offenses will all but force the poet to summarize. At that point we will hear something like the familiar formula "Sūr Dās says, unless one sings to the Lord," or as I have translated here, "Sūr Dās says, sing to the Lord, sing or else. . . ." Whatever follows—always a statement of perdition—invariably ends the song. More recent poems in the *Sūr Sāgar* sometimes find a way to sweeten the message with a note of optimism at the end, but in older poems the bleakness is unmitigated. In the example above, poetic closure underscores this totality. Error and illustration, the poet's life and the life of the animal world to which he increasingly turns for analogy, meet in open confrontation in the last phrase of the song: "you're feeding your tail to the viper of time."

Is there a message of salvation here? Only the very mention, in song, of the song of the Lord permits the song to come to an end. That mention is negative, of course—*bhagavant bhajan* BINU: "*unless* one sings to the Lord," "*without* singing of the Lord"—but even a negative mention allows the song to arrive at its own subject and thus conclude. Alternatively this can be phrased strictly in terms of memory, so that the penultimate phrase is something like "without remembering Hari" (*hari sumiran binu*), and the effect is the same: an act of memory is completed even in the profession of forgetfulness, and closure is at hand. For a singer that closure is the analogue of salvation: it brings both release and fulfillment. And as the subject of these songs makes clear, Sūr would have us all be singers.

In this case, which is more extreme than most, we have a group of songs that explicitly lead us to believe that they are *not* songs to the Lord, not *hari bhajans*, yet by virtue of what finally happens in them they become *hari bhajans*; and it is the medium itself, the act of remembering what had been forgotten, that turns forgetting to recall. They become songs and remembrances of Hari through the aesthetic necessity of closure. At that point *bhagavant bhajan,* "singing of the Lord," or some alternative expression must enter the poem, however backhandedly (*binu,* "without, unless") if the song is to be a song at all.

This is a specific necessity if the song in question is to be a *pad* and thus to take its place in Sūr's poetic repertoire. The convention of including the poet's signature at the end of every *pad* necessitates a change of perspective, however slight. In a *pad* whose diction is entrusted to one or another of the figures in Krishna's world, as Sūr's normally are, the mention of the poet's name very often provides a double reading for the last line, or at least a hint of one. At one level its message still pertains to the speech of the character concerned; at another level it is Sūr's, or concerns him.

Such a change of voice is not possible in Sūr's poems of petition since there, at least according to the conventions of the *vinaya* genre, the poet is speaking for himself. Yet he must insert his signature all the same, and that act opens a tiny space in the syntax that makes the experienced listener expect the intrusion of another voice, at least as an overtone. If one reads the message that immediately follows the signature for what it literally says, it seems the poet rejects this possibility and attempts to hold himself and his audience to the compelling force of the rest of the poem: *bhagavant bhajan BINU*. But the act of signing the poem creates a bond between the singer and the Lord that suggests another valency altogether. Here we have *sūr dās bhagavant bhajan,* "Sūr Dās's song of the Lord," as we have "Sūr's Lord" (*sūr prabhu, sūr syām,* and the like) in numerous other poems. It is almost impossible that a hint of this redeemed association between the singer and his God will not be felt, since in the original the two words are directly juxtaposed. This is despite the warning (*binu*) that crashes in afterward and realigns the meaning with the gloomy sentiment expressed in the rest of the poem: "Sūr Dās says, unless one sings to the Lord. . . ." This hint of redemption—for everything in the poem but the very barest structural feature of the genre itself militates against it—is Sūr's own analogue to the cry of Ajāmil. Ajāmil, the Brahmin, had lost all sense of his own calling and reestablished contact with the Lord only by chance at the moment of death, his own closure, when the son to whom he cried for help happened to bear the name of God: Nārāyaṇ. In these poems of despair Sūr also turns his head away, but in the end we hear the sound of salvation anyway.

As I say, this is the extreme case. The saving power of many of Sūr's songs is much more obvious. They are an ocean of poetry that undulates with the name and deeds of the Lord. But even in the corpus as a whole the plaintive note of the loss of Krishna echoes with persistent force: *viraha* and *vinaya* are the dominant moods of the early *Sūr Sāgar*. Throughout the collection, it seems, there is no other way to make the absent Krishna present than to give one's voice to song. Such a presence remains covert, of course. Sūr is hardly willing to compromise the truth by pretending that God resides in the individual soul, only waiting to be discovered by a process of consciousness alteration such as Ūdho recommends. That would be an empty presence and an ersatz salvation. No, Krishna is genuinely gone—both from the *gopīs* who remember him and from the common people who have forgotten him. The hope of reunion in some far-off Kurukṣetra, a hope that later contributors to the *Sūr Sāgar* were unable to withstand, is misplaced. What hope there is, is here.

Sometimes Sūr proclaims it outright, in words such as we have already heard (S 235):

> *Songs to Hari work great wonders:*
>
> They elevate the lowly of the world,
> who celebrate their lofty climb with drums.
> To come to the feet of the Lord in song
> is enough to make stones float on the sea.
> No wonder that even the meanest of the mean—
> hunters and harlots—can mount the skies,
> Where wander the infinite company of stars,
> where the moon and the sun circle around,
> And only Dhruv, the polestar, is fixed,
> for he as a lad had sung his way to Rām.
> The Vedas are verses, testaments to God—
> hearing them makes the saints saintly and wise—
> And what about Sūr? I sing too.
> O Hari, my shelter, I've come for your care.

But it is much more characteristic for the message of song as salvation to be implicit. That is why it has been necessary to approach the subject as circumspectly as we have in this chapter. Since Sūr was wholly engaged in the act of seeking salvation through song, he rarely stood outside to comment on the process itself: it would have distorted the deed. Such an external, neutral voice would have vitiated his poetry, turned it to prose. Hence what we have in the vast sweep of the *Sūr Sāgar* is a series of performative utterances.[12] Not merely descriptions or comments, they seek to bring about that of which they speak: the *gopīs* yearn for Krishna with the hope, somehow, of bringing him back, and the poet longs for salvation with the same end in mind. The medium, in all cases, is song. Song is the inveterate discipline that makes the Lord present even when he is absent, and it includes within its scope both poems that have a definite narrative context—in some sense *saguṇa* poems—and those that do not, that flow directly out of the

12. On this notion of J. L. Austen in the context of *viraha* poetry, see Karine Schomer, "Mahadevi Varma and the Chayavad Age of Modern Hindi Poetry: A Literary and Intellectual Biography" (Ph.D. diss., University of Chicago, 1976), pp. 332–33.

rigid, boundless need of the poet himself—in some sense their *nirguṇa* complement. The act of coming to expression in song for the sake of God is itself the final subject of the *Sūr Sāgar* and its reason for being.

Perhaps it is especially appropriate, then, as we saw at the very beginning of our study, that nothing of Sūr remains but his poems. These poems *are* Sūr Dās. As performative utterances, they work their own salvation, calling up in the hearer, and doubtless in the poet too, a reality that would not otherwise be there. At one level, of course, this is Krishna, the absent present God. But at another it is the poet himself, who also would not be but for the act of having committed himself to song. There would be no Sūr Dās if we could not hear him. As tradition has so correctly said, everything else about him is blind.

Who, then, is Sūr Dās, and what salvation does he herald? He is a poet separated from the fundament of his own being by a cause he does not fathom, and connected to it only by the slippery thread of language. If he does not sing, what can he do? If he does not sing, what is he? So he sings. Like the forlorn people of Braj who are tied to Krishna only by memory, he sings songs of loss and lapse; in them he acts to be.

"By the rivers of Babylon," the psalmist said, "we sat down and wept when we remembered Zion. . . . How could we sing the Lord's song in a foreign land?"[13] But that psalmist did sing—even when he said he could not, even when he said there was no proper musical bone in his body—and we remember his words today. So it is for Sūr. In poem after poem we find him still in exile. Yet he sings of the Lord, he sings of his Babylon, and in some not quite comprehensible way the song succeeds in restoring his long-lost, shining Jerusalem.

13. Psalm 137.1 as translated in *The New English Bible: The Old Testament,* pp. 865–66.

Sūr Dās with his one-stringed instrument (*ektār*). Modern painting by Warish Khan after the Moghul style typified in the school of Shah Qalam. Courtesy of Laurent Aubert, Geneva.

Notes on the Translations

WHILE A detailed presentation of manuscript readings for poems contained in the early *Sūr Sāgar* must await the publication of a critical edition, certain information about poems translated in this book concerns the reader more immediately. Each poem fully translated is listed here in the order in which it appears in the text. The manuscripts in which it is to be found are then cited, together with any notes that may be required to explain to readers of the standard Nāgarīpracāriṇī Sabhā edition why translations made here differ from what the printed text would seem to imply. I am greatly indebted to Kenneth E. Bryant for devising a computerized first-line index to poems included in old manuscripts of the *Sūr Sāgar,* which provided easy and complete access to the manuscript information included here.

P. 31. *They say you're so giving, so denying of yourself*

MANUSCRIPTS: J1, B2, B3, U1, J2, J4, A1. Sabhā 135. The verse order given here is not quite that of the Sabhā. Lines 3–4, concerning Vibhīṣan and Rāvaṇ, are translated in the order given them in J1, B2, U1, J2, and J4, which reverses that of B3 and A1, the sequence offered in the Sabhā edition. All manuscripts agree in placing the verse concerning Prahlād (or alternatively Sudāmā) after these two, except J2, which lists it as verse 3. The translation given here accords with the Sabhā text in verse 1, and with the preponderance of manuscripts. The reading is not entirely secure, however, since the two oldest manuscripts (J1, B2) include the name of Rām in the title line, though at different points, and U1 inserts that of Hari. In Sabhā verse 3 (here v. 4), the word *sar* is to be replaced by *kar,* as shown in all manuscripts except J1 (*karam*); the meaning changes little. The word *jan,* absent in all manuscripts, is to be subtracted from the Sabhā's verse 4 (here v. 3). Later in the same line I have retained the old J1 reading *pūr bali* (cf. Sabhā *purabalī*), which seems to be at the root of *purabilī* (B3, cf. A1) and *pūrab pīti* (B3, cf. J4), rather than following the more formulaic *prem prīti* (U1, J2). The personnel in verse 5 are entirely different from what the Sabhā version suggests. Again I follow J1 (*prahilād kī pratigyā pārī surapati kīnhau jāni*; cf. B2, U1), to which J2 and J4 are similar except that they interpret the deliverance of

Prahlād as a matter of mercy (*kripā bhaī*) rather than as the fulfilling of a promise or vow. Only B3 and A1 support the Sabhā's mention of Sudāmā at this point (A1: Śrīdāmā). Reference to Indra is made in J1, B2, U1, and J2, but not J4, which follows the Sabhā reading after the caesura.

NOTES: Sudāmā was a penurious boyhood friend of Krishna who went to him after he had become monarch of Dvaraka and was given, on returning to his native Braj, every comfort imaginable. The four fruits of life are the four ultimate aims for which one can strive: *kāma, artha, dharma,* and *mokṣa*—pleasure, gain, righteousness, and release. Krishna's teacher, Sāndīpan, had had no male progeny until Krishna intervened with fate. Vibhīṣan, brother of Rāvaṇ, had in his heart always sided with Rām, his brother's foe, and was rewarded for his faithfulness when Rām defeated Rāvaṇ in battle and installed Vibhīṣan on the throne of Laṅkā. Rām is one of the avatars of Viṣṇu, other than Krishna, who is implied in this poem (and explicitly mentioned in J1 and B2); the other is Narasiṅh, who came to the aid of young Prahlād and saved him from death at the hands of his father, thus honoring Prahlād's unwavering devotion. Indra was made wise after he angrily opposed the worship of Krishna at Mount Govardhan—formerly the residents' praise had been directed to him—and was accepted into the ranks of Krishna's worshippers even though he had rained destruction on him and his associates for seven days and nights. By citing this history of mercy on the part of his Lord, as he does in many other *vinaya* poems, Sūr Dās hopes to shame Krishna into granting a boon to him as well. Normally what he asks for is salvation or acceptance in some form.

P. 32. *Now I am blind; I have shunned Hari's name.*

MANUSCRIPT: folio 102a of Hindi manuscript no. 1359/14, *pad saṅgraha,* in the Maharaja Man Singh Pustak Prakash Research Centre, Jodhpur. Because this manuscript, written at Ahipur (i.e., Nagaur), does not form a part of the Sabhā edition, I present the full text below:

aj hõ andh hari nā̃m na let
māyā moh bhrami sūjhat nahī̃ vūjhat
āye nar sīs siroruh set
sakucit aṅg utaṅg bhaṅg dij
drig jal śravat urāhat het
kari sutant maṃjār āṣ lāu
krīḍat kāl nahī̃ laṣat acet
mrig bijhun kai kāj man jaisāi
mānāu race bijhukā ṣet
sūr dās sa bhagavant bhajan bin
parai muṇḍi mudagir jam bet

As is common in manuscripts of this period, no distinction is made between *ṣ* and *kh*. In verse 2, *nar* is visually the more plausible reading, but the orthography for *bhar* in this manuscript is only slightly different and would make somewhat better sense. *Sa* in the final verse appears to be the product of dittography, as is particularly suggested by its being the last consonant in one line of the manuscript and the first in the next.

NOTES: The "tears," or more literally "water" (*jal*), in verse 3 are not signs of emotion; watery eyes are a common phenomenon among the aged in India. The continued attention to eyes in verse 4 is explicit, but in verse 5 it is merely understood. The scarecrows Indian farmers construct—primarily to ward off deer rather than crows—typically have heads made of inverted pots to which eyes have been affixed. The poet may intend a contrast between the proverbial agility of the deer, a quickness often associated with eyes, and these unmoving specimens. The final line, with its formulaic quality, applies equally to the speaker of the poem and to those whom he addresses. "Death" here is the god Yama (*jam*), but death's presence has already been suggested by the term *kāl* in verse 4, which means both "time" and "death." *Het* (v. 3) and *bet* (v. 6) are slightly problematical. I have interpreted the former as *hetī* and the latter as broadly redundant with *mudagir*.

P. 40. *Viṣṇu, from his sacred mouth*

MANUSCRIPTS: none. Sabhā 225.

P. 55. *I've hurried on over, for the news has come*

MANUSCRIPTS: U1, B4, A1, U2. Sabhā 639. The manuscripts diverge from the Sabhā text substantially in the order in which they present the verses. B4 and A1 appear to have the full six-line poem, reordering the Sabhā verses as follows: 1,2,4,5,3,6. U1 and U2 agree with this sequence, but omit verses from it. U1 has 1,2,5,6; U2 has 1,2,5,3,6. The B4/A1 version translated here is close to that of the Sabhā, except in the following places: verse 2 concludes *ā̃gan vajati vadhāī*; verse 3 (here v. 5) concludes *varanau kahā vaḍāī* (cf. U2, but A1 has *vanāī* as the last word); verse 4 (here v. 3) begins *kahīe kahā kahat nahi āvai*; and verse 6 reads as follows: *sūr dās prabhu antarjāmī nand suvan sukh dāī.*

P. 60. *Wayfarer, see how the dark Jumna's blackened.*

MANUSCRIPTS: B1, B2, B3, U1 (twice), J4, A1, K1. Sabhā 3809. In a number of respects the manuscripts depart from the Sabhā version. In verse 3, the words *giri, dhaṃsi,* and *taraph* all appear in some manuscripts, but in each case an argument can be made that an alternative is to be preferred. *Giri* (J4, K1) should be replaced by some form of *janu,* as in all other manuscripts except A1, which has the synonymous *māno.* The change has the effect of removing or at least muting the suggestion that the Jumna's posture as a love-distraught woman fallen from her bed is to be compared with the Jumna's thunderous descent from the mountains to the plain. *Dhasi,* "crashed" (B3, J4, A1, K1) yields to *dhuki,* "fainted" (B1, B2, U1); and *taraph/talaph,* "destroyed" (B3, A1, K1) to *talapi,* "bed" (B1, B2, U1). *Bal janu* deserves note as an important variant for some form of *bārū* in verse 4, and *pūr* for *cūr* in the same line, but for reasons of sense I have retained the Sabhā reading in both cases. This is to favor B3, J4, A1, and K1 over B1, B2, and U1, contrary to normal practice. In verse 5, almost all manuscripts have *pulin manu* in place of *kul par*; and I have interpreted *pañkaj* (lotus) as a single word, though the word from which it is built, *pañk* (mud), is also to be stressed, as the Sabhā editors have done. In verse 6, *ati* replaces *gati* in all manuscripts except A1 and J4, which lack either; *tahā̃* and *mati* are the most frequent substitutes for the Sabhā's *ati.* Verse 7, finally, should contain the phrase *cakaī vyāj vakati hai,* various forms of which are found in all manuscripts, in place of *cakaī piy ju raṭati hai*; *phen* (B1, B2, B3, K1, and fol. 100 of U1) is to be substituted for *bhaī*; and *āhārī* (B1, U1, cf. K1, U1) for *anuhārī* (B3, *Sabhā*).

NOTES: The sheldrake (*cakaī,* Skt. *cakravāka*) is a bird that spends the night separated from its mate. See Daniel H. H. Ingalls, *An Anthology of Sanskrit Court Poetry: Vidyākara's "Subhāṣitaratnakoṣa,"* p. 501. Kenneth Bryant has translated the Sabhā version of this poem in *Poems to the Child-God,* p. 202.

P. 61. *Ūdho, the memory of Braj never fades*

MANUSCRIPTS: none. Sabhā 4774. Note that the first two lines of Sabhā 4890 (J4, K1) and Sabhā 4775 (no manuscripts) are closely related to their counterparts here.

P. 65. *"Who are you, my fair one?" the Dark One asks.*

MANUSCRIPTS: none. Sabhā 1291.

NOTES: For alternate translations, see Bryant, *Poems to the Child-God,* p. 187; B. B. L. Sharmā, "Rādhā of Sûradāsa," in *Suradasa, A Reevaluation,* ed. Nagendra, p. 113; and Usha Nilsson, *Surdas,* pp. 25–26.

P. 69. *Nothing, today there was nothing I could do.*

MANUSCRIPTS: See the following entry. Sabhā 4911.

P. 70. *Nothing, nothing, there was nothing I could do*

Manuscripts: J1, B1, B2, B3, U1, B4, J2, J4 (once fully, once partially), A1. An additional occurrence is reported in J4, but the page is missing. Sabhā 2498, 4911. As explained in chapter 3, the basic text of S 2498 is closer to the manuscript versions of this poem than is S 4911. Crucial elements in S 4911 that do not appear in the manuscripts are the following: *nahī̃* in verse 3, *na* in verse 4, and *na* in verse 5. *Binu* in verse 7 appears only in B3, J2, J4, and A1, and *prabhu* is omitted from line 8 only in B2, J2, J4, and A1. In addition, several words that contribute to the tone of the poem as understood in its "Kurukṣetra" guise are absent in the oldest manuscripts: *āju* is altogether lacking in verse 1, and *nij* is found only in the B3, B4, J4, and A1 versions of verse 6. J1, B1, B2, and U1 have *jiy* or *jīy* instead, which accounts for the translation "soul" and underscores the spokeswoman's point that her emotions proceed through a logic of their own, without her control—precisely the opposite of the sense of personal responsibility that *nij* would imply. The phrase *hā̃u rahī ṭhagī sī* (S 4911.2) is absent in all manuscripts, which approximate the reading of S 2498 instead. In J1, B1, B2, and U1, the order of verses 5 and 6 is reversed from what it appears in either S 2498 or S 4911, and the translation of S 2498 follows the revised order. The remaining manuscripts present verses 5–6 in the order in which they appear in the Sabhā edition. These same manuscripts (B3, B4, J2, J4, A1) agree in beginning what they count as verse 5 in the same manner as S 4911: *kaṃcukī tā̃i* (with orthographic variations). The older tradition, however, disagrees about the word to be paired with *kaṃcukī* (B1: *phaṭi*; B2: *kaṭi*; U1: *phal*). In the case of J1, one has a different phrase altogether (*praphulit man*). There is fair variation in the interpretation of verse 7, but B1, B2, and U1 agree, as follows: *gurajaṇ sakuc kachu na sakal kari suni mati bidhi sajani.* J1 is in agreement beginning at *suni,* but fails to give a reading for the portion before the caesura.

P. 71. *Rukmiṇī asks, "Which maid, my dear"*

Manuscripts: B1, B3, U1, B4, J4, A1, K1. Saghā 4904. The B1 version, translated here, differs from that given by the Sabhā in only two respects significant to the meaning. In verse 4 the word *ṭhag* occurs, rather than the less specific *yahai,* and verse 8 ends with the phrase *var dhyā̃ citavanī ḍorī.*

P. 72. *Rādhā, how brilliant your shining face*

Manuscripts: B1, B2, U1 (twice), B4, J2, J3, J4. Sabhā 2320. This poem depends so strongly upon the use of specific similes that even in cases where the Sabhā's choice of words is not that indicated by the old manuscripts, the meaning is little affected. The Sabhā's *bank* in verse 2, for instance, is absent in the manuscripts, which instead fill out the meter with *pragaṭ* (or *pragaṭī*, U1: fol. 68) or *bāṭ* (J4); but its meaning is restored in the next verse, where all manuscripts except B4 and J2 contain the word *kuṭil* (B4 has *vikaṭ*; J2, *bank*). In verse 1 they are unanimous in preferring *ati* to the Sabhā's *birājat*, except folio 68 of U1, which has the interesting variant *śrī tāi*, on which compare S 2314.6 in manuscript. The one serious deviation caused to the translation by adhering to the manuscripts comes in verse 5. It appears in the translation as line 6, since verses 3–5 are distributed over four lines rather than three. The Sabhā reads *gati maimant nāg jyau nāgari*, which evidently compares the movement of the clever, urbane Rādhā to the slow, rhythmic gait of an elephant—a frequent simile in Indian poetry. The problem is that *gati*, "gait," is found only in J3, evidently as a reinterpretation of *ati*, which is found in folio 68 of U1 and in J2. *Ati* makes no reference to movement, and neither does the word found in the remaining manuscripts; some form of *manu* (B1, B2, B4, J4, and fol. 54 of U1). The verb perhaps compensates, since all manuscripts have *āvati* or *āvat* in place of the Sabhā's *nāgari*, but one is left with the problem that the slow gait of the *gajagāminī* is not that of an elephant in rut, which is clearly specified by the term *maimant* in all manuscripts (except J4: *matt*). I have therefore preferred to translate by emphasizing what is usually meant when reference is made in love poetry to an elephant in rut: the strong perfume exuded from the temples to attract the mate.

P. 73. *She's found him, she has, but Rādhā disbelieves*

MANUSCRIPTS: J1, B1, B2, B3, U1, B4, J2, J3, J4, A1. Sabhā 2741. There is considerable difference of opinion as to what the proper verse order for this poem should be. I have translated according to the order that predominates in the oldest manuscripts (J1, B2, U1, B4, J2; also B1, except that it omits v. 4.) The Sabhā version replicates the order followed in A1, and resembles that of B3 except that B3 has omitted the fourth verse, which, curiously, is also absent in the 1976 edition of the Sabhā *Sūr Sāgar* through a typographical error. J3 and J4 present a six-verse poem, omitting Sabhā lines 5 and 6; a marginal notation in J3 reinserts these after Sabhā's verse 3, restoring the poem to its more usual length. Because the Sabhā version tends to agree with B3, A1, J3, or J4 against the remaining manuscripts, there are several discrepancies with respect to what is translated here. I have read *sacu* rather than *sukh* (B3, A1, Sabhā) in verse 2, and *baḍhāvati* rather than *banāvati* in Sabhā verse 6 (here, v. 4), though J1 and B2 have *vadhāvati*. I adopt *kihi* (J1, B3, B4, A1; cf. B1, U1, B2) *yah* (J1, B1, B3, U1, A1) in place of *ke hiy* (Sabhā; cf. J3, J4: *jo hiy*) in verse 7. In Sabhā verse 4 (v. 6 here) I have followed

A1 and the Sabhā in interpreting the overwhelmingly predominant *saci* as *saṃci,* producing the translation "hoard" rather than "truth."

P. 74. *Away! Go back to where you spent the night!*

MANUSCRIPTS: J1, B1, B2, U1, B4, J4, A1, K1. Sabhā 3122. Most manuscripts (B1, B2, U1, B4) support the Sabhā's *nahī* in verse 1, but J1 and K1 omit it. A1 transforms it into a part of the variant *tanu.* In verse 3, the Sabhā's verb *birājat* is found in none of the manuscripts, all of which have some form of *banyau hai* except for K1's *jamyo hai.* The difference is significant because *banyau* and *jamyo* suggest the imprint of a necklace now gone, whereas *birājat* (shines) might suggest an actual one. That this is an imprinted necklace, not a real one, explains why it is "stringless" (*binahī sūtra,* B1, cf. B2, U1, A1, K1; *binu gunahī,* J1, B4, cf. Sabhā). Only the original's jewels, not its string, were sufficiently large or sharp to have left a mark in Krishna's chest. *Maṇi/mani* (J1, B1, B2, U1) is probably to be preferred to the Sabhā's *ur* (so B4, A1, K1) in verse 3, and *caturi* (B1, B2, B4, J1) to *catur* (U1, K1, Sabhā) later in the line. In the following verse the Sabhā's verb *bithurī* should be replaced with mention of Krishna's rumpled clothing (*ambar* in all except J1, which reads *ori*). All manuscripts mention it, whereas only B1, B2, U1, and B4 mention his hair (*alak*); the others take the occasion to specify further the nature of Krishna's clothes. In verse 5, all manuscripts agree in preferring some form of *bhāi,* here translated "passion," to the Sabhā's *bhalāi*; an original *bhāī* or *bhāi* evidently explains U1's *bhaī.* There is the familiar difference of opinion as to *bhavan* (J1, B2, K1, Sabhā) or *bhuvan* (B1, U1, B4) in the word just preceding. Although the Sabhā's *alas* in the last line is found in none of the manuscripts, it accurately renders the sense of *nīd* in B1, B2, and U1. J1 and B4, however, have *lol* and *cāru* respectively; K1 suggests *sajal*; and A1 introduces a different phrase altogether.

P. 75. *Seeing the Dark One is like staring in the dark*

MANUSCRIPTS: B1, B2, B3, U1, B4, J3, J4, A1. Sabhā 2742. In the first two lines, B1, B2, and B4 describe an all-night vigil with the Dark One. His name, Syām, is the first word in the poem, and the last three words in the second line read *sakal* (B2: *sayal*) *nisi jāgat.* The latter phrase is retained, though sometimes broken apart, in B3, J3, J4, and A1; but *syām* is dropped from line 1 in these manuscripts. The basic reading for the first part of line 2 is *kahā karau raṇ rañg nayan mere,* though *raṇ* is altered to *nar* in B4 and to *rati* in B3, J3, and J4. The meaning of verses 3–4, if not always their word order, is close to that of the Sabhā in all manuscripts except B4 and J4, which present verses 3–5 in different orders. In verse 5, the Sabhā's *śrī* is missing from the manuscripts; *saneh* is replaced by *sanāh* in all manuscripts except J3 (*grah*); and *anurāgat* yields to *pratirājat* except in B3 and A1. B1 presents what must be close to the original version of the last line: *itai mān sūr mere locan sab hī māh syām sukh māgat* (so B2, cf. B4). The Sabhā version of the poem is different enough from that translated in chapter 3 to warrant its own translation:

She gazes at him as if she cannot see,

Even though he stands transfixed by one aim:
  a singular stare; no eyelid intervenes.
His, like Kāma's, is a handsome sight,
  and hers is radiance no measure can trace.
They're intimate rivals, like Arjun and Karṇa,
  and neither will ever consider surrender:
She in her feminine finery arrayed,
  and he with his limbs oiled in amorous armor.
Sūr says her militant eyes thirst for plunder:
  more and still more of the joy of her lover.

NOTES: Although the original poet preferred the immediacy of the first-person quotation, the shift from it to third-person speech and back was evidently experienced as difficult in subsequent years. The two most recent of the old manuscripts to contain this poem, J3 and A1, carry the third-person perspective over into the last line by transforming "my eyes" (*mere locan*) into "these eyes" (*ye locan, ai locan*). In the Sabhā version, the first-person dimension has been eliminated altogether, particularly by means of an alteration in the second line that removes, once again, "my [battlefield] eyes" (*raṇ raṅg nayan mere*). A translation of the poem that results appears above.

P. 75. *"Hari has come, at last he's come!"*

MANUSCRIPTS: B1, B2, B3, U1, J3, J4, K1. Sabhā 4721. Little of substance separates the manuscript versions of this poem from the text offered by the Sabhā editors. All manuscripts, for instance, have *kachu* rather than *ati* as the second word in verse 3, and most (B1, B2, U1, J3, J4) prefer *bikal* to *birah* (B3, Sabhā) soon after (K1 has *hṛde*). Adjustments such as these are minor. The most significant problem for the meaning, perhaps, comes in the final line. The manuscripts seem undecided as to whether it is Rādhā or Ūdho who has lost the power of speech and mental functioning, or both. The Sabhā version removes the unclarity by assigning the speechlessness to Ūdho and the loss of faculties to Rādhā, but the ambiguity of the manuscripts can be sensed from a representative example: *sūr dās prabhu kahī na jāi kachu hū ajāṇ matihīnī* (U1).

P. 76. *Ever since your name has entered Hari's ear*

MANUSCRIPTS: J1, B1 (twice), B2, U1, B4, J2, J3, J4, A1. Sabhā 3399. Most of the shifts that the manuscripts require a student of the Sabhā text to observe are small. In verse 3 one must read *suhṛd* rather than *surabhi,* in accord with all manuscripts except J2 (*sang*). Verse 7 begins with some form of the noun *tarapaṇ* rather than the verb *tarapat,* and in verse 8 one has the possibility of reading *kṛs gāt sakal añg* (U1, cf. B1, B2, A1) rather than *kṛs gāt sakal vidhi* (B4, cf. J1, J3, J4, Sabhā). In the first part of line 5 the manuscripts reveal a fair latitude in what they understand to be the correct word to pair with *raci: paci, param,* and *ruci* are all options, in addition to *rucir,* which the Sabhā shares with B4 and J4. Later in the line, however, the manuscripts are all but unanimous in choosing *pāṭh* to complement the earlier *pīṭhi,* rather than the Sabhā's *gān.* The exceptions are B4, which repeats *pīṭh,* and J4, which has *gā̃n.* All manuscripts provide a different ending for verse 7 than the Sabhā presents. Each of them has some version of *bipra bhoj bolat bisrām,* with J2 as the only noteworthy exception: it substitutes *bhajan* for *bhoj.*

P. 76. "*Give me, Kānh, a shawl for my shoulders.*"

MANUSCRIPTS: B1, B2, U1, J3, J4, A1. Sabhā 2609. All manuscripts except A1 read *megh ko ḍambar* rather than *megh āḍambar* in verse 3, giving the moment a soberer cast than it has in the Sabhā version. The second part of verse 5 is at variance with the Sabhā: *jin ko ant na pāyo kinar* (B1, U1, J3, cf. A1; missing in B2). The translation of verse 6 reflects the version given in B1: *sūr dās sañg lakhī na jāi kachu khāt gvāl sāmar.* Other manuscripts, however, transpose the word *sañg* to the latter part of the line (*khāt gvāl sañg sāmar*). Given that arrangement, the line could also be understood to convey the idea that even such special persons as those listed in verse 5 are not vouchsafed a vision of Krishna eating with his cowherd friends.

P. 77. "*Rādhā, a look at your loveliness has him*"

MANUSCRIPTS: B1, B2, U1, B4, J2, J3, J4, A1 (twice). Sabhā 3067. I have alluded in chapter 3 to the important disparity between the final couplet of this poem as it appears in the Sabhā edition and as it appears in the old manuscripts. All manuscripts read *dūtikā* rather than *rādhikā* in verse 11, and all but one give some form of *kahe bacan* as its corresponding verb, followed by *sūr prabhu* at the beginning of line 12. Only J3 and J4 read approximately *suni suvacan bilās sūr ruci* as the Sabhā does. Other variations are of much less serious consequence. *Bhae bhay* in verse 4 should read either *bhae suni* or *suni bhae,* since only J3 and J4 support the Sabhā reading. B2 and B4 prefer *raṇadhīr/ranadhīr* to *ranavīr/raṇabīr/ranabīr* (J3, J4, A1, Sabhā) at the end of verse 5; J2 has *ranabhīr.* In verse 8 the martial imagery is strengthened by reading *jāṇi/jāni jadupati* (B1, B2, U1, B4, J2, J3, J4) rather than *dekhi giridhar.* A1 presents slight variants: *jāni vrajapati* in folio 1 and *dekhi yadupati* in folio 64. J2 and folio 64 of A1 read *gūpāl* or *gupāl* rather than *dayālu* in verse 10, but the remaining manuscripts stand with the Sabhā. B1 and U1 omit verses 5 and 6.

P. 80. *Listen, let me tell about Bṛṣabhānu's daughter*

MANUSCRIPTS: B4, J3, J4. Sabhā 2732. The manuscript readings are not generally different from those given by the Sabhā, but in two respects there is a significant divergence. First, Sabhā verses 11–14 are lacking in B4, J3, and J4. Since their inclusion seems required by the *nakh-śikh* convention, however, I have retained them in the translation. Second, the manuscripts reverse the order of Sabhā verses 7–8 and 9–10; hence the translation does the same. The Sabhā ordering is made possible by introducing verse 9 with the words *tā bic,* which has the effect of putting the forehead mark on an exact plane with the eyebrows. In the manuscripts, however, this mark is given its more natural position slightly above the eyebrows, and the verses describing it are given a correspondingly prior position. The verse numbered by the Sabhā as verse 9 (v. 7 in the manuscripts and the translation here) begins with a reference to the hair that has, according to its sequence in the manuscripts, just been described. The words *sundar alak* replace the Sabhā's *tā bic banī.* Additional alterations that affect the translation are minor: the existence of the word *pragaṭī* in verse 6 rather than *pasarī,* and of *vāri* at the end of line 10 (line 8 in B4, J3, J4, and the translation here) rather than *pāri.*

NOTES: The Three Cities' Foe (*tripurāri*) is Śiva, who is famed for his ascetic practices, among which that of sitting for extended periods of time under the hot sun and surrounded by fires is well known. The god's white color is from the ash that he smears on himself, another ascetic attribute. The poem refers to the ambrosial nectar (*amṛt, sudhā*) of the moon on two occasions. The idea is that the full moon is made to glow by this immortal substance, with which it shares a common name (*som*). The moon holds the liquid of immortality like a vessel, whose profile can be seen when it wanes toward its crescent shape. As the moon waxes and wanes, the vessel progressively fills and empties.

P. 82. *When Rādhā turns her mindful gaze*

MANUSCRIPTS: B1, B2, U1, B4, J3, J4, K1. Sabhā 2379. A number of differences between the manuscripts and the Sabhā text are of consequence to the meaning of the poem and its translation. In verse 2, the words beginning with *upacati* in the Sabhā edition are replaced with close approximations of the following, from B1: *rājati hai dvai sasi cār cakor.* The only appreciable variants are U1's *sis* and B2's *sās* for *sasi;* K1's *lāgat* for *rājati;* and, rather surprisingly, *āṭh* for *cār* in J3 and J4, which doubles the number of *cakor* birds. Verse 4 in the manuscripts corresponds to the Sabhā version, but verses 3, 5, and 6 diverge sufficiently from the printed text to warrant full quotation. Verse 3 is *saras madhup vai mukh le lobhī ḍol madhup jug jor* (B1, U1, B4, cf. B2), with minor variants near the beginning of the line in J3 (*sarasi ja mukh*), J3 (*saras madhup e mukh*), and K1 (*sāras mukh madhu*). Allowing for orthographic and inflectional variations, all manuscripts agree in presenting verse 5 as *līyai manorath rajanī āve vāḍhī ārati bhor,* except that U1 drops the first letter of *rajanī* and B4 substitutes *manohar* for *manorath* and *vālā* for *vāḍhī.* Verse 6 is *sūr dās prabhu ihai dasā din dampati vit cit cor.* Variants are U1's *sadā* and K1's *disā* for *dasā,* and J3's *baṃchit* for *dampati.* Probably we should understand *cit cit* rather than *vit cit* in B4 and J3; and J4 reads *cit vit* (or *citavit*).

NOTES: "The clever one who is wed to Passion" (*rati nāgar*) is Kāma. His name translates "Love" or "Lust"; that of his wife, Rati, translates "Passion." The reference in this context is not just to Kāma, of course, but to Krishna. The proverbial *cakor* bird lives only on the ambrosial light shed by the moon, which fits well with the present image since the moon, with its roundness and soft glow, is a frequent simile for a lovely face. A number of somewhat later poems, but still well within the "early" group, bear thematic comparison with this one: S 3088, 3274, *pariśiṣṭ* 93.

P. 86. *Why this sudden burst to bloom?*

MANUSCRIPTS: B1, B2, U1, B4, U2. Sabhā 2314. Verse 3 is substantially different in manuscript from the Sabhā version. I am translating *mūh kamān madan sar sādhi bigasit badan ju ādhe,* which all manuscripts approximate but for *mauh* (B4) or *mōh* (B1) at the outset and B4's substitution of *tilak* for *madan.* Verse 4 begins *citavani cāru bak avalokani* in all manuscripts. In verse 5, B1, U1, and U2 have *suk* in place of *siv* (B2, B4, Sabhā), and all manuscripts except B2 (*sobh*) have *simbhu* or *sambhu* rather than *sem. Śrī* is unanimously preferred to *sivā* in line 6.

P. 94. *Gopāl has slipped in and stolen my heart, friend.*

MANUSCRIPTS: J1, B1, B2, B3, U1, B4, J2, J3, J4, J5, A1. Sabhā 2490. The Sabhā edition departs from the best manuscript traditions only in relatively minor matters, few of which greatly alter the translation. Among those that might are the possible substitution of *ko jānai hari* (J1, J2, J3, J5) for *ko jānai ju* (in the remainder, cf. Sabhā) in verse 2, and of *bhuvan* for *bhavan* in verse 3 (so J1, B1, U1, B4). The word "wit" in verse 7 translates *bacan cāturī* (J1, cf. B1, U1, J3) rather than the Sabhā's *sahit saṃcyau paci.* In the last line *chiḍāi* is to be preferred over Sabhā's *curāi,* which only J2 approximates, but this changes the meaning little. The phrase that follows immediately is something like *citai hasi citabit,* not the Sabhā's *citai cit sajani.* The translation "look" construes *citabit* (U1, cf. B1, B3, A1) as *citavat,* as does J2, but this solution is not altogether satisfactory. B2 and B4 have adopted entirely different readings (*mohan, antar*), and J1 reads *citai haṃs vrat.*

P. 94. *I know, I know what fine qualities you have*

MANUSCRIPTS: J1, B2, U1, B4, J3, J4, A1, U2. Sabhā 3255. The almost identical readings of J1 and U1 are not always easy to rationalize: I have hewed to the readings that preponderate in other manuscripts, as reflected in the Sabhā edition, at the end of lines 1 and 2 (*bhare* and *ḍhare* rather than *nure* and *rure*) and in line 6 (*samujhi* raher than *sumuki*). Important manuscript departures from the Sabhā edition are the following: some version of *bali jāū̃* to replace *man mohan* in verse 2; *alas badan chabi* (J1, U1, cf. B2), as translated here, or *ālas bas sab* (J3, U2, cf. J4, A1) in place of *aru sram ālas* in verse 3; and *kāi tum kusal kisor nand nand sut* (J1, U1, but the second *nand* is probably to be excised as in B4, cf. B2) as against *tum ati kuṭil kisor nand sut* (J3, J4, U2, A1, cf. Sabhā) in verse 5. Verse 4, in which the translation follows J1 and U1 (cf. B2, B4) is sufficiently altered to bear quoting in its entirety: *candan tilak milyau vāhā bandan kām kuṭil kaṃc nakh ughare.* J3 and J4 (cf. U2, A1) present the line in a somewhat different shape: *candan tilak lagyo miṭi bandan syā̃m subhag tan nakh ughare.*

P. 95. *Every rhythm pulses to a different beat*

MANUSCRIPTS: B1, B2, B3, U1, J4, A1. Sabhā 3815. B2 inserts verse 5 before verse 3, but all other manuscripts support the Sabhā's verse order. In most other respects also the Sabhā is close to the manuscripts. The order of words varies considerably from manuscript to manuscript in verse 4, but the meaning is the same. The Sabhā's *kapūr* (camphor) in verse 5 is only found in J4; instead one has *kumkumā jal ur* (B1, cf. B2, U1) or *sīr kumkumā* (A1, cf. B3). Finally, only B2 supports the Sabhā's *amṛt bel* in verse 7; the rest have some form of *yah rati amrit latā suni sūrij* as the first portion of that line.

P. 95. *Seeing that Nanda has returned*

MANUSCRIPTS: J3, J4, K1. Sabhā 3746. In verse 1, all manuscripts have *jāni* rather than the Sabhā's *dekhi.* The conclusion of the line is problematical; I have translated *havai* (J3) *na* (K1) in place of the Sabhā's *lain* (so J4). Lines 3 and 4 depart somewhat from the Sabhā version in both manuscripts. The K1 reading, approximated in J3 and J4, is: *kahā rahyo navanītacor mero pūchat nāri naī/ tihi chin praphulit ati kumumedini māno mūlahū hem haī.*

P. 96. *The season of rains has come*

MANUSCRIPTS: B1, B2, B3, U1, A1. Sabhā 3935. U1 breaks off in the middle of the fifth verse, and A1 stops at the end of the fourth; B1, B2, and B3 contain the full poem. Alterations of word order and vocabulary affect the meaning that emerges from the Sabhā version only in the last line, where only A1 strongly suggests that Krishna will respond to the *gopī*'s plea and come to Braj. It uses the verb *āvahi* (cf. Sabhā *āvai*). Preferable is the more straightforward protest of B1: *sūr sabithā jaisai jāṇaigau jādo rāi.* B2 repeats this, but substitutes *suthith* for *subithā;* A1 has *sumati.*

P. 102. *Mādhav, give ear to what love is in Braj.*

MANUSCRIPTS: U1, J4, K1. Sabhā 4762. The order of verses translated here is that of U1 and J4, also adopted by the Sabhā. K1 places verses 5–6 before verses 3–4. The penultimate line is problematical in both manuscripts. Only J4 displays the Sabhā's *saneh arpan,* which I have translated. K1 approximates it with *sameh un kai,* but U1 has *samet ā̃nanu.* In the last line the word "love" translates not the Sabha's *prem,* which appears in neither manuscript, but U1's and J4's *bhajan,* i.e., *bhakti.* On the relation between these latter two, see chapter 6. K1 has *śobhā.* Other small departures from the Sabhā edition are the substitution of *vūjhi* for *sodhi* in verse 2 and the use of *dekhi* in place of *sumiri* in verse 6.

P. 104. *It's a wondrous thing to live in Braj*

MANUSCRIPT: U1. Sabhā 4174. Divergencies between the readings of U1 and the Sabhā's version are minimal—nothing more substantial than U1's *gāvat sujas harī ko* to replace *gāvat jas hari pī kau* in verse 5.

NOTES: Cf. S 4187,4339. Kānh is a familiar vernacularization for Krishna. The buttermilk (*chāch*) tax refers to the episode of the *dān līlā,* in which Krishna refused to let the *gopīs* pass on the path to Mathura where they were bound to sell their milk products. They could do so only if first they let him taste their goods.

P. 105. *If Hari dwells in each of us, within*

MANUSCRIPTS: J1, B1, B2, B3, U1, J2, J3, J4, A1, U2. Sabhā 4408. The meaning presented by the Sabhā version is changed in only one detail by the manuscript evidence: *aṃcal,* in verse 6, must be omitted, since no manuscript contains it. The phrase in which it occurs reads instead *giri kar kyō̃ na dharī* or a close analogue, except for two substitutions in regard to *kyō̃: kō̃* in U1 and *kayai* in B3. A noteworthy variant for *ham* in verse 4 is *hā̃si* or *hasi* (J1, J3, J4), and J1 is allowed to read *jarī* as the final word in verse 8 because it has not that but *barī* at the end of line 3. All other manuscripts read *bharī* in verse 8, with the exception of J3 (*barī*).

NOTES: Cf. S 4461. Indra is the god most closely associated with rain. The phrase "he lifts not a finger" is a reference to the episode in which, to protect Braj from Indra's rainy ravages, Krishna lifted up Mount Govardhan so that his cowherding friends and their animals could take shelter under it. Some versions of the story have it that he held the mountain up on a single finger, though the term here is merely *kar* (hand). The line contains a gentle pun on the word *giri,* which is both the noun "mountain" and the verb "to fall," here translated "crumble." A second pun is added in the Sabhā edition by means of the term *aṃcal,* which refers to an upper garment but also echoes *acal,* another term for mountain. *Giri aṃcal* would then mean both "the mountain fell" and "our garments fall away," alluding to the fact that as the *gopī*s cry, their tears are so plentiful that the upper portion of the cloth wrapped about them slips down under the weight of the deluge. The term I have translated with the words "yearning" and "[scorched with] separation" is *viraha.*

P. 106. *He's gone—to Mathura, I hear.*

MANUSCRIPTS: B1, B2, U1, J2, J3, J4. Sabhā 3599. In the first four verses the manuscripts are in close accord with the Sabhā edition, with the exception of the word *sukṛt,* at the beginning of verse 3. B1, B2, U1, and J2 adopt this rather than the Sabhā's *saṅkit;* J3 and J4 have *sakṛt.* Verses 5 and 6 are at substantial variance with the Sabhā's version. With the exception of J3 and J4, which take an entirely different course, all manuscripts have some approximation of *suphalak sut aise kari chāḍi* rather than *nandanandan tau aise lāgau* in verse 5, and *ko* rather than *kab* in verse 6, to fit the change of subject. The simile is as given by the Sabhā in B1 and U1 (*jyau jal purain pāt*), but B2 and J2 read *bin* in place of *jyau,* which changes the meaning substantially. Some commentators have interpreted the simile in a different way from that presented in the translation here, thinking that it makes a comparison between the splendid isolation of the lotus on a pond and Krishna's indifference to the *gopī*s in Mathura. That would be possible, but perhaps less likely, if one understood the subject of the sentence as Akrūr rather than Krishna.

NOTES: The son of Suphalak (Skt. Śvaphalka) is Akrūr, the messenger whom Kaṃsa sends from Mathura to fetch Krishna. The Sabhā version and two manuscripts (J3 and J4) do not mention him, leaving the *gopī* to focus her sense of loss on Krishna alone. It is worth quoting the variant of verses 5 and 6 presented in J3 and J4. Reading with J3, *ur dhakadhakī tab hi tẽ lāgī agam janāyo gāt / sūr dās svāmī ke calibāi jyau jantrī bin jantr sakāt.* The sense is something as follows:

Ever since I've learned that he's lost and gone
  my heart has begun this pounding:
Sūr Dās says, with my master away
  I'm like an instrument with no one to play.

P. 106. *Nandakumār's no longer in Braj.*

MANUSCRIPTS: B1, B2 (twice), B3, U1, J2, J4, A1. Sabhā 4004. The manuscripts are in fair unanimity, though sometimes B3 and A1 break off in an independent direction. They lack verses 5 and 6 altogether, and J4, which is closest to the Sabhā version, occasionally goes another. The translation reflects the readings of B1, B2, J2, and U1. These diverge from the Sabhā text at the following respects. In verse 2, *sukh sāgar* replaces the Sabhā's (and J4's) *sujān sakhi;* B3 and A1 have *sukh dāyak* instead. The line ends *tan ko priy pratihār* (U1; cf. B1, B2, B3), not as the Sabhā has it (cf. J2, J4). With minor variants, all manuscripts begin verse 4 with *ab tā binu,* as translated here, rather than *tā din tāi* (J4, Sabhā). All manuscripts except J2 and J4 prefer *bhavan* to *bhuvan* in verse 4, as does the Sabhā; for the reverse preference, see Sabhā 2490.3. In verse 5, *man haṭak* is more secure than *kachu aṭak* (J4, Sabhā); and all manuscripts agree that the final word in the line is to be understood as some form of *siṅgār,* not *agār.*

P. 107. *Having seen Hari's face, our eyes are opened wide.*

MANUSCRIPTS: J1, B1, B3, U1, J2, J4. Sabhā 4184. The manuscripts are in close agreement and present only minor departures from the Sabhā text, most of which are synonyms for what the Sabhā gives. One should read *aṭak* in place of *haṭak* early in verse 8, to avoid the repetition in the Sabhā's version. All manuscripts do so except B3, which is independent: *kare kahā ai kahe na mānat.*

P. 108. *Follow your own advice, why don't you?*

MANUSCRIPTS: J1, B1, B2, B3, U1, J2, J4, J5. Sabhā 4501. This poem is one of the more difficult to present because it exists in two distinct rescensions. In one (J1, B3, J5), the order is that of the Sabhā edition, with the complication that in the oldest manuscript of this group, J1, lines 5 and 6 have been conflated so that most of line 6 is missing. In the other rescension, the one translated here, the order of verses changes markedly at just this point. The lines numbered 5 and 7 in the Sabhā text are reversed, and the vocabulary of line 8 is somewhat altered, though the meaning remains essentially the same. At two points the manuscripts in both rescensions give readings that contrast to the ones that appear in the Sabhā version. In line 4, one should probably read *auru mṛg chālā* (J1, so B1, U1, cf. B2) rather than *mālā mṛg chālā* (B3, J5), but in any case not *mekhalā selī* with the Sabhā. B1, B2, and U1 give the following construction of what is translated here as verse 5, contrasting to the Sabhā's verse 7, and other manuscripts are in fair agreement: *udhau kahau su sā̃cī jānu bariṣā badhati pā̃camī gājai.* J1 has an appropriate *avadhi* in place of *badhati.*

NOTES: Aside from its decorative role, collyrium has the effect of enabling the eyes to open and close more easily. Ūdho wears none, has "unanointed eyelids," which is appropriate to his status as a yogi and is in accord with the frequent yogic practice of keeping the eyes closed, but contrasts to the *gopīs*' ability to keep their eyes constantly open (as other yogis attempt to do) in the hope of Krishna's return. Certain schools of meditative practice cultivate the awareness of an interior sound, but on that score too the *gopīs* have Ūdho bested, since their awareness is flooded by the fifth tone of the scale (*pā̃camī*)—the dominant, the sol—which is traditionally held to have amorous associations and therefore has a particular connection with the monsoon season, when separation from one's lover is most keenly felt. The mention of a whistle made from an animal's horn (*siṅgī*) in line 4 evokes the image of a Nāth Yogī, but the staff (*daṇḍ*) and antelope's skin (*mṛg chālā*) are more widely used among ascetics. The Sabhā's mention of an old cloth worn around the neck or waist (*mekhalā selī*) would consolidate the image of a Nāth Yogī, but the phrase does not appear in the old manuscripts. A more specific depiction of Ūdho as a Nāth Yogī can be found in the somewhat more recent S 4311, translated on page 146.

P. 109. *First teach yourself, you black honeybee*

MANUSCRIPTS: B3, U1, J2, J3, J4, A1. Sabhā 4231. Only minor variants set the manuscripts apart from the Sabhā version. Among the more meaningful are *kharo* in place of *mahā* in verse 2 (only J3 and J4 have *mahā*); *caranani* instead of *karanani* in verse 3 (the manuscripts are unanimous); and the possibility of favoring *kamal nayan ke saṅg* (B3, J2, A1) over *nandanandan ke saṅg* (U1, J3, J4) in verse 4.

P. 110. *Ūdho, hearts like ours can't change*

MANUSCRIPTS: B3, U1, J2, J4, A1. Sabhā 4346. In two places B3 and A1 present alternatives to the more predominant tradition (U1, J2, J4) that is accurately conveyed in the Sabhā edition and translated here. In B3 and A1 the final portion of line 3 in *hā hā triya lekhe nirmūl* and line 5 concludes with the words *koṭi yatan jo kīje.*

P. 111. *Those Mathura people, they're rife with vice.*

MANUSCRIPTS: J1, B1 (twice), B3, U1, J4, A1, K1, U2. Sabhā 4208. The manuscripts are not widely divergent and are in general accord with the Sabhā readings. In verse 3, however, one should probably prefer something like J1's *āye hai kahiyat braj udhau* to the Sabhā version, since the latter is supported only by the manuscript group consisting of B3, A1, and K1. In line 5, similarly, *sambhog* is to be preferred to *samyog,* which only those three manuscripts display, along with other changes in line 5 that the Sabhā does not reflect.

P. 112. *Ūdho, yoga is something we've had to endure*

MANUSCRIPTS: J4, J5, K1. Sabhā 4311. In contrast to normal practice, I have translated the version of this poem given in a single manuscript: K1. The order of verses that it presents differs somewhat both from what one finds in J4 and J5, which agree with one another, and in the Sabhā edition. All are in agreement through verse 8. At that point K1 adopts a sequence of verses that are numbered by the Sabhā as follows: 15–16, 9–10, 13–14, 17–18. J4 and J5 have the following sequence after verse 8: 11–12, 9–10, 15–16, 13–14, 17–18. In the translation given here, verses 15 ("The Lord of Passion . . .") and 13 ("Where, oh where . . .") each occupy two lines rather than the usual one. The couplet omitted by K1 (Sabhā vv. 11–12) should come directly after verse 8, according to J4 and J5, completing with definitive specificity the comparison between the *gopīs* and the Nāth Yogīs. It might be translated as follows:

> The senses seem senseless, and tasteless their joys,
> to those whose yogic penance is to fill with love's void,
> And tongues trained to taste the delights of love's banquet
> now shout out the sounds of Lord Gorakh, forlorn.

Here and there differences of wording pull the translation away from the Sabhā version. Among these are *sapnā* (dreams) in verse 3 rather than *sām jaṭ* (J5) or *sab tan* (J4, Sabhā); *karavar* (so J4, J5: "loss, misfortune," here translated "love's wound") in place of *karatal* in verse 7; *mantra* ("secret words") with the Sabhā but against J4 and J5 (*prem*) in verse 15; *ramat na* ("not in pleasure") with J5 but against J4 and the Sabhā in verse 9; and *tatva* (so J4, cf. J5: "worth") as a replacement for the Sabhā's *tumahī* in verse 17. K1 has *kahiyau jai sades,* i.e., *sandes* (message) at the end of verse 16 rather than J4's *andes* or J5's *ādes,* both of which become more appropriate as situated in those manuscripts than *ādes* is in the Sabhā version since they lead to the command the Sabhā has placed in verse 14. Finally, K1 chooses the adjective *jhūṭho* (useless, used-up) for the concluding phrase in verse 18 rather than the Sabhā's *phokaṭ* or J5's *chūchau,* both of which contrast to J4's *pūran.*

P. 132. *Master, my mind is absent and lost.*

MANUSCRIPTS: B2, U1, B4, J4. Sabhā 103. Lines 3–6 are given in different orders in different manuscripts, and none agrees with the Sabhā version. I have followed the oldest manuscript, B2, in which verses 5–6 are reversed with respect to the Sabhā edition. The Sabhā order for verses 3–6 is altered as follows in U1: 5, 4, 6, 3; B4 and J4 have 5, 6, 4, 3. The first half of verse 5 is difficult in U1 (*kavan kājī*) and B2 (*kāl kāval kāraṇ*), so I have accepted the versions of B4 (*kavar kuvar kāraṇ*) and J4 (*kor kor ke kāj*); cf. Sabhā.

P. 133. *My soul, abandon the blandishments of flesh.*

MANUSCRIPTS: J1 (twice), B2, U1, B4, J4, J5. Sabhā 59. The Sabhā reading *ant hi kapaṭ* (v. 2) differs from all manuscripts, which have *ant ki pās,* as translated here, with one exception: J1 (fol. 51). I follow J1 (fol. 51), U1, B4, and B2 in reading *anaṅg taraṅg* rather than the Sabhā's *antar gahat* at the beginning of verse 3.

P. 135. *Soul, turn your back on those who shun the Lord.*

MANUSCRIPTS: B3, U1, J2, J4, J5, A1. Sabhā 332. The Sabhā version of this poem is longer by two lines than any contained in the manuscripts, with the exception of U1, whose entry is yet a line longer than the Sabhā's. In U1, however, there is considerable confusion. At verse 6 its rhyme scheme changes entirely, and the lines that follow are strange to any recorded elsewhere; moreover verse 2, which parallels the Sabhā's, is a marginal insertion. The remaining manuscripts agree in omitting lines 2 and 6 of the Sabhā's edition, giving the six-line poem translated here. Because the poem is constructed entirely of stock images, there is very little alteration in meaning even if individual words and phrases vary from one manuscript to another. The one minor substantive variant comes in verse 5 (Sabhā v. 7). Whereas B3 and A1 display the Sabhā's reading *pāhān patit,* as translated here, J2 has *pāpī pāhān* and J4 and J5 have *jyau pāhān.* To arrive at the Sabhā's version, the following lines should be inserted after verses 1 and 4 respectively:

The company of those who think of evil things
  and sully the singing of God's songs.

Or an elephant—why bother to bathe it in the stream?
  It will only turn to its accustomed bath of mud.

Pp. 137, 149. *Syām is solely the patron of the poor.*

MANUSCRIPTS: B2, U1, B4. Sabhā 19. The version of B2 and U1, translated on p. 137, is ordered quite differently from the Sabhā's version, which follows that of B4 translated on p. 149. U1 and B4 agree in assigning the half-line concerning Kubjā to verse 3, though they differ in other respects. The Sabhā, however, avoids mention of Kubjā in both lines 3 and 5. It seems to follow B4's *sācī prīt cātak* in verse 5 and to give an analogue of B2's *hari jī prīti ka lāhik* or U1's *hari jī pati ke lāhak* in verse 3. B2 omits the line in which Kubjā occurs, probably inadvertently, since the result is a five-line poem. Mention of other variants is made in the text.

P. 139. *Nandanandan has bought me, redeemed me*

Manuscripts: B4, J4. Sabhā 171. The translation accords with the Sabhā version, which is close to both manuscripts, but several points deserve mention. J4 reverses the order of verses 3 and 4; B4 agrees with the Sabhā sequence. In verse 4, the meaning of J4's *cakra ke cihn* is the same as Sabhā's *mudrā cakra,* whereas B4 has *līlā cakra.* In verse 6 both manuscripts prefer a designation of Krishna (J4: *svāmī;* B4: *prabhu)* to Sabhā's *kāu* and vary independently in other respects, but B4's meaning, despite its reading *vāy* for *khāi,* is close to the Sabhā's.

P. 140. *Now I have danced too much, Gopāl.*

Manuscripts: J1, B2, B3, U1, B4, J4, J5, A1, U2. Sabhā 153. The Sabhā text is in general quite close to this critical reconstruction, except that the position of lines 4 and 6 is reversed. There are a few additional contrasts. In verse 3, "sham" translates *ḍimbh* (J1, B4) or *ḍambh* (U1, J4; cf. *ḍāmbh,* J5, and *hambh,* B2) and replaces the Sabhā's *mahā* (so B3, A1, U2). In the same verse *bāndhe* (J1, cf. B4) is preferred to *bājat* (Sabhā, cf. B3, J4, J5, A1, U2). In verse 6, *ke* (or *kī*) is chosen over the Sabhā's *dai,* for which there is no manuscript authority. Verse 7 reads *sabahī kalā kāchi dikhalāi aru pūraṇ agh jāl* with B2 and U1 (cf. B4), rather than the later version (B3, A1, and U2) adopted by the Sabhā.

Notes: This translation is much indebted to the one offered by Kenneth E. Bryant for the Sabhā version in *Poems to the Child-God,* pp. 205–6, as a number of borrowed words and phrases make evident.

P. 143. *Life has filtered away in a thousand tiny bothers—*

Manuscripts: J1, B2, B3, U1, J2, J4, J5, A1, U2. Sabhā 292. In verse 3, the manuscripts refer in various ways to a trap set by knotting together pieces of grass. As against Sabhā's *gā̃ti,* J1 reads *kā̃s bā̃ḍhyau* and B2 has *kandī.* The others are content with a variant of the more general term *phand.* J1, J2, J4, and J5 support the Sabhā's *māyā,* but B2, B3, U1, A1, and U2 prefer *moh,* "delusion." The translation of verse 5 reflects *kāchi* (Sabhā, B2, J5), which would account best for the variants *nāc* (J1) on the one hand and *kachi* (U1, J2) on the other. B3, U2, and A1 share a totally different line in verse 5, and J4 omits it altogether.

P. 144. *Life goes well for those who sing of Hari.*

MANUSCRIPTS: U1, B4, J4, J5. Sabhā 233. One scribe (J5) has corrected the last line to produce a reading that would accord with the first translation given. He substitutes *mili* for *prabhu*: *sūr dās mili sādh samāgam.* Among other manuscript variations, perhaps the most noticeable occurs in the title line. Only J5 agrees with the Sabhā in making *rām* the object of the verb "to sing." U1 and J4 have *hari gun;* B4 has *gopāl hi.*

Pp. 145, 176. *Songs to Hari work great wonders*

MANUSCRIPT: B2. Sabhā 235. It is unfortunate that the single manuscript in which this poem occurs is B2, since that scribe often gives weak, even demonstrably mistaken readings. *Sis* for the Sabhā's *sasi* and *har* for *aru* in verse 5 seem to be cases in point, and a puzzling *a* is found in *adham nīc a vyādh gaṇikā* (v. 4), replacing the Sabhā's *ajāmil aru bhīl ganikā.* Although B2's refrain establishes song (*bhajan*) as the subject of the poem in the same words as the Sabhā's does, there is less direct emphasis on singing as such in the body of the *pad* than in the Sabhā version. Instead of *bhajan kau paratāp* in line 3, B2 has *hari kai caraṇ kau paratāp;* rather than *nigam jākau sujas gāvat* in line 7, B2 has *ved jākī sākhi bolai.*

NOTES: The reference to the power of devotional song in verse 3 evidently concerns the prayer offered to Rām by Jāmbavān, as reported in various versions of the *Rāmāyaṇa.* In it he sings of Rām's power to ferry all beings across the sea of life, which then inspires the bears and monkeys in Rām's entourage to believe that they can float trees and great rocks on the ocean, creating the bridge to Laṅkā that was required for Rām's army to rescue Sītā.

P. 147. *What did you do to deserve that day?*

MANUSCRIPTS B2, B3, U1, J4, J5, A1. Sabhā 77. The Sabhā version is quite close to that preserved in the majority of the manuscripts, as translated here. B2 and U1 occasionally present minor exceptions, as at the beginnings of verses 4, 6, and 8; U1 omits line 7. Variations between B3, J4, J5, and A1 scarcely affect the meaning at any point. In verse 4, I have followed B3, J4, and A1 (and therefore the Sabhā) more closely than B2 and U1, which have *dharati āpu gagan bāy tej racyo tan* (U1). In verse 5, no manuscript includes mention of the Sabhā's *sraun.* The translation of the first half of verse 8 is based on the following: *sūr suhṛd mani īsvar agraj gani.* The word *suhṛd* appears in B3, A1, and J5 and can be inferred to have been the basis of B2's *sai de.* U1 also seems to have had *suhṛd* in a source. It reads *sūr dāsu hridai,* but the spelling *dāsu* is somewhat uncharacteristic for this scribe; *dās* is more normal. It appears he has inserted *dā* before an original *suhrid.* This leaves J4 as the one genuinely dissenting version: *sūr hṛdai mā̃hi.* The word *mani* appears in B2, B3, U1, and A1, and is to be preferred over *mā̃hi* or *mahi* (J4, J5) or *māni* (Sabhā). One must follow B2, U1, and J4 in reading *agraj gani* rather than *antaryāmī* with B3, A1, and the Sabhā. If one had followed the Sabhā's version, closer to B3 and A1, the last line might have been translated:

So listen, fool, release and erase
  your cheating, lying, willful ways:
Sūr Dās says, your companion is God,
  the friend who knows each inner mood.

P. 150. *Today's the showdown, and I'm not going to flinch*

MANUSCRIPTS: U1, B4, J2, J4, A1. Sabhā 134. The translation follows U1 and J2, whose readings are in tolerable agreement with each other and not markedly different from those supplied in the Sabhā edition. From this J4 occasionally diverges, and B4 and A1 more frequently. All manuscripts read *ek kod* in verse 1 rather than the Sabhā's *ek-ek,* except A1, which has simply the deficient *ek.* In verse 2, *nāgar* (U1, J2) is to be preferred to the Sabhā's *mādhau* (so A1). None of the manuscripts supports the Sabhā's *nacyau* in verse 4—in U1 and J2 one finds *kahyau* instead—and the preceding word, *ughari,* is found ony in U1 (*ughāri*). J2 substitutes the mildly divergent *ubhari* at this point, and the others, as if to avoid scandal, adopt quite different readings. Sabhā's verse 5 approximates U1, J2, and J4, except for *kat apanī,* for which should be substituted *tum hī to* (U1, J2, cf. J4). The first half of the last line is reconstructed as *sūr dās tab hī pai uṭhihāu,* which is U1's reading but for *tab* (U1: *jab*) and is approximated in J2 and, somewhat less closely, J4. No manuscript confirms the Sabhā's repetition of the concept *patit* in verse 6.

NOTES: Kenneth Bryant translates the Sabhā's version of this poem in *Poems to the Child-God,* p. 206. The present translation is indebted to his at several points. The poem seems to imply that the core of Hari, his adamantine inmost jewel (*hari hīrā,* v. 5), is to be understood as his ability to rescue the fallen. This is the foundation for his most exalted reputation and the reason that his self-confidence is rightly destroyed if Sūr is too great a sinner for him to save.

P. 151. *I, only I, am best at being worst, Lord*

MANUSCRIPTS: U1, B4, J2, J4, J5. Sabhā 138. All manuscripts depart from the line order established in the Sabhā edition by inserting after the first verse a distant cousin of Sabhā's verse 5. For that verse U1 reads *vār na kou saṅg calat hāu calat savani mai līkau.* Other manuscripts adopt slightly different phrasings, most with *segh karan* (*sedh karan*?) instead of *saṅg calat.* I follow U1 in verse 5, a stronger reading than that given in the remaining manuscripts. Not all of the four cardinal sinners mentioned in U1 are the same as those listed in Sabhā's verse 3. On their identities, see below.

NOTES: In verse 5, the vulture (*gīdh*) is Jaṭāyu, who fought to prevent Rāvaṇ from carrying away Sītā in the *Rāmāyaṇa* but was mortally wounded in the combat. Rām performed his obsequies and ushered him into heaven. The prostitute (*ganikā*) to whom reference is made is probably Piñgalā. Various stories are told about prostitutes of this name. According to one, Piñgalā was granted salvation despite her moral laxity on the basis of teaching her parrot to repeat the name of Rām. According to another, a prostitute called Piñgalā attempted to lure away the righteous Rām himself, was cursed by Sītā, but then forgiven by Rām through the granting of a birth in the presence of Krishna in her next life. It is likely that the poet had in mind specific persons such as Jaṭāyu and Piñgalā in referring to the hunter (*byādh*) and the tyrant (*nṛpati,* "king") as well, but their identities are not plain to me. It would also be possible to construe this list in a more general way—"vultures, hunters, tyrants, whores"—since these are roles in life that imply ethically questionable acts.

P. 156. *In the realm of the fallen, Hari, I am king*

MANUSCRIPTS: J4 (twice). Sabhā 144. In verse 3, the J4 versions differ from the Sabhā's at two points: they have *ras bhṛtya* or *ras bhṛtti* instead of *ru subhat* and *kaṣī* instead of *khaḍga.* The Sabhā reading is also attractive:

> Appetite is this land's appropriate name,
> desires are the warriors, their weapons the senses.

J4 prefers the ironic *sumati* to the Sabhā's *kumati* (bad advice) in verse 4, and verse 6 is markedly different. J4 (fol. 291) reads: *bhūpati gyā̃n bhagyo nij mū taji asat sāmati pati īs.* Folio 295 corrects the verse, I believe, by reading *bhū* for *mū* and *sañgatti* for *sāmati.* Note that the Urdu *phauj* in the Sabhā version disappears. In line 7, J4 versions read *mahī* for *mayā, jīte* for *bandī,* and *bandī* for *māgadh.* The last line is: *sūr birad nij gaḍh kari rākhyo ant kāl kīvār* (or, *kī bār*).

P. 164. *Danced, I have danced before you*

MANUSCRIPTS: J1, B2, B3, U1, B4, J4, J5, A1. Sabhā 174. The Sabhā's *bahut* (v. 1) is absent in the manuscripts, all of which have some form of *hū* or *hõ* except for B4 and J4 (*hī*). In verse 2, I have translated B3's *suni din dāni dayālu dev maṇi,* which is approximated in J4 and A1 and, with the substitution of *muni* for *maṇi,* in U1, B4, and J5. J1 and B2 read *damodar* (i.e., *dāmodar*) in place of *dev maṇi*. Other significant departures from the Sabhā's edition are to read, with most manuscripts, some version of *jal thal mahi* (J1) instead of *jāne māi* in verse 3 and to adopt *gūḍh* in place of *kāchi* in verse 4.

NOTES: It is tempting to accept Mātāprasād Gupta's suggestion that *baḍ* in verse 2 is to be understood as *biḍ* (Skt. *viṭa*), a voluptuary, buffoonish companion at a dissolute, sensuous court, rather than as *baḍ*, "twaddle, palaver," though all manuscripts except J4 give either *baḍ* or *vaḍ*. Mātāprasād Gupta, ed., *Sūrsāgar,* p. 146.

P. 165. *I'm pleading with you to turn, hear this wretch*

MANUSCRIPTS: U1, J4, J5. Sabhā 42. In general, the manuscripts are close to the Sabhā reading. Occasionally vocabulary differs, but the meaning is essentially the same, as in the case of *saṭī* for *lakuṭi* (v. 2), *asaṅkhit* (J4, J5, cf. U1) for *kari kari* (v. 5), and *man* for *ātmā* (v. 6). The substitution of some version of *jamunikā dai mukh* for *karāvati prabhu jū* in verse 4 and *kul badhu* for *par-badhū* in verse 8 clarifies the meaning. I follow the Sabhā in preferring *mahā mohinī* (U1) to *moh rūpī mohinī* (J4, J5) in verse 7 and in choosing *pati* (J4, J5) in verse 9 over the metrically awkward *mahīpati* (U1), perhaps a product of dittography.

P. 169. *Unless we love the Lord we're like dogs and pigs*

MANUSCRIPTS: U1, J2, J4, J5. Sabhā 357. All manuscripts reverse the order of Sabhā lines 2 and 3. Verse 2 (Sabhā v. 3) contains a difficult expression replacing the Sabhā's *gīdhinī.* It appears in various manuscripts as *gahahuvā, gahaduvā, gahadūvā,* and *gahaḍūvā,* and is probably to be rationalized, as Mātāprasād Gupta has done, with the meaning "owl" (Gupta, *Sūrsāgar,* p. 292). The manuscripts lack the male-female pairs that the Sabhā presents in this line. The three animals mentioned in verse 3 (Sabhā v. 2) are found in J2, J4, and J5; U1 lacks the mongoose; none has the Sabhā's mouse (*mūsā*). U1 concludes the poem by listing the names of four animals without syntax: camels, bullocks, donkeys, and water buffaloes. The Sabhā version makes place for an element of syntax (*manau*) by failing to mention the donkey, but the list given in the remaining manuscripts is more convincing still. The two well-tempered domestic animals are omitted, as Thomas Ridgeway has pointed out to me, leaving the more disagreeable camels and asses; and a full syntax is provided, appropriate to the poem's conclusion: *jyāu ũṭ khar vaise* (J4, cf. J2).

P. 173. *Time after time I've deceived myself*

MANUSCRIPTS: B3, B4, J2, J4. Sabhā 326. None of the manuscripts directly supports the Sabhā's *avani* in verse 3, but their meaning is probably not far removed. *Mṛchan* (B4, J4) and *machan* (B3) seem best construed as having to do with dry land (Skt. *mṛtsnā, mṛtsnam*), as their stand-in *avani* implies, rather than with fish; J2 has *acan.* In verse 4, the Sabhā's *tin māi* approximates B4's *tin pahi,* but *jan jan pai* (B3, J2, cf. J4) is probably to be preferred. In the second half of verse 8, I have followed J2 (*kāl byāl gahi pūch khavāyo;* cf. B3) against B4 and J4 which, though divergent, more closely approximates the Sabhā version: "you'll find yourself bitten by the viper of time."

Sūr Dās sings for Krishna. Poster illustration printed by S. S. Brijbasi & Sons, Bombay.

Glossary

Ajāmil: legendary Brahmin who forsook home and family obligations for a dissolute life with a prostitute, but was nevertheless granted salvation by Viṣṇu/Krishna

Arjun: one of the Pāṇḍava brothers and a chief protagonist in the *Mahābhārata,* in whose service Krishna acted as adviser and charioteer

aṣṭachāp: "eight seals," the eight poets, including Sūr Dās, who are most highly revered in the Vallabha Sampradāy

Balarām: Krishna's elder brother

bel: the wood-apple tree, sacred to Śiva, whose fruit is considered in traditional Indian pharmacology to have various medicinal properties

bhagat: see *bhakta*

bhagavant bhajan: singing to or of God

Bhāgavata Purāṇa: ninth- or tenth-century Purana whose description of Krishna's life subsequently became the standard scripture for many Vaiṣṇavas

bhajan: song or singing addressed to God

bhakta: one who is devoted to, who loves God

Bhaktamāl: early (ca. 1600 A.D.) hagiographical anthology focusing on the lives of medieval Indian saints

bhakti: devotion, love, love of God or by God

bhramargīt: songs of, or to, the bee, addressed by the *gopīs* to Ūdho on his visit to Braj

Bījak: a collection of the verse of Kabīr made by members of the Kabīr Panth, centering in the eastern Hindi-speaking regions

bintī: request, plea; see *vinaya*

binu (Hindi *binā*): without, unless

Braj: deriving from the Sanskrit *vraja,* "cowherd encampment"; hence the grazing country where Krishna grew up, in the environs of (but considered by many not to include) Mathura

Braj Bhāṣā: dialect of Hindi spoken in Braj and for four centuries the most familiar idiom for Hindi poetry

Brindavan (Brindāvan): basil forest where Krishna is said to have danced the *rās;* now a pilgrimage center consecrating the spot, on the Jumna north of Mathura

Bṛṣabhānu: father of Rādhā

Caitanya: Bengali Brahmin saint (1486–1533 A.D.) considered by his followers an incarnation of Rādhā and Krishna, who rejected traditional brahminical learning in favor of simply reciting the names of Krishna

cakor: mythological bird said to feed only on moonbeams

campā: tree known for both its beauty and its fragrance, which is anomalous in that its flowers do not attract bees

Caṇḍīdās: fifteenth-century (?) Bengali lyricist, some of whose poems are dedicated to Krishna

devanāgarī: the script in which Sanskrit and Hindi are normally written

Dhruv: prince who as a boy withdrew from his royal status and joined a group of sages, practicing stern austerities in the hope of gaining a favor from Viṣṇu. This was accomplished when Viṣṇu, seeing the child's devotion, raised him to celestial status, where he can be seen today as the polestar.

Dvaraka (Dvārakā): city on the western coast of India over which Krishna reigned in his mature years

ghī: clarified butter

Gokul: place where Krishna spent his infancy, identified in the Vallabha Sampradāy with a village across the river from Mathura

Gopāl: cowherd; title of Krishna

gopī: one of the cowherding women or girls of Braj

Govardhan: the sacred mountain of Braj, located west of Mathura

Govardhannāthjī: Krishna as "Lord of Mount Govardhan," which he is said to have lifted; the image of Krishna originally installed in the temple atop the mountain

Hari: title of Viṣṇu/Krishna, frequently interpreted as meaning "the one who takes away" sin or evil

Harirāy: fourth-generation descendant of Vallabhācārya who composed a commentary on the *Caurāsī Vaiṣṇavan kī Vārtā;* traditional dates 1590–1715 A.D.

Indra: tempestuous king of the gods in Vedic times who, though he retained the title, was demoted in subsequent Indian religious history. Especially associated with thunder and storms, he showered seven days of rain on the people of Braj in response to a change in their religious practice, whereupon Krishna lifted Mount Govardhan to shelter them

Jāmbavān: the wise king of the bears who aided Rām in his campaign to conquer Laṅkā

Jaṭāyu: vulture who fought Rāvaṇ to prevent him from abducting Sītā

Jumna (Sanskrit, Yamunā): the great river of Braj, conceived as a female divinity and sister of the Ganges

Kabīr: the most influential *nirguṇa* poet of medieval North India; traditional dates 1440–1518 A.D.

Kām (Kāma): god personifying *kām* (Sanskrit, *kāma*), love in the sense of desire, particularly sexual desire

Kaṃsa: demonic king who usurped the throne of Mathura, archenemy of Krishna

Kānh: corruption of "Krishna" and familiar name for him
Karṇa: half-brother of the Pāṇḍavas who took the side of the Kauravas in the *Mahābhārata* war out of a special rivalry with Arjun, whom he vowed to kill but by whom he himself was slain
Kosala (Kośala): territory in the Gangetic basin of which Ayodhyā was the capital and the family of Rām the rulers
Kubjā: hunchback, specifically the hunchback woman who greeted Krishna with unguents upon his arrival in Mathura, whereupon Krishna removed her deformity
kumkum: powder applied by women as decorative marks to their foreheads; at best, made of saffron
Kurukṣetra: place northwest of Delhi that was the site of the battle of the *Mahābhārata* and the spot where, according to some, Krishna reunited briefly with his loved ones from Braj
līlā: play, both in the sense of "fun" or "game" and in the sense of "drama"; especially the activity of God, since it is motivated by no concern for reward
Madan: intoxicating; a name of Kām
Mādhav: a title of Krishna whose derivation is disputed. Usually it is taken as a patronymic referring to Madhu, a putative Yādav ancestor of Krishna
Madhuban: small pilgrimage site and place of retreat near Mathura; sometimes the term is also used to refer to the Mathura region in general
Mahābhārata: the Great Epic of India, detailing the internecine struggle between the Pāṇḍavas and their cousins, the Kauravas
mān: mood of anger, pique, or sulking felt on the part of a woman who believes herself to have been mistreated by her lover
Manmohan: beguiler of the heart (or mind); a title of Krishna
Mathura (Mathurā): ancient trading and pilgrimage center on the Jumna south of Delhi, at the heart of (but by many not considered a legitimate part of) Braj
Māyā (*māyā*): magic or illusion, depending upon one's point of view; that power by means of which Viṣṇu or Brahman adumbrates the phenomenal world; often personified as female
Mīrā Bāī: legendary princess of Citor to whom substantial amounts of Hindi, Rajasthani, and Gujarati verse are attributed; traditional dates 1547–1614 A.D.
Mohan: winsome, beguiling; a title of Krishna that sometimes stands in for a longer title: Madanmohan, "the one who beguiles [even] Kām"
Muralī: Krishna's flute, personified as a woman
Nāgarīpracāriṇī Sabhā: institution established in Benares for the advancement of literature written in Indian languages, especially Hindi
Nāmdev: fourteenth or fifteenth century lower-caste Maharashtrian *sant* to whom poems in both Hindi and Marathi are attributed
Nanda: foster father of Krishna in Braj, husband of Yaśodā
Nandakumār: son of Nanda; i.e., Krishna

Nandanandan: the joy of Nanda; a title of Krishna
Nārāyaṇ: title of Viṣṇu/Krishna
naṭ: a class of acrobats and impromptu performers with whom Krishna is sometimes associated
Nāth Yogī: one of a group of renunciants who trace their spiritual lineage back to Gorakhnāth
Navanītapriyajī: Krishna as "the one who is fond of fresh butter"; tutelary deity of Viṭṭhalnāth, housed originally at Gokul
nirguṇa: without qualities; the view that God cannot be positively conceived
nirguṇī: advocate of *nirguṇa bhakti*
pad: verse form involving lines of variable length whose final syllables either adopt a single rhyme or rhyme by couplets, and whose final or penultimate line normally includes the signature (*chāp*) of the composer
Pāṇḍavas: one faction in the great war described in the *Mahābhārata*
Piṅgalā: prostitute who was granted a seemingly unearned salvation
Purana (*purāṇa*): one of a group of texts that recount the great events that happened of old (the literal meaning of the word is "old"), among them the story of Krishna
puṣṭimārga: the way of grace and fulfillment; the term designating the soteriology of Vallabhācārya
Pūtanā: demoness with poisoned breasts whom Kaṃsa deputed to suckle the infant Krishna
Rādhā: the most beloved among Krishna's milkmaid sweethearts, often considered as fully his consort
Rādhikā: diminutive of Rādhā
Rām (Rāma): Rāmacandra, usually counted the seventh avatar of Viṣṇu and the last to precede Krishna; occasionally also Balarām; and often, especially in the phrase *rām nām,* a general designation for God
Ramāpati: lord (or husband) of Ramā; i.e., Lakṣmī; a title of Viṣṇu/Krishna
rās: Krishna's circle dance with the *gopī*s
rās līlā: Krishna's circle dance with the *gopī*s and the musical dramas that take as their starting point the imitation of that dance
Rukmiṇī: chief queen of Krishna as king of Dvaraka
sabad (*śabda*): the interior "word" by means of which the *satguru* reveals himself to those he chooses
Sabhā: Kāśī Nāgarīpracāriṇī Sabhā, publishers of the currently standard edition of the *Sūr Sāgar*
sādh (*sādhu*): good, righteous, therefore a term used by Sūr as a synonym for *sant;* in modern parlance, a religious ascetic
saguṇa: with qualities; the view that divine beings can be known and properly worshipped through their attributes
saguṇī: advocate of *saguṇa bhakti*
sākhī: a witnessing; the term applied to the trenchant couplets of Kabīr
sampradāy: teaching tradition, religious community, especially one of the

communities who consider themselves to have been established by religious figures in sixteenth-century Braj

saṅgrahātmak: organized according to groupings, especially those having to do with incidents in Krishna's life and genres of poetry addressed to him

sant: good, true; a term commonly used to describe poets and devotees of the *nirguṇa* persuasion in medieval North India but which had a somewhat wider application at the time

satguru (*sadguru*): the interior "true teacher" whose veneration is a hallmark of the *sant* tradition

satsaṅg: the community of "the good," those who worship the Lord; in later parlance, a religious gathering of those whose beliefs and practice follow *sant mat,* the perspective thought to be shared by such great *sant*s as Kabīr and Nānak

satsaṅg: the community of "the good," those who worship the Lord; in later parlance, a religious gathering of those whose beliefs and practice follow *sant mat,* the perspective thought to be shared by such great *sant*s as Kabīr and Nānak

Sītā: wife of Rām

Śiva: great god of the Hindu pantheon, who combines the contradictory properties of pure asceticism and pure eroticism, but who in Braj is usually understood as prototype of the former

skandha: heap, pile; the designation used for the twelve books of the *Bhāgavata Purāṇa*

skandhātmak: organized according to *skandha*

śloka: the most familiar form of Sanskrit verse

Śrī: the goddess who personifies fortune, luck, auspiciousness; consort of Viṣṇu

Subodhinī: commentary on the *Bhāgavata Purāṇa* by Vallabhācārya

śuddhādvaita: true non-dualism; the general term that designates the philosophy of Vallabhācārya

Śuk: intellectually talented son of Vyās whose entire life was spent in search of saving knowledge, for the sake of which he endured long study, far journeys, and severe ascetic practice

sumiran (Hindi, *smaraṇ*): memory, remembering; therefore, in a devotional context, worship or attention

Syām (Śyām): dark; a title of Krishna

tamāl: flowering tree chosen for comparison with Krishna because of its black bark

tilak: auspicious mark applied to the center of the forehead, often in a specifically religious setting

tulsī: a bush or small tree that is a member of the basil family and is considered to be sacred to Viṣṇu/Krishna

Tulsī Dās: major Hindi poet and devotee, principally, of Rām; traditional dates 1543–1623 A.D.

Ūdho (Sanskrit, Uddhava): messenger Krishna sends from Mathura to

Braj to urge the *gopīs* not to pine after him, but rather to recognize his presence in their hearts by means of yogic discipline and refined knowledge

Vaiṣṇava: worshipper of Viṣṇu or any of his avatars, including Krishna and Rām

Vallabha, Vallabhācārya: saint and philosopher who traveled to Braj and whose descendants became the leaders of the Vallabha Sampradāy; traditionally considered the guru of Sūr Dās and dated to 1478–1531 A.D.

Vallabha Sampradāy: religious community that takes Vallabhācārya as its founder

vārtā: conversation, account; a genre of prose, often including poetry as well, in which the early sectarian works of the Vallabha Sampradāy were written

Veda: literally "knowledge," the collective name of the most ancient Hindu scriptures

Vidur: the wisest man in the *Mahābhārata,* but a halfbreed because born of a union between Vyās, who was a Brahmin, and a Śudra woman. Krishna visited him in his humble hut and accepted peelings offered him by Vidur's wife, who was at home alone and was thoroughly flustered by the visit of so great a personage

Vidyāpati: Sanskrit and Maithili poet, many of whose compositions concern Krishna; traditionally dated 1352–1448 A.D.

vikram: i.e., *vikram saṃvat,* the indigenous dating system most frequently employed in India; said to be calculated from the victory of Vikramāditya of Ujjain over the Śakas in the first century B.C.

vinaya: petition; a genre of verse in which the poet addresses complaint, petition, and/or praise to God

viraha: the separation of loved ones and the anguish it causes

virahiṇī: woman who is a victim of *viraha*

Viṣṇu: great god of the Hindu pantheon, for Vaiṣṇavas the ultimate summation of divinity. Krishna is either considered one of his avatars or, more familiarly in Braj, coextensive with him

Viṭṭhalnāth: second son of Vallabhācārya, generally credited with having fixed the ritual and social organization of the Vallabha Sampradāy; traditional dates 1551–1640 A.D.

viyoga: disjunction, separation; especially the separation of lovers

viyoginī: woman who is a victim of *viyoga*

Vyās: the legendary sage who is said to have narrated the *Mahābhārata* and to have arranged the Puranas

Yādav: clan formed by the descendants of Yadu, of which Krishna is a member

Yaśodā: foster mother of Krishna in Braj, wife of Nanda

Bibliography

Abbott, Justin, E., and N. R. Godbole, trans. *Stories of Indian Saints: English Translation of Mahipatti's Marathi Bhaktavijaya.* 2 vols. Poona Scottish Mission Industries, 1934.

Abū l'Faẓl 'Allāmī. *The Ā'īn-i Akbarī.* Translated by H. Blochmann. 1871. Delhi: Aadesh Book Depot, 1965.

Agnihotrī, Śail Bālā. *Sūr-Sāhitya kā Manovaijñānik Vivecan.* Kanpur: Abhilāṣā Prakāśan, 1977.

Al Badāonī. *Muntakhabu-t-tawārīkh.* 1898–99. 3 vols. Translated and edited by George S. A. Ranking, W. H. Lowe, and T. Wolseley Haig. Delhi: Idarah-i-Adabiyat-i-Delli, 1973.

Allchin, F. R., trans. *The Petition to Rām.* London: George Allen & Unwin, 1965.

———. "The Place of Tulsī Dās in North Indian Devotional Tradition." *Journal of the Royal Asiatic Society* (1966), parts 3 and 4, pp. 123–40.

Ānandavardhana. *Dhvanyāloka.* Benares: Haridās Sanskrit Series, 1940.

Ārya, Rāmsvarūp, and Girirājśaraṇ Agravāl, eds. *Sūr Sāhitya Sandarbh.* Bijnaur: Sūr Paṃcśatī Samiti, 1976.

Ātreya, Kamalā. *Ādhunik Manovijñān aur Sūr-Kāvya.* Sahibabad: Vibhū Prakāśan, 1976.

Bahura, Gopal Narayan. "An Introduction to the Pothīkhānā of Jaipur." *I A V R I Bulletin* 7 (1979): 20–29.

———, and Kenneth E. Bryant, eds. *Pad Sūrdās kā/The Padas of Sūrdās.* Jaipur: Maharaja Sawai Man Singh II Museum, 1984.

Barth, Karl. *Church Dogmatics.* Translated by G. W. Bromiley and T. F. Torrance. Vol. 1, part 2. Edinburgh: T. and T. Clark, 1956.

Barthwal, P. D. *The Nirguṇa School of Hindi Poetry.* Benares: Indian Book Shop, 1936.

Barz, Richard. *The Bhakti Sect of Vallabhācārya.* Faridabad: Thomson Press, 1976.

(*Bhāgavata Purāṇa*) *Śrīmadbhāgavata.* Benares: Paṇḍit Pustakālay, 1965.

Bhāradvāj, Jagdīś. *Kṛṣṇa Kāvya mẽ Līlā-Varṇan.* New Delhi: Nirmalkīrti Prakāśan, 1972.

Bhārat Bhūṣaṇ "Saroj." *Sūrdās: Ek Adhyayan.* Delhi: Regal Book Depot, 1964.

Bharati, Pushpa. *Soordas, the Blind Bard Who Sang about Lord Krishna.* Bombay: India Book House Education Trust, n.d.

Bhātī, Deśrājsiṅh. *Sūr kī Kūṭakāvya.* New Delhi: Aśok Prakāśan, 1970.

———. *Sūrdās aur unkā Sāhitya.* Agra: Vinod Pustak Mandir, 1977.

Bhaṭnāgar, Rāmratan. *Sūr Sāhitya kī Bhūmikā.* Allahabad: Rāmnārāyaṇlāl Benīmādhav, 1964.

Brajbāsī Dās. *Braj Vilās.* Bombay: Khemrāj Śrīkṛṣṇadās, 1953.

Briggs, George Weston. *Gorakhnāth and the Kānpaṭha Yogīs.* 1938. Delhi: Motilal Banarsidass, 1973.

Brown, C. Mackenzie. *God as Mother: A Feminine Theology in India.* Hartford, Vt.: Claude Stark, 1974.

Bryant, Kenneth E. "The *Bhramargīt* of Sūrdās." Paper presented to the conference on "The *Sant* Tradition," Berkeley, Calif., 1978.

———. *Poems to the Child-God: Structures and Strategies in the Poetry of Sūrdās.* Berkeley and Los Angeles: University of California Press, 1978.

Bryce, Winifred, ed. *Women's Folk-songs of Rajputana.* New Delhi: Government of India, 1964.

Bühler, Georg, trans. *The Laws of Manu.* 1886. New York: Dover, 1969.

Buitenen, J. A. B. van. *Rāmānuja on the Bhagavadgītā.* 1953. Delhi: Motilal Banarsidass, 1968.

Burghart, Richard. "The Founding of the Ramanandi Sect." *Ethnohistory* 25, no. 2 (1978): 121–39.

———. "Wandering Ascetics of the Rāmānandī Sect." *History of Religions* 22, no. 4 (1983): 361–80.

Callewaert, W. M. *The Sarvāṅgī of the Dādūpanthī Rajab.* Leuven: Katholieke Universiteit, 1978.

———, ed. *Early Hindī Devotional Literature in Current Research.* Leuven: Katholieke Universiteit, 1980.

Caturvedī, Javāharlāl. "Sūrsāgar ka Vikās aur uskā Rūp." In *Kanhaiyālāl Poddār Abhinandan Granth,* edited by V. S. Agrawala, pp. 119–32. Mathura: Akhil Bhāratīya Braj Sāhitya Maṇḍal, 1953.

———. *Sūrdās: Adhyayan-Sāmagrī.* Mathura: Akhil Bhāratīya Braj Sāhitya Maṇḍal, 1959.

———. *Mahākavi Śrīsūrdās aur unkā Kṛtattva.* Agra: Sūr-Smārak Maṇḍal, 1962.

Caturvedī, Paraśurām. *Uttarī Bhārat kī Sant-Paramparā.* Allahabad: Leader Press, 1972.

Caturvedī, Sītārām. *Mahākavi Sūrdās aur unkī Pratibhā.* Allahabad: Hindi Sāhitya Sammelan, 1978.

———, ed. *Sūr-Granthāvalī.* 5 vols. Benares: Akhil Bhāratīya Vikram Pariṣad, 1974–76.

Cauhān, Vidyā. *Lokgītõ kī Sāṃskṛtik Pṛṣṭibhūmi.* Agra: Pragati Prakāśan, 1972.

Citrāv, Siddheśvarśāstrī. *Bhāratvarṣīya Prācīn Caritrakoś.* Poona: Bhāratīya Caritrakoś Maṇḍal, 1964.

Cohen, Richard J. "Sectarian Vaishnavism: The Vallabha *Sampradaya*." In *Proceedings of the South Asia Seminar, 1981–1982*. Philadelphia: University of Pennsylvania Press, 1984.

Copḍā, Sudarśan. *Bhakta Kavi Sūrdās*. Delhi: Hindi Pocket Books, 1979.

Czuma, Stanislaw. *Indian Art from the George P. Bickford Collection*. Cleveland: Cleveland Museum of Art, 1975.

Dayāl, Rāmeśvar. *Madhyayugīn Kṛṣṇa-Bhakti Paramparā aur Lok-Saṃskṛti*. Delhi: Pāṇḍulipi Prakāśan, 1975.

Devendrakumār. *Bhramargīt aur Sūr*. Kanpur: Grantham, 1967.

Dimock, Edward C., Jr. *The Place of the Hidden Moon*. Chicago: University of Chicago Press, 1966.

Dournon-Taurelle, Geneviève, recorder. *Inde. Rajasthan. Musiciens professionels populaires*. Ocora, OCR 81, 1973?.

Dowson, John. *A Classical Dictionary of Hindu Mythology and Religion, Geography, History, and Literature*. London: Routledge and Kegan Paul, 1968.

Dūbe, Udayśaṅkar "Śil." "Sūrsāgar kā ek Durlabh Prati." *Braj Bhāratī* 22, no. 3 (1968): 4–17.

Dvivedī, Hazārīprasād. *Madhyakālīn Dharma-Sādhanā*. Allahabad: Sāhitya Bhavan, 1970.

———. *Sūr Sāhitya*. New Delhi: Rājkamal Prakāśan, 1973.

———. *Kabīr*. New Delhi: Rājkamal Prakāśan, 1976.

———. *Nāth Sampradāy*. Varanasi: Naivedya Niketan, n.d. [1966].

Dvivedī, Kedārnāth. *Kabīr aur Kabīr-Panth*. Allahabad: Hindī Sāhitya Sammelan, 1965.

Eliade, Mircea. *Yoga: Immortality and Freedom*. Translated by Willard R. Trask. Princeton: Princeton University Press, 1970.

Falk, Nancy A. and Rita M. Gross, eds. *Unspoken Worlds: Women's Religious Lives in Non-Western Cultures*. San Francisco: Harper and Row, 1980.

Finnegan, Ruth. *Oral Poetry: Its Nature, Significance and Social Context*. Cambridge: Cambridge University Press, 1977.

Garcin de Tassy. *Histoire de la Littérature Hindouie et Hindoustanie*. 1870. 3 vols. New York: Burt Franklin, 1968.

Garg, Lakṣmīnārāyaṇ. *Sūr-Saṅgīt*. 2 vols. Hathras, U.P.: Saṅgīt Kāryālay, 1958–59.

Garga-Saṃhitā. Translated into Hindi by Pt. Śyāmsundar "Suman." Bombay: Bholeśvar Pustak Bhaṇḍār, n.d.

Glasenapp, Helmuth von. "Die Lehre Vallabhâcāryas." *Zeitschrift für Indologie and Iranistik* 9 (1933–34): 268–330.

Gosvāmī, Jīva. *Śrī Śrī Gopālacampū*. 2 vols. Edited and translated into Hindi by Syāmdās. Brindavan: Śrīharinām Saṅkīrttan Maṇḍal, 1968–70.

Gosvāmī, Lalitācaran. *Śrī Hit Harivaṃś Gosvāmī: Sampradāy aur Sāhitya*. Brindavan: Veṇu Prakāśan, 1957.

Govindadās. *Braj aur Braj Yātrā*. Delhi: Bhāratīya Viśva Prakāśan, 1959.

Gross, Neil. "Paradoxes of Krishna in the Poetry of Surdas." Master's thesis, Columbia University, 1978.

Growse, Frederic Salmon. *Mathurá: A District Memoir.* 3rd ed. Allahabad: North-western Provinces and Oudh Government Press, 1883.
Gupta, Dāmodardās. *Sūrdās.* Delhi: Hindī Sāhitya Saṃsār, 1962.
Gupta, Dīndayāl. *Sūrdās.* Delhi: Hindī Sāhitya Saṃsār, 1962.
———. *Aṣṭachāp aur Vallabh-Sampradāy.* 2 vols. Allahabad: Hindī Sāhitya Sammelan, 1970.
Gupta, Jagdīś. *Kṛṣṇa Bhakti Kāvya.* Allahabad: Gautam Printing Press, 1968.
Gupta, Mātāprasād. "Sūr Sāgar kī Bhūmikā." Edited by Udayśaṅkar Śāstrī. *Bhāratīya Sāhitya* 13, no. 1–2 (1968): 43–94.
Gupta, R. D. "Priyā Dās, Author of the *Bhaktirasabodhinī.*" *Bulletin of the School of Oriental and African Studies* 32, no. 1 (1969): 57–70.
Guptā, Uṣā. *Hindī ke Kṛṣṇa Bhakti Kālīn Sāhitya mẽ Saṅgīt.* Lucknow: Lucknow University, 1959.
Gurū Granth Sāhib, Ādi Śrī. 4 vols. With Hindi commentary by Manmohan Sahagal. Lucknow: Bhuvan Vāṇī Trust, 1978–82.
Hargulāl. *Sūrsāgar mẽ Lok Jīvan.* Delhi: Hindī Sāhitya Saṃsār, 1967.
Hartz, Richard Alan. "A Metrical Translation of Selected Maithili Lyrics of Vidyapati." Master's thesis, University of Washington, 1979.
Hawley, John Stratton. "The Early *Sūr Sāgar* and the Growth of the Sūr Tradition." *Journal of the American Oriental Society* 99, no. 1 (1979): 64–72.
———. "Krishna in Black and White: *Darsan* in the Early *Sur Sagar.*" *Journal of Asian and African Studies* 15, no. 1–2 (1980): 43–58.
———. *At Play with Krishna: Pilgrimage Dramas from Brindavan.* In association with Shrivatsa Goswami. Princeton: Princeton University Press, 1981.
———. "*Yoga* and *Viyoga:* Simple Religion in Hinduism." *Harvard Theological Review* 74, no. 2 (1981): 1–20.
———. *Krishna, the Butter Thief.* Princeton: Princeton University Press, 1983.
———, and Donna Marie Wulff, eds. *The Divine Consort: Rādhā and the Goddesses of India.* Berkeley: Berkeley Religious Studies Series, 1982.
Hein, Norvin. *The Miracle Plays of Mathurā.* New Haven: Yale University Press, 1972.
Hess, Linda. "Studies in Kabir: Texts, Traditions, Styles and Skills." Ph.D. diss., University of California, Berkeley, 1980.
———. *The Bījak of Kabir.* In collaboration with Shukdev Singh. San Francisco: North Point Press, 1983.
Holland, Barron, ed. *Popular Hinduism and Hindu Mythology.* Westport, Conn.: Greenwood Press, 1979.
Ingalls, Daniel H. H. "Śaṁkara on the Question: Whose Is *Avidyā.*" *Philosophy East and West* 3, no. 1 (1953): 69–72.
———. *An Anthology of Sanskrit Court Poetry: Vidyākara's "Subhāṣitaratnakoṣa."* Cambridge: Harvard University Press, 1965.
Jhā, Narendra. *Bhaktamāl: Pāṭhānuśīlan evam Vivecan.* Patna: Anupam Prakāśan, 1970.
Johanns, Peter, S. J. *Vers le Christ par le Vedanta.* Translated by Michel Ledrus. 2 vols. Louvain: Museum Lessianum, 1932.

Juergensmeyer, Mark, and N. Gerald Barrier, eds. *Sikh Studies: Comparative Perspectives on a Changing Tradition.* Berkeley: Berkeley Religious Studies Series, 1979.

Jyotī, Līlā. *Sūrdās aur Potnā: Vātsalya kī Abhivyakti.* Bangalore: Vidyā Mandir Hindi Book Center, 1976.

Kabīr. *Bījak.* With commentary by Khemrāj Śrīkṛṣṇadās. Bombay: Śrīveṇkaṭeśvar Press, 1968.

Karmakar, R. D. "Comparison of the Bhāṣyas of Śaṅkara, Rāmānuja, Keśavakaśmirin and Vallabha on Some Crucial Sūtras." *Annals of the Bhandarkar Oriental Research Institute* 1, no. 2 (1920): 105–27.

Kavirāj, Kṛṣṇadās. *Śrī Caitanya-caritāmṛta of Kṛṣṇadāsa Kavirāja Gosvāmī.* Commentary by A. C. Bhaktivedanta Swami. 3 vols. New York: Bhaktivedanta Book Trust, 1974–75.

Kinsley, David. "The Image of the Divine and the Status of Women in the *Devī-bhāgavata-purāṇa.*" Paper presented to the American Academy of Religion, New York, 1979.

Kumār, Vacandev, ed. *Sūr: Vividh Sandarbhõ mẽ.* Varanasi: Kiśor Vidyā Niketan, 1979.

Lester, Robert C. *Rāmānuja on the Yoga.* Madras: Adyar Library and Research Centre, 1976.

Lord, Alfred. *The Singer of Tales.* Cambridge: Harvard University Press, 1960.

Lorenzen, David N., ed. *Religious Change and Cultural Domination.* Mexico City: Colegio de México, 1981.

McGregor, Ronald Stuart. *Nanddas: The Round Dance of Krishna and Uddhav's Message.* London: Luzac and Co., 1973.

McLeod, W. H. *Gurū Nānak and the Sikh Religion.* Oxford: Clarendon Press, 1968.

———. *The Evolution of the Sikh Community.* Delhi: Oxford University Press, 1975.

———. *The B40 Janam-Sakhi.* Amritsar: Guru Nanak Dev University, 1980.

———. *Early Sikh Tradition: A Study of the Janam-Sākhīs.* Oxford: Clarendon Press, 1980.

Mahābhārata. Edited by V. S. Sukthankar. 19 vols. Poona: Bhandarkar Oriental Research Institute, 1927–59.

Mani, Vettam. *Purāṇic Encyclopaedia.* Delhi: Motilal Banarsidass, 1975.

Manusmṛti. Commentary of Meghātithi. 2 vols. Calcutta: Manasukharāy Mor, 1967 and 1971.

Marfatia, Mrudula I. *The Philosophy of Vallabhācārya.* Delhi: Munshiram Manoharlal, 1967.

Masson, J. L. and M. V. Patwardhan. *Aesthetic Rapture.* 2 vols. Poona: Deccan College, 1970.

Matisoff, Susan. *The Legend of Semimaru, Blind Musician of Japan.* New York: Columbia University Press, 1978.

Miller, Barbara Stoler. "Rādhā: Consort of Kṛṣṇa's Vernal Passion." *Journal of the American Oriental Society* 95, no. 4 (1975): 655–71.

Misra, Janardan. *The Religious Poetry of Sūrdās.* Königsberg: Albertus-Universität, 1934.

Miśra, Rāmcandra. *Sant Nāmdev aur Hindī Sāhitya.* Farrukhabad: Śailendra Sāhitya Sadan, 1969.

Mītal, Dvārkāprasād. *Hindī Sāhitya mẽ Rādhā.* Mathura: Javāhar Prakāśan, 1970.

Mītal, Prabhudayāl. *Sūrdās Madanmohan: Jīvanī aur Padāvalī.* Mathura: Agravāl Press, 1958.

———. *Gosvāmī Harirāy jī kā Pad-Sāhitya.* Mathura: Sāhitya Saṃsthān, 1962.

———. "Sūr Kṛt Padõ kī Sabse Prācīn Prati." *Nāgarīpracāriṇī Patrikā* 67, no. 3 (1962): 262–67.

———. *Braj kā Sāṃskṛtik Itihās.* Delhi: Rājkamal Prakāśan, 1966.

———. *Braj kī Sāṃskṛtik Yātrā.* Mathura: Sāhitya Saṃsthān, 1966.

———. *Braj ke Dharma-Sampradāyõ kā Itihās.* Delhi: National Publishing House, 1968.

———. *Braj kī Kalāõ kā Itihās.* Mathura: Sāhitya Saṃsthān, 1975.

Nābhājī. *Śrī Bhaktamāl.* Lucknow: Tejkumār Press, 1961.

Nāgarīpracāriṇī Sabhā. *Khoj Reports.* Benares: Nāgarīpracāriṇī Sabhā, 1902–9.

———. *Hastalikhit Hindī Pustakõ kā Saṅkṣipt Vivaraṇ.* 2 vols. Varanasi: Nāgarīpracāriṇī Sabhā, 1964.

Nagendra, ed. *Suradasa, A Reevaluation.* New Delhi: National Publishing House, 1979.

———, and K. D. Sharma, eds. *Sūradāsa, His Mind and Art.* Chandigarh: Bahri Publications, 1978.

The New English Bible: The Old Testament. London: Oxford and Cambridge University Presses, 1970.

Niemann, Grahame. "The Bhāgavat Daśam Skandh of Bhūpati." *I A V R I Bulletin* 8 (1980): 3–8.

Nilsson, Usha. *Surdas.* New Delhi: Sahitya Akademi, 1982.

O'Connell, Joseph T. "Gaudiya Vaisnava Symbolism of Deliverance (*uddhara, nistara* . . .) from Evil." *Journal of Asian and African Studies* 15, no. 1–2 (1980): 124–35.

Ojhā, Dharmanārāyaṇ. *Sūr-Sāhitya mẽ Puṣṭimārgīya Sevā Bhāvanā.* Allahabad: Śodh Sāhitya Prakāśan, 1973.

Omprakāś. *Madhyayugīn Kāvya.* New Delhi: Arya Book Depot, 1973.

Orr, W. G. *A Sixteenth-Century Indian Mystic: Dadu and His Followers.* London: Lutterworth, 1947.

Pāṇḍey, Siddhanāth. *Saṅkṣipt Sūrsagar.* Meerut: Sāhitya Bhaṇḍār, 1975.

Parekh, Bhai Manilal. *Sri Vallabhāchārya.* Rajkot: Bhagavata Dharma Mission, 1943.

Parīkh, Dvārkādās, ed. *Caurāsī Vaiṣṇavan kī Vārta.* Mathura: Śrī Bajaraṅg Pustakālay, 1970.

———, and Prabhudayāl Mītal. *Sūr-Nirṇaya.* Mathura: Sāhitya Saṃsthān, 1962.

Ramanujan, A. K. *Hymns for the Drowning: Poems for Viṣṇu by Nammāḻvār.* Princeton: Princeton University Press, 1981.

Rāvat, Candrabhān. *Sūr Sāhitya: Nav Mūlyā̃kan.* Mathura: Javāhar Pustakālay, 1967.

Redington, James D. "The Meaning of Kṛṣṇa's Dance of Love According to Vallabhācārya." Ph.D. diss., University of Wisconsin-Madison, 1975.

Richardson, Edwin Allen. "Mughul and Rajput Patronage of the Bhakti Sect of Maharajas, The Vallabha Sampradaya, 1640–1760 A.D." Ph.D. diss., University of Arizona, 1979.

Saksenā, Nirmalā. *Sūrsāgar Śabdāvalī.* Allahabad: Hindustānī Academy, 1962.

Sangar, S. P. "Some Aspects of Sixteenth Century Hindu Society as Reflected in the Literature of Sur Das." *The Research Bulletin of the University of the Panjab* 34, no. 2 (1962): 1–27.

Śarmā, Harbanślāl. *Sūr aur unkā Sāhitya.* Aligarh: Bhārat Prakāśan Mandir, 1971.

———. *Sūr-kāvya kī Ālocanā.* Aligarh: Bhārat Prakāśan Mandir, n.d.

———, ed. *Sūrdās.* Delhi: Rādhākṛṣṇa Prakāśan, 1969.

Śarmā, Kṛṣṇadev, ed. *Vidyāpati aur unkī Padāvalī.* Delhi: Aśok Prakāśan, 1976.

Śarmā, Munśīram. *Sūrdās kā Kāvya-Vaibhav.* Kanpur: Grantham, 1971.

Śarmā, Rājnāth. *Bhramar Gīt-Sār.* Agra: Vinod Pustak Mandir, 1976.

Śarmā, Śrīnivās. *Sūrdās aur unkā Bhramargīt.* New Delhi: Aśok Prakāśan, 1972.

Śāstrī, Udayśaṅkar, ed. "Sūrsāgar kī Sāmagrī kā Saṃkalan aur uskā Saṃpādan." *Bhāratīya Sāhitya* 17, nos. 1–2 (1972): 73–101.

Śāstrī, Ved Prakāś. *Śrīmadbhāgavat aur Sūrsāgar kā Varṇya Viṣay kā Tulnātmak Adhyayan.* Agra: Sarasvatī Pustak Sadan, 1969.

Satyendra. *Braj-Sāhitya kā Itihās.* Allahabad: Leader Press, 1967.

———. *Pāṇḍulipi Vijñān.* Jaipur: Rājasthān Hindī Granth Akādamī, 1978.

Sazanova, Natal'ia Mikhailovna. *Voprosi Indiiskol Filologii.* Moscow: Izdatel'stvo Moskovskogo Universiteta, 1974.

———. *Surdas Krishnayana* [*Die Volkskultur von Braj und das poetische Schaffen des Dichters Sūrdās*]. 2 vols. Translated by Roland Beer and N. M. Sazanova. Leipzig: Gustav Kiepenheuer, 1979.

Schomer, Karine. "Mahadevi Varma and the Chayavad Age of Modern Hindi Poetry: A Literary and Intellectual Biography." Ph.D. diss., University of Chicago, 1976.

———. *Mahadevi Varma and the Chhayavad Age of Modern Hindi Poetry.* Berkeley and Los Angeles: University of California Press, 1983.

———, and W. H. McLeod, eds. *The Sants: Studies in a Devotional Tradition of India.* Berkeley: Berkeley Religious Studies Series and Delhi: Motilal Banarsidass, forthcoming.

Seṭh, Jagannāth, ed. *Sūrdās: Vividh Sandarbhõ mẽ.* Calcutta: Śrī Baḍābājār Kumārsabhā Pustakālay, 1979.

Shah, J. G. *Shri Vallabhacharya: His Philosophy and Religion.* Nadiad: The Pushtimargiya Pustakalaya, 1969.

Sheth, Noel. "The Justification for Kṛishṇa's Affair with the Hunchbacked Woman." *Purāṇa* 25, no. 2 (1983): 225–36.
Singer, Milton, ed. *Krishna: Myths, Rites, and Attitudes.* Chicago: University of Chicago Press, 1966.
Singh, Ram Adhar. *Syntax of Apabhraṃśa.* Calcutta: Simant Publications India, 1980.
Siṅh, Sudarśan. *Śri Kṛṣṇa Bāl Mādhurī.* Gorakhpur: Gita Press, 1965.
———. *Anurāg-Padāvalī.* Gorakhpur: Gita Press, 1968.
———. *Virah-Padāvalī.* Gorakhpur: Gita Press, 1969.
———. *Sūr-Vinay-Patrikā.* Gorakhpur: Gita Press, 1970.
———. *Śri Kṛṣṇa Mādhurī.* Gorakhpur: Gita Press, 1971.
Smith, Bardwell L., ed. *Hinduism: New Essays in the History of Religions.* Leiden: E. J. Brill, 1976.
Smith, Wilfred Cantwell. "The Crystallization of Religious Communities in Mughul India." In *Yād-nāme-ye Irāni-ye Minorsky*, ed. Mojtaba Minori and Ijar Afshar, pp. 1–24. Tehran: Tehran University, 1969.
———. "Introduction to World Religion." Lectures, Harvard University, 1969, 1971.
———. *Towards a World Theology.* Philadelphia: Westminster, 1980.
Snātak, Vijayendra. *Rādhāvallabh Sampradāy: Siddhānt aur Sāhitya.* Delhi: National Publishing House, 1968.
Snell, Rupert. "Scriptural Literature in the Rādhāvallabha Sampradāya." *I A V R I Bulletin* 4 (1978): 22–30.
Spink, Walter. *Krishnamandala, a Devotional Theme in Indian Art.* Ann Arbor: Center for South and South East Asian Studies, University of Michigan, 1971.
Śrī Govardhannāth jī ke Prākatya kī Vārtā. Bombay: Śrī Veṇkaṭeśvar Press, 1905.
Srivastava, S. N., ed. *Surdas: Poetry and Personality.* Agra: Sur Smarak Mandal, 1978.
Śukla, Govardhannāth, ed. *Paramānand Sāgar.* Aligarh: Bhārat Prakāśan Mandir, n.d.
Śukla, Rāmbahorī. *Kāvya-Pradīp.* Allahabad: Hindi-Bhavan, 1976.
Śukla, Rāmcandra. *Sūrdās.* Varanasi, 1948.
Śukla, Viśvanāth. *Hindī Kṛṣṇa Bhakti Kāvya par Śrīmadbhāgavat kā Prabhāv.* Aligarh: Bhārat Prakāśan Mandir, ca. 1966.
Sūr Dās. *Sūr Sāgar.* 5th ed. Lucknow: Newal Kishore Press, 1882.
———. *Sūr Śatak Pūrbārdh.* Edited by Bhāratendu Hariścandra. Patna and Bankipur: Khaḍgabilās Press, 1899.
———. *Sūrsāgar.* Edited by Jagannāthdās 'Ratnākar' et al. 1st ed., vol. 2 (but vol. 1 never appeared). Benares: Nāgarīpracāriṇī Sabhā, 1934. Subsequent eds.: vol. 1, 1972; vol. 2, 1976.
———. *Śrīsūrsāgar.* Edited by Radhākṛṣṇadās. Bombay: Khemrāj Śrīkṛṣṇadās, 1957.
———. *Sūrsāgar Sārāvalī.* Edited by Prabhudayāl Mītal. Mathura: Agraval Press, 1958.

———. *Sāhitya Laharī*. Edited by Prabhudayāl Mītal. Mathura: Sāhitya Saṃsthān, 1961.

———. *Sūrsāgar ke Sau Ratna*. Edited and commentary by Prabhudayāl Mītal. Mathura: Sāhitya Saṃsthān, 1962.

———. *Sūr-Sāgar*. Edited by Javāharlāl Caturvedī. Calcutta: Śrīnand Mīnānī, 1965.

———. *Sūrsāgar*. Edited by Mātāprasād Gupta and prepared for publication by Udayśaṅkar Śāstri. *Bhāratīya Sāhitya* 15, no. 1–2 (1970): 145–472; 16, no. 1–2 (1971): 149–84; 17, no. 1–2 (1972): 155–96; 17, no. 3–4 (1972): 195–203; 18, no. 1–2 (1973): 145–205; 18, no. 3–4 (1973): 163–210; 19, no. 1–2 (1974): 159–208; 19, no. 3–4 (1974): 173–220.

———. *Sūrsāgar Saṭīk*. Vol. 1. Edited and translated (into Hindi) by Hardev Bāhrī and Rājendra Kumār. Allahabad: Devbhāratī Press, 1974.

———. *Sūr-Paṃcśatak*. Edited and commentary by Manmohan Gautam. Delhi: Sūrya-Prakāśan, 1976.

———. *Sūrsāgar*. Edited by Mātāprasād Gupta and prepared for publication by Udayśaṅkar Śāstrī. Agra: Agra University, 1979.

———. *Pad Sūrdās kā/The Padas of Sūrdās*. Edited by Gopal Narayan Bahura and Kenneth E. Bryant. Jaipur: Maharaja Sawai Man Singh II Museum, 1984.

Sūrdās: Ek Viśleṣaṇ. New Delhi: Government of India (Ministry of Information and Broadcasting), 1978.

Swann, Darius L. "Three Forms of Traditional Theatre of Uttar Pradesh, North India." Ph.D. diss., University of Hawaii, 1974.

Sweeney, Amin. *Authors and Audiences in Traditional Malay Literature*. Berkeley: Center for the Study of South and Southeast Asia Studies, University of California, 1980.

Śyāmsundardās et al., eds. *Hindī Śabdsāgar*. 11 vols. Varanasi: Nāgarīpracāriṇī Sabhā, 1965–75.

Ṭaṇḍan, Hariharnāth. *Vārtā-Sāhitya*. Aligarh: Bhārat Prakāśan Mandir, ca. 1960.

Ṭaṇḍan, Premnārāyaṇ. *Brajbhāṣa Sūr-Koś*. Lucknow: Lucknow University, 1950.

———. *Sūr kī Bhāṣā*. Lucknow: Hindī Sāhitya Bhaṇḍār, 1957.

———. *Sūr-Sārāvalī: Ek Aprāmāṇik Racanā*. Aminabad: Hindī Sāhitya Bhaṇḍār, 1961.

———, ed. *Sūrdās kī Vārtā*. Lucknow: Nandan Prakāśan, 1968.

Ṭhākaur, Manmohan, ed. *Sūrdās Paṃcśatī Samāroh*. Calcutta: Sūrdās Paṃcśatī Samāroh Samiti, 1978?.

Thiel-Horstmann, Monika, ed. *Bhakti in Current Research, 1979–1982*. Berlin: Dietrich Reimer Verlag, 1983.

Thoothi, N. A. *The Vaishṇavas of Gujarat*. Calcutta: Longmans, Green and Co., 1935.

Thrasher, Allen W. "Mandana Miśra on the Indescribability of *Avidyā*." *Wiener Zeitschrift für die Kunde Südasiens* 21 (1977): 219–37.

Tivārī, Pāras Nāth, ed. *Kabīr Granthāvalī*. Allahabad: Prayāg Viśvavidyālay, 1961.

Tivārī, Śaśi. *Sūr ke Kṛṣṇa: Ek Anuśīlan.* Hyderabad: Milind Prakāśan, 1961.

Tripāṭhī, Rāmnareś, ed. *Grām-Sāhitya.* 2 vols. Sultanpur: Hindī Mandir, 1951–52.

Tulsī Dās. *Rāmcaritmānas.* Gorakhpur: Gita Press, 1947.

———. *Vinaya Patrikā.* With the Hari-toṣiṇī Ṭīkā of Viyogī Hari. Allahabad: Lokbhāratī Prakāśan, 1977.

Tulsī *Sāhib. Ghaṭ Rāmāyaṇ.* 2 vols. Allahabad: Belvedere Printing Works, 1976–77.

Upādhyāy, Kṛṣṇadev, ed. *Bhojpurī Lok-Gīt.* 2 vols. Allahabad: Hindī Sāhitya Sammelan, 1954, 1966.

Vājpeyī, Nand Dulāre. *Mahākavi Sūrdās.* Delhi: Rājkamal Prakāśan, 1976.

Vājpeyī, Nārāyaṇ Prasād. *Sūr Dās ke Dārśanik Vicār.* Delhi: Jñānabhāratī, 1969.

Vallabhācārya. *Śrī Subodhinī* [*kā Hindī Anuvād*]. Translated into Hindi by Phatahcand Vāsū Śāstrī et al. 11 vols. completed. Jodhpur: Śrī Subodhinī Prakāśan Maṇḍal, 1966–75.

———. *Kṛṣṇaṣodaśagranthāḥ.* Bombay: Nirnaya Sagar Press, n.d.

Vālmīki. *Rāmāyaṇa.* Baroda: Oriental Institute, 1960.

Varmā, Dhīrendra. "A Note on the MSS of the Sūr Sāgar." *Allahabad University Studies* 3 (1926): 291–307.

———. *Vicār-Dhārā.* Allahabad: Sāhitya-Bhavan Limited, 1957.

Varmā, Vrajeśvar. *Sūrdās: Jīvan aur Kāvya kā Adhyayan.* Allahabad: Lokbhāratī Prakāśan, 1979.

———. *Sūr-Mīmāṃsā.* New Delhi: Oriental Book Depot, n.d.

Vatsyayan, Kapila. *Traditional Indian Theatre: Multiple Streams.* New Delhi: National Book Trust, 1981.

Vatuk, Ved Prakash, and Sylvia Vatuk. "The Ethnography of *Sāng*, A North Indian Folk Opera." *Asian Folklore Studies* 26, no. 1 (1967): 29–51.

Vaudeville, Charlotte. *Bārahmāsā.* Pondichéry: Institut Français d'Indologie, 1965.

———. *Pastorales par Soûr-Dâs.* Paris: Gallimard, 1971.

———. "The Govardhan Myth in Northern India." *Indo-Iranian Journal* 22 (1980): 1–45.

———. *Kabīr.* Vol. 1. Oxford: Clarendon Press, 1974. Vol. 2, forthcoming.

Vrajvallabhśaraṇ, Govindśaraṇ Śāstrī, and Premnārāyaṇ Śrīvāstav, eds. "Śrīrādhā-Aṅk." *Śrīsarveśvar* 23 (1966): 7–12.

Wadley, Susan Snow. "The Rains of Estrangement: Understanding the Hindu Yearly Cycle." Paper presented to the American Anthropological Association, Los Angeles, 1978.

Westcott, G. H. *Kabir and the Kabir Panth.* Cawnpore: Christ Church Mission Press, 1907.

White, Charles S. J. *The "Caurāsī Pad" of Śrī Hit Harivaṁś.* Honolulu: University Press of Hawaii, 1977.

Wulff, Donna M. "Drama as a Mode of Religious Realization: The *Vidagdhamādhava* of Rūpa Gosvāmin." Ph.D. diss., Harvard University, 1977.

———. "*Rasa* as a Religious Category: Aesthetics and Supreme Realization in Medieval India." Paper presented to the conference honoring Wilfred Cantwell Smith, Center for the Study of World Religions, Harvard University, 1979.

Yāmunācārya. *Gītārthasaṃgraha.* English commentary by V. K. Ramanujachariar. Madras: Sri Ranganatha Paduka, 1971.

Zvabitel, Dusan. "The Development of the Baromasi in the Bengali Literature." *Archiv Orientalni* 29 (1961): 582–619.

Poems Translated from the *Sūr Sāgar*, by English Title

ALL POEMS TRANSLATED from the *Sūr Sāgar* in their entirety are listed here according to the numbers given them in the Nāgarīpracāriṇī Sabhā edition. Poems only partially translated or bearing another signature than Sūr's are not listed. The last poem listed (*) is not included in the Sabhā edition.

Poems Translated from the *Sūr Sāgar*, by Hindi Title

THE FOLLOWING IS a list of poems translated from the *Sūr Sāgar* in their entirety in this book. The index is arranged alphabetically according to the devanagari system. For ease of use, the first line as given in the Nāgarīpracāriṇī Sabhā edition has been adopted rather than a critically reconstructed version. The one poem with * was not included in that edition.

Index

Abhinavagupta, 116
Abu'l Fazl, 22–24
Acrobat, 143, 159, 165–66
Advaita Vedānta, 109
Ā'īn-i-Akbarī, 22–24
Ajāmil, 131–32, 175
ajānyo, 152
Akbar, 10, 17–18, 24
Akrūr, 15, 103, 106, 192
Alīkhān Paṭhān, 7
Allchin, F. R., 116, 125, 128, 157
Alterations in poems, 69–70, 79, 84, 142–43, 148–49
Āḻvārs, 28
Anger. See *mān*
Animal and human natures, 132–41, 156, 169, 201
antarjāmī/antaryāmī, 26, 56
Antelope, skin of, 193–94
Anthologies, 127–30
Anup Sanskrit Library, 44, 48
anurāg, 46–49
Apabhraṃśa, 30
Arjun, 137, 149, 186
Arrow of *sabad,* 135–36
Arts. See *bhajan;* Dance; *kalā;* Song
Asceticism. See *sanyās;* Yoga; Vallabha on
aṣṭachāp, 6–7, 12
Audience, knowing, 73, 75
avadhūt, 124
avidyā, 139–40, 164. See also *ajānyo*
avigat, 122
avināsī, 122

B1, dating of, 44
Bābā Rām Dās, 23
Bahura, G. N., 36
bājīgar, 165–66
bāl poems, 46, 48–49
Balarām, 47–48, 60, 102
Bansal, Nareś Candra, 28
bārahmāsā, 114
Barth, Karl, 117–18
Barthwal, P. D., 125
Barz, Richard, 5–7, 10
Battle of love, 74–75, 77–78, 186–87
Beauty. See Rādhā, beauty of
Bee, 73, 82, 99, 104, 109, 113. See also *bhramargīt;* Ūdho
bhagat. See *bhakti*
Bhagavad Gītā, 41, 102
bhagavant bhajan, 168, 174–75, 180
Bhāgavata Purāṇa, 2, 86, 98, 115, 127; as taught to Sūr Dās, 19; and *Sūr Sāgar,* 37–41, 44–45, 53
bhaj-, 168–69
bhajan, 102, 143–44, 167–71, 174–75, 180, 187, 191; and *bhakti,* 168–69
Bhaktamāl, 15–17, 22–23, 126
bhaktavatsal, 58, 142–43
bhaktavatsaltā, 131
Bhaktavijaya, 15
Bhaktavinod, 14–15
bhakti, 47–48, 58, 102, 121–27, 137, 164, 167–69; and *bhajan,* 168–69
Bhaktirasabodhinī, 23. See also Priyā Dās
Bhaviṣyottara Purāṇa, 67
Bhojpuri, 114
bhramargīt, 47–49, 62, 98–114, 118, 121–22, 124, 136, 163
Bhūpati, 40
Bibliothèque Nationale, 24
Bird of the soul, 132
Birth of Krishna. See Krishna, birth of
Black, 47, 60, 109, 135–36

PUBLICATIONS ON ASIA
OF THE HENRY M. JACKSON SCHOOL
OF INTERNATIONAL STUDIES

1. Boyd, Compton, trans. and ed. *Mao's China: Party Reform Documents, 1942–44*. 1952. Reissued 1966. Washington Paperback-4, 1966. 330 pp., map.
2. Siang-tseh Chiang. *The Nien Rebellion*. 1954. 177 pp., bibliog., index, maps.
3. Chung-li Chang. *The Chinese Gentry: Studies on Their Role in Nineteenth-Century Chinese Society*. Introduction by Franz Michael. 1955. Reissued 1967. Washington Paperback on Russia and Asia-4. 277 pp., bibliog., index, tables.
4. *Guide to the Memorials of Seven Leading Officials of Nineteenth-Century China*. Summaries and indexes of memorials to Hu Lin-i, Tseng Kuo-fan, Tso Tsung-tang, Kuo Sung-tao, Tseng Kuo-ch'üan, Li Hung-chang, Chang Chih-tung. 1955. 457 pp., mimeographed. Out of print.
5. Marc Raeff. *Siberia and the Reforms of 1822*. 1956. 228 pp., maps, bibliog., index. Out of print.
6. Li Chi. *The Beginnings of Chinese Civilization: Three Lectures Illustrated with Finds of Anyang*. 1957. Reissued 1968. Washington Paperback on Russia and Asia-6. 141 pp., illus., bibliog., index.
7. Pedro Carrasco. *Land and Polity in Tibet*. 1959. 318 pp., maps, bibliog., index.
8. Kung-chuan Hsiao. *Rural China: Imperial Control in the Nineteenth Century*. 1960. Reissued 1967. Washington Paperback on Russia and Asia-3. 797 pp., tables, bibliog., index.
9. Tso-liang Hsiao. *Power Relations within the Chinese Communist Movement, 1930–34*. Vol. 1: *A Study of Documents*. 1961. 416 pp., bibliog., index, glossary. Vol. 2: *The Chinese Documents*. 1967. 856 pp.
10. Chung-li Chang. *The Income of the Chinese Gentry*. Introduction by Franz Michael. 1962. 387 pp., tables, bibliog., index.
11. John M. Maki. *Court and Constitution in Japan: Selected Supreme Court Decisions, 1948–60*. 1964. 491 pp., bibliog., index.
12. Nicholas Poppe, Leon Hurvitz, and Hedehiro Okada. *Catalogue of the Manchu-Mongol Section of the Toyo Bunko*. 1964. 391 pp., index.
13. Stanley Spector. *Li Hung-chang and the Huai Army: A Study in Nineteenth-Century Chinese Regionalism*. Introduction by Franz Michael. 1964. 399 pp., maps, tables, bibliog., glossary, index.

14. Franz Michael and Chung-li Chang. *The Taiping Rebellion: History and Documents*. Vol. 1: *History*. 1966. 256 pp., maps, index. Vols. 2 and 3: *Documents and Comments*. 1971. 756 and 1,107 pp.
15. Vincent Y. C. Shih. *The Taiping Ideology: Its Sources, Interpretations, and influences*. 1967. 576 pp., bibliog., index.
16. Nicholas Poppe. *The Twelve Deeds of Buddha: A Mongolian Version of the Lalitavistara*. 1967. 241 pp., illus. Paper.
17. Tsi-an Hsia. *The Gate of Darkness: Studies on the Leftist Literary Movement in China*. Preface by Franz Michael. Introduction by C. T. Hsia. 1968. 298 pp., index.
18. Tso-liang Hsiao. *The Land Revolution in China, 1930–34: A Study of Documents*. 1969. 374 pp., tables, glossary, bibliog., index.
19. Michael Gasster. *Chinese Intellectuals and the Revolution of 1911: The Birth of Modern Chinese Radicalism*. 1969. 320 pp., glossary, bibliog., index.
20. Richard C. Thornton. *The Comintern and the Chinese Communists, 1928–31*. 1969. 266 pp., bibliog., index.
21. Julia C. Lin. *Modern Chinese Poetry: An Introduction*. 1972. 278 pp., bibliog., index.
22. Philip C. Huang, *Liang Ch'i-ch'ao and Modern Chinese Liberalism*. 1972. 200 pp., illus., glossary, bibliog., index.
23. Edwin Gerow and Margery Lang, eds. *Studies in the Language and Culture of South Asia*. 1974. 174 pp.
24. Barrie M. Morrison. *Lalmai, A Cultural Center of Early Bengal*. 1974. 190 pp., maps, drawings, tables.
25. Kung-chuan Hsiao. *A Modern China and a New World: K'ang Yu-Wei, Reformer and Utopian, 1858–1927*. 1975. 669 pp., transliteration table, bibliog., index.
26. Marleigh Grayer Ryan. *The Development of Realism in the Fiction of Tsubochi Shōyō*. 1975. 133 pp., index.
27. Dae-Sook Suh and Chae-Jim Lee, eds. *Political Leadership in Korea*. 1976. 272 pp., tables, figures, index.
28. Hellmut Wilhelm. *Heaven, Earth, and Man in the Book of Changes: Seven Eranos Lectures*. 1976. 230 pp., index.
29. Jing-shen Tao. *The Jurchen in Twelfth-Century China: A Study of Sinicization*. 1976. 217 pp., map, illus., appendix, glossary, bibliog., index.
30. Byung-joon Ahn. *Chinese Politics and the Cultural Revolution: Dynamics of Policy Processes*. 1976. 392 pp., appendixes, bibliog., index.
31. Margaret Nowak and Stephan Durrant. *The Tale of the Nišan Shamaness: A Manchu Folk Epic*. 1977. 182 pp., bibliog., index.
32. Jerry Norman. *A Manchu-English Lexicon*. 1978. 318 pp., appendix, bibliog.
33. James Brow. *Vedda Villages of Anuradhapura: The Historical Anthropology of a Community in Sri Lanka*. 1978. 268 pp., tables, figures, bibliog., index.

34. Roy Andrew Miller. *Origins of the Japanese Language*. 1980. 217 pp., maps, bibliog., index.
35. Stevan Harrell, *Ploughshare Village: Culture and Context in Taiwan*. 1982. 234 pp., maps, illus., glossary, bibliog., index.
36. Kozo Yamamura, ed. *Policy and Trade Issues of the Japanese Economy: American and Japanese Perspectives*. 1983. 332 pp., index.
37. Bruce Cumings, ed. *Child of Conflict: The Korean-American Relationship, 1945–1953*. 1983. 335 pp., index.
38. Chan Hok-lam. *Legitimation in Imperial China. Discussions under the Jurchen-Chin Dynasty, 1115–1234*. Forthcoming.
39. Harold F. Schiffman. *A Reference Grammar of Spoken Kannada*. 1983. 177 pp., bibliog., index.
40. John Stratton Hawley. *Sūr Dās: Poet, Singer, Saint*. 1984. 233 pp., illus., glossary, bibliog., indexes.
41. Alison Black. *Nature, Artifice, and Expression in the Philosophical Thought of Wang Fu-chih*. Forthcoming.